T

WRONG

GIRL

BY MIKE DEROSA

Dedication

This book commemorates both times in my life when I had to be the best version of myself. First, when I served as a U.S. Navy Submariner with the sharpest guys in the world. Second, when I tried to be worthy of my perfect little person, my Sharon, my darling wife.

CONTENTS

THE WRONG GIRL
PROLOGUE

A meeting was held after World War Two had ended, which would determine the fate of the world. The Allies, as they were known, had won that horrible war and met in Yalta to pretty much divide up the planet, each getting his cut.

FDR, a lifelong politician, had no real killer instinct and just spewed toothless rhetoric that allowed enough time for Stalin to fearlessly occupy Poland. Since the war had virtually bankrupted the British Empire, Churchill sat by as well, as he was in no position to control a raging Ioseb Jughashvili.

The secure future of the Atlantic Charter and all of Eastern Europe was frittered away as a sick, weak, and naïve American President desperately tried to retain some sort of legacy while the Iron Curtain was about to be slammed down like a hot hammer on an anvil.

Lost in the grand scheme of these lofty negotiations between governments was the rage living in the souls of individuals whose lives and families had been destroyed by that war. There were the remnants of so many Jewish families, now wisps of smoke, who begged for a country of their own.

The few and tattered French Resistance fighters, whose towns were wiped from the earth, wept silently over the blackness of their once beautiful countryside.

What of the hundreds of thousands of soldiers' families forever missing their loved ones at Christmas dinner in a home whose sadness will never go away?

Oh, yes, these three great conquerors held themselves up as "the good guys" and rulers of the future while virtually ignoring their other ally, China.

The China that helplessly screamed while being raped at Nanking. The same China that saw 250,000 countrymen murdered because they would not turn over Doolittle's Raiders to the enemy.

The same China that was condemned to biological destruction by the despicable Unit 731, which retreated unpunished into the shadows of history.

The Chinese government wondered where was their piece of the pie. Where was their invitation to Yalta? True, they had their own internal squabbles between Chiang Kai Shek and Mao. They held meetings between the Nationalists and Communists to try and arrive at one government. Neither condition should have negated an invitation to Yalta, but no invitation came.

Unfortunately, these internal squabbles led to an all-out civil war in 1947, with one government establishing itself in Taiwan and the other retaining the mainland.

But, beyond the concerns of the government, what of the many young children, now grown, who witnessed the horror of invasion and occupation in places like Ihwang, Nencheng, and a hundred other small towns?

What of the children who heard the cries of their fathers being burned alive and their mothers raped over and over and over by a vengeful enemy bent on nothing but destruction? What of THEIR loss and seething needs for revenge?

There were some individuals, some patriots, and some who had prepared their entire lives to repay a debt owed to the world. The collective Chinese memory may be a long one, but a boy who watches his father soaked in kerosene and set ablaze never, ever forgets.

Yes, some members of these particular families haven't forgotten how the world turned its back and let China's enemies destroy her and eventually sat back and let her tear herself apart politically.

They will never forget that when the fat markets and resources of the post-war world were being divided up, China was betrayed and offered no seat at the table.

The West may have forgotten, but the Chinese certainly have not. Would they develop some long-range plan to make things, right? Sometimes, you use your opponent's power against him.

So, what was it that empowered the enemy? Money, profit, political power? Then, become indispensable as a producer of the goods that fuel their economies. Open the vastness of China as a market and become indispensable as a trading partner.

No invitation to ride the bus at Yalta? Well, then they would DRIVE the bus at Panmunjom and The Paris Peace Accords. Maybe the world prefers China as an adversary? Maybe, it's time for China to make its move. Maybe, it's time to be the bride and not a bridesmaid.

Maybe, one of these wronged individuals, now grown and wealthy beyond measure, had been getting even one step at a time for many years. He searched his own withered face in the mirror and figured he had time enough for one last thrust.

Were he successful, his efforts would bring him a prize he could offer his country to use as the old Celts would the Fragarach or Retaliator. A sword built by the gods that can cut through anything and whose inflicted wounds cannot be healed....

He had, offhandedly, intimated that such a prize would be his pleasure to deliver to those who ran his country, but his generosity was refused. Those same leaders were his long-standing friends, who were once starving and lost along with him. Now, they were the very political giants who were hesitant to walk the world stage as fearsome characters and competitors.

No, they preferred the dance of dialogue and diplomacy rather than threats and disagreement. They seemed to have forgotten the hellishness of the war and all that had been taken from them.

Well, he had not forgotten, and he would go it alone since he had the means, organization, and will to fight on.

Bolin Li pulled the old Zippo lighter out of his pocket for maybe the millionth time. Bolin, a Chinese name that means "gentle rain," had been a good and gentle boy born to a loving family.

His was the aforementioned little town of Ihwang, 500 miles or so southeast of Wuhan, and it had been a happy place in the summer of 1942. A happy place right up until the Japanese Army officers rode in on their booted horses, leading an army of devils.

They had a mission, after all, these representatives of The Empire of Japan: investigate the rumor that one of those Doolittle assassins was hiding in this town, find him, make the residents pay for daring to stand against their great empire, and drag him back to Japan.

Impeccable in his uniform, the officer in charge directed his men, all wearing loincloths, to forcibly enter and search the houses. The men of Ihwang protested, and the shooting and slashing began; no warning, no negotiating, no time to even grasp what was happening.

With bayonets fixed to their rifles, the soldiers kicked in the doors, pulled women and children out of the way, and looted every item of value they didn't break.

Bolin's little friend, Zhen, a name that ironically means "greatly astonished," stood still in silent terror out in front of his own home. Bolin had never forgotten that one last look of astonishment on his friend's face when the shiny, bloody sword cleaved his head open like a ripe melon right down through the chin.

Bolin couldn't move. The sound of the guns, the horses, and the screams of the crowd were all too much. His mother, Ai Li, grabbed his arm, and they started to run. She pulled him headlong, and he had difficulty breathing with all the swirling dust. He could barely keep his balance.

Heading nowhere in particular, they were bumped and jostled by the panicking mob of neighbors and friends, all desperate to save themselves and their loved ones. People fell left and right, either from colliding with the others or from the bullets fired directly into the crowd.

A rifle butt whizzed over Bolin's head and caught his mother square in the face. Blood spurted from her nose and mouth as she seemingly passed out and fell to the ground releasing his hand. Three soldiers were immediately on her and tore every strip of clothing away as each took his turn.

She was silent through it all, her eyes fixed on him, and Bolin still, after all these years, couldn't decide if she was already dead or just refused to give them the satisfaction of her pleas. He ran.

Father Anthony Fredrickson, the long-time Irish Catholic Missionary they had all come to love, stood in the street with both hands held in supplication to the Japanese commander. He begged for the violence to stop, but the stuffy officer handed him a small shiny object, the very Zippo lighter Bolin now held and rubbed with a thumb.

He still remembers the look on the old priest's face as he held the lighter close to his failing eyes. He turned it over in his now wrinkled hands. He toyed with the striker and felt the cold brass of the U.S. Army crest on the side, now well-worn.

He struck the spark a few times and let his thoughts run back, back, back. He was there again. He could see it, smell it, hear that little "clink" sound all again for the millionth time.

"Where is the man who owns this?" the Japanese officer asked in very good English while plucking the lighter from Fredrickson's hand.

"I know of no such man."

"You lie, Father. This belonged to an American flier who helped bomb Japan. He and his crewmates crashed somewhere nearby.

Some came here to this very town and were helped by these very people." He swept the crowd with a graceful arc of one arm.

Fredrickson tried stalling while he thought of what to say next. He haltingly asked the commander, "Where…did you, uh, get that lighter?"

Lieutenant Yamazuki pulled his sword and pointed it across the street at the man whose arms were now held by two loinclothed soldiers.

Fredrickson knew him. Of course, it was little Bolin's father who had allowed the owner of that lighter to live with his family while he recuperated. The lighter was given as a token of thanks, but now it was a death sentence.

Yamazuki said that if Fredrickson admitted what he knew, the elder Li alone would be arrested, and the violence in the town would stop. If he continued with this lie, then the repercussions would continue.

"Better to sacrifice one man than the entire village," Father Fredrickson thought. He remembered his religious lessons in the Seminary about the valiant Sicarii rebels at the Siege of Masada. One man volunteered his soul to save those of his fellows. One man would have to die now.

"Very well, yes," he said in the resignation of the inevitable. "That flier was here. He was treated medically and was taken away by other Americans." That was another lie, and Yamazuki knew it. Fredrickson was just trying to keep the Chinese rescuers out of it.

Yamazuki smiled and gently said, "Thank you, Father. Step back, now."

The soldiers held both of Li's arms straight out to the side, and Yamazuki's sword traced a figure eight in the air, cleanly removing one arm and then the other.

The screams didn't last long as the sudden loss of blood caused the elder Li to mercifully lose consciousness and fall to the street right at the feet of his petrified son.

The soldiers then doused Bolin's dad with kerosene. Yamazuki struck the lighter and threw it to set a stunned and shocked Bolin's not-quite-dead father ablaze. Little Bolin Li peed himself and began to scream. His little voice was lost in the madness and died away amidst the screams of so many.

The violence did not stop as promised but intensified. As it turned out, for two weeks, the soldiers stayed drunk and raped every female from age 10 to 65.

They looted every building and burned everything they did not consume or steal. They killed anything alive, and the human bodies were strewn among the rotting carcasses of cows, pigs, horses, and any other creature who had once been alive. They even burned the crops in the fields before moving on.

Somehow, in the chaos of the murders of his parents, Bolin had stood seemingly invisible to the killers around him. He was only 4, and little at that, so he must not have been even worthy of a glance downward.

He bent and picked up the ignominious lighter lying in the dust of the street. Now, 78 years later, he rubbed it again between thumb and forefinger as though a genie would come forth and make it all go away.

He remembered running all that day and well into the night. He spent that rainy first night under the bridge that joined his town with the next where his Uncle Chen was magistrate. He waited until morning and crossed the bridge tentatively as, oddly, the only sound was the crackle of the fires that consumed the village.

He was cold and hungry, shaking with shock. He needed help and wanted the comfort of Uncle Chen's house.

He found his uncle at home, but Uncle Chen had been tied to a chair and shot dead. He was sitting there now, facing the door, looking at little Bolin Li as though ready to welcome him in.

There was food on the table, but it was all covered in spattered blood. Bolin Li ate it anyway. There was water in the barrel at the end of the counter, and although unsure, he drank it anyway. Even at this young age, he had made up his mind to live. Oh, yes…he would live, and someday, he would get even.

It took another 32 years, but by then, a now-grown Bolin Li had become very successful in the pharmaceutical business, as it were. He had contacts all over the Pacific Rim and lots of people who wanted to work for him and become his friend. They would do his bidding either for the money or just to avoid the anger of Bolin Li, as he was renowned for doling out the most brutal of punishments.

One of those contacts, a distributor in Japan, had finally located for him the commodity he had been searching for all this time: a now civilian Daichi Yamazuki. Yes, THAT Yamazuki. The once LT.

Yamazuki who killed his father, killed his best friend, and ordered the destruction of his entire childhood. It was time for the reckoning. The former Lieutenant Daichi Yamazuki had left the Army after the war and spent the entire time since as a mid-level code enforcer in the city of Koriyama.

North and east of Tokyo, Koriyama was a beautiful place, but Yamazuki had a reputation as a thug who demanded bribes. He certainly wasn't above accosting poor business owners for sex or goods if money was not to be had. The good people of Japan, if there were any in that hellish country, wouldn't miss him.

One day, Yamazuki was approached at his usual Ramen lunch place by a beautiful, sexy Japanese girl who asked to join him. She said she was here to make good on her mother's debt for code infraction charges if that was alright.

She apologized that they were unable to pay in cash, but perhaps he would accept another form of payment. She undid the top two buttons of her blouse while speaking and offered a lecherous and probably drunk Yamazuki her best come-hither smile.

He looked her over slowly. His eyes lingered on her luscious lips and full bosom. "She must be part American," he thought. Probably the spawn of one of those thug occupiers the Yankee Army had left behind to rob his country. She put a hand on his arm and slid closer.

Whispering now, her lips brushed his ear. "I have a car outside and a suite reserved nearby." She was leaning so close to him that he was staring down her blouse as she spoke. The scent of her was intoxicating, and he quickly finished his wine. He was all tingly inside and took her hand as he hurriedly exited the restaurant.

Yamazuki hadn't even gotten to the sidewalk when he was bashed on the head and thrown into a waiting van. Ten hours later, he woke up in one of Bolin Li's warehouses with ropes tied to his wrists and his arms outstretched.

He was stripped down to his underwear and T-shirt, one sleeve just touching the dragon tattoo on his left bicep. He slowly focused on one arm, then the other, and shook his head to wake up.

Bolin Li stood before him and spoke in English with a very upbeat tone, "Welcome back to China, Lieutenant Yamazuki!"

Yamazuki looked at Li, to his hands, and back again. He pulled on the ropes and shook them madly.

"What is going on here? Who are you? What do you mean by

"China," he screamed in Japanese. "Do you know who I AM?"

"No, no, English, please. I have heard you speak English before, and I know you have an excellent command of the language," he said in an exaggeratedly condescending tone.

Yamazuki shook his head one more time, trying to clear the cobwebs from the drugs and the dizziness from the blow. He was starting to focus on the smiling face before him, trying to figure out just what was going on.

"Oh, yes, I know who you are very, very well. I made your acquaintance a long time ago."

Bolin stepped back and took note of how different Yamazuki looked. Age, alcohol, and the scars of battle all helped to take the shiny starch out of the Army officer he first encountered all those years ago. Yamazuki, quiet now, looked Bolin over and tried to figure out just who the hell this bastard was.

"Rather than offer lengthy explanations. Let me show you something that might help you remember the day we met."

Bolin Li held out the old Zippo lighter.

"I was very little the first time I saw you holding this."

Bolin could see the clarity of memory wash over the face of LT. Yamazuki. He knew that lighter. He remembered that day. He just now realized why his arms were outstretched…

Amazingly, that was 46 years ago, but the human skin that was made into the blotter upon which Bolin Li worked every day still seemed fairly vibrant.

The stitching between each piece was perfect, and even the dragon tattoo ink was clear and the design vivid. It took a while to peel every inch of it off a screaming and begging Yamazuki. It's amazing what you can do when you take your time and concentrate.

Money and contacts gave Bolin Li access to everything, and he loved the technology that was his key to it all. Lots of vengeance to dole out. The money bought him people who would do anything he asked, and his total lack of pity ensured their cooperation.

Those who were not motivated by money were easily motivated by pain or violence. If not to them personally, then to their loved ones. Many ways to get what you wanted in this world; the war had taught him that.

He had made lots of friends willing to upload software, for example, that allowed his satellites to access computer systems and electronic grids of all types. It was only a few seconds of work, and the rewards were remarkable.

Some of his "friends" were motivated by piles of money, while others placed real value on the release of a dear relative from some unfortunate situation.

As the opportunities presented themselves, the access he gained easily facilitated the hacking that caused the self-destruction of facilities such as the reactor at Chornobyl.

Once the cooling system low-level alarms and interlocks were disabled and the primary coolant allowed to drain, the reactor was doomed.

Death and destruction soon followed, and no one had any inkling there were reasons and intentions behind it all. After all, he owed debts to entire countries, and he was going to pay them off.

He thought back to that day when he had been discovered by the roaming Chinese gangs looking for food and valuables once the Japanese had left. His life had been spared by a woman named Qing Shan, whose men had wanted to cook and eat him. They were starving, and any vestige of decency and morality were concepts long dead.

Qing Shan came upon the men stripping what was left of Bolin's pee-soaked clothes and were about to cut his throat when she screamed at them to stop. She backhanded one of the men, who turned out to be her brother, and said they would not become the animals the Japanese had proven themselves to be.

She picked Bolin from the ground and helped sort out the smelly rags he was wearing. He searched her face and saw the same agony and desperation he imagined was on his face as well.

"Xie Xie," he said in gratitude, and she asked if he would like to travel with them. Of course, he said he would. After all, he had no one and nothing. They almost ate him, for God's sake; better to be with them than against them.

So, for the next two years, he tried to keep up with them as they wandered the countryside, trying to find food and shelter. Once in a while, they would come across something of value left behind by the enemy.

Food stores, Sake, and forgotten uniforms were like gold to them. They ate whatever they could find as months grew to years. Eventually, the war ended. They had made their way to Beijing and were placed in one of the camps set up by the Communists.

Here, they were fed, checked over by doctors, had a roof over their heads to sleep, and all they had to do was listen to the "lessons" offered every day right before meals. No food unless you sat and listened, so they sat and listened. Mao this, Mao that; the devil Shek, stuff like that. It always led to rice and vegetables, so they didn't mind.

After a month, they had had enough of the indoctrination and started to steal food and whatever else they could stockpile in preparation for leaving. There were only six willing to go, and Qing Shan was one. They pledged lifelong loyalty to one another and promised to stick together no matter what. Bolin was almost seven years old now and thought of these other youngsters as his family.

None older than 16, they had witnessed their villages burned, parents killed or taken away, and the lives they knew gone in a moment. They were afraid and angry at the same time. They had nothing but each other and decided that was how it was going to be.

They would leave tomorrow, so there would be just one more night of looking for stuff to take with them. That was when destiny showed up as one of their numbers slid through a window and into the makeshift medical ward.

He grabbed the cardboard box on the desk and headed out the door to get back to the group. Qing Shan met him and was so excited to see a package that looked new and undamaged. She said she was hoping for canned pineapples but found only glass bottles of pills and some bandages. A large red cross adorned each little package.

None of them could speak English, let alone read it, and even if they did, words like Quinine and Flagyl were WAY outside of their comprehension. Classic meds to treat Malaria and Dysentery, these pills would have been a tremendous help to all the poor sufferers in this camp alone. On the black market, however, they were REALLY valuable.

The next night, right after lessons and their meal, each kid put a box of pills in every pocket, and they hit the road. Over the next few weeks, they came upon missionaries here and there willing to trade for these pills. Sometimes, there were American dollars; sometimes, just food. Always, there was something else to steal and sell.

One thing tends to lead to another, and this little band of kids grew into a little band of young adults who always had drugs to sell. Time passed, and a lifetime in pharmaceutical distribution had grown into a global empire. Payment in scraps of food or the odd dollar here and there had given way to electronic transfers in the billions.

Payment also took the form of property, favors, promises, and people. Their lives were dedicated to any purpose Bolin Li and his empire assigned them. Such wealth and influence gave him the fuel to assault America with Opioids and Fentanyl. It also helped him develop the greatest one-two punch; a punch nobody would see coming.

Buying the right people, uploading the right virus, and hacking the digital safety protocols at the lab in Wuhan unleashed the first punch on a world that turned away from him as a boy. A world that offered no friendship for his country in its time of need. The first punch would make them sick, but the next was the final catalyst to make them all go away.

He rubbed that lighter again, and indeed, the genie had come forth and was out in the world right now, ready to even up the score.

One more card to play, and his little American angel was the dealer. She would not fail; she had been properly motivated. The video of her mother tied to a chair while the hair was burned off her head had done the trick. Obey, and your mother will be released. Fail and, well, you know.

1

It's the last night in port for the US Navy Fast Attack submarine USS DODGE CITY. She had been enjoying an extended Liberty Call in England training alongside her Royal Navy Submarine counterparts. Six weeks in Portsmouth had been a fun and exciting time for the crew, many of whom had never set foot in a foreign country.

She had been in the shipyard in Connecticut for the last year and a half, being overhauled and reinvented by incorporating the first fully integrated Artificial Intelligence system the Navy ever put on a nuclear submarine.

This system was tied into every key system, from Propulsion to Sonar Master Target tracking, to Fire Control, Weapons Delivery, and Navigation. Auxiliary systems like atmosphere monitoring, inventory, trim systems, ECM, Global Link-up, and Communications were also engaged.

Not only was every system on the boat monitored, but the crew was monitored, as well. Each man had been chipped, and his health status, location, reliability, and level of exhaustion were all monitored by the AI. This was the first time this was ever done before, and it had to be run by the JAGs to see if there was some rights infringement. In reality, military people have FEWER rights than your average civilian.

Being chipped was presented to the men as a new level of health monitoring. Since the Navy loved us so much, they wanted to keep a closer eye on us and make sure we were all OK.

In other words, they were VolunTOLD about getting chipped. A quick shot in the thumb and forefinger web of the left hand and a chip the size of a grain of rice was planted.

I describe the DODGE CITY as "Reinvented" because this sub was originally commissioned into the US Navy over 3 decades ago as the USS ALBUQUERQUE (SSN706) and had served as SUBLANT's "go to" boat; even earning the nickname "Sure Shooter" for 12 out of 12 Tomahawk hits launched into Kosovo.

She had been a special boat crewed with special men, and now she was at the tip of the spear once again.

Removed from the active rolls of Naval Ships in 2015, ALBUQUERQUE was towed to Electric Boat in 2018 and was reborn as USS DODGE CITY (SSAIN 1). The "Submersible Ship Nuclear 706" hull number was now "Submersible Ship Artificial Intelligence Nuclear 1" as she was the first boat of, hopefully, a new class of Attack Submarines.

Along with the name change, her new AI was unlike anything seen before at sea. Her entire Combat Systems suite had been gutted, reimagined, and rebuilt.

No longer outfitted with a standard Torpedo Room, weapons delivery would be through 50 horizontally-mounted launch tubes. These tubes had been configured between the superstructure and the HY-80 pressure hull, which had been retooled and necked-down Forward to look more like a rifle cartridge casing than a tube.

This whole underwater weapon delivery system, nicknamed the "Wheel Gun" (slang for a six-shooter) by the crew to play on the Dodge City theme, was reminiscent of a revolver in that these tubes were the big moving parts of a cylindrical, rotatable weapons stowage/delivery system.

Encapsulated weapons, such as Tomahawk cruise missiles, Harpoon cruise missiles, the new MK100 Lingering capable mine, plus the old reliable MK48 ADCAP torpedo, were tube loaded through a hatch that flipped open like a revolver loading gate.

Weapons no longer needed a plug-in "A" cable, either, to talk to Fire Control. The advantage here was a reduction in the number of hull penetrations as the weapons were programmed telemetrically.

The original 4 MK63 tubes had been removed along with the Ejection Pumps, WRTs, and torpedo stowage racks. This entirely new space was used as a SEAL Team prep center.

Additional food storage space originally built below the Torpedo Room had been converted into an extended battery compartment redesigned to house the bigger and better ship's battery. This also helped to offset the weight change to the ship with all that heavy weapons handling equipment being removed.

A contest had been held to name this revolutionary Artificial Intelligence system, and the new Hospital Corpsman, HM1 Adams, had won with the name: "Military Autonomous Target Tracking and

Digitally Integrated Life-support, Logistic, and Operational Nexus."

Yeah, it seems a little long, but there are a few things in play that make it all understandable...Dodge City was the setting of the famous TV show, "Gunsmoke," and everyone involved with this boat enthusiastically embraced the Gunsmoke theme.

Even the Navy Detailers at BUPERS in D.C., the people that cut orders for sailors to go from one Duty Station to the other, had gotten into the whole Gunsmoke thing and were searching for the right names to staff DODGE CITY.

Other entries in the contest included such predictable as "Cyberdine Systems Model 101" from The Terminator movie. That one was from Bobby, The Dog Faced Boy, in A-gang, while "HAL" was sent in by The Texas Tripod, real name ET2 Margeson, who earned his nickname for having the biggest cock onboard.

Anyway, you might recall that "Doc Adams" was the name of the town doctor in the TV show, so the guy that details Corpsmen cuts orders for Petty Officer First Class Richard Adams to serve as DODGE CITY's "Doc," as sailors refer to their Corpsman.

Petty Officer Adams had grown up watching reruns of the show and just loved it. His contest-winning name for the AI system, when reduced to an anagram, spells out MATT DILLON, the central character of the show.

Over in the MS, or Mess Specialist detailing office, they found Chief Petty Officer Theresa Russell was due for orders. Well, Chief Russell was one of the first enlisted women to qualify in Submarines, the concept of which was a big bone stuck in the throat of the purists who regarded submarine duty as the last bastion of the all-male warrior ethos.

Somewhere, sometime, probably during Obama's administration, the military became something of a Social Experiment, and more Progressive ideals were put in play.

Even policies like "Don't ask, don't tell," which allowed gays to serve in secret were formally overturned. Women were being assigned to more combat-oriented roles rather than just medical or administrative ones as before.

Russell was a ground-breaker, and now, here she was, the only female onboard in a sea of testosterone and hardons. For some reason, the military refuses to acknowledge that putting boys and girls in close proximity usually results in fucking and ruined careers.

3

As part of this great social awakening, women were assigned to Submarine Duty. Yes, Chief Russell was one of the first female sailors to earn her Dolphins, but whose orders to DODGE CITY were less about her abilities or accomplishments and more because she shared a last name with Kitty Russell, the Marshal's love interest in Gunsmoke.

On her first day aboard, right after morning quarters, where she was introduced to the crew by the CO, Chief Russell made it a point to announce, "I'll kill any of you motherfuckers that calls me Kitty." She said it with a wry smile on her face, but most of the guys figured she was serious.

She had a buzz cut on one side of her head, and if she completely shaved off the hair on that side, you could see a tattoo of a mean-looking orange cat riding a Harley and firing a machine gun. Since the Navy didn't go for visible head tattoos, she kept enough hair grown in to cover it.

She had kind of a "man-ish" way of walking that made people wonder if she was a dyke or not, and at around 5 feet ten and 160 pounds, it made it hard to envision her as a fragile girly-girl, so, everyone just went with dyke and let it go.

Besides, she just looked like she could probably kick most of the crew's asses, so it wasn't worth teasing her about it or even bringing it up, but it did draw a line between her and everybody else.

DODGE CITY had been here in Portsmouth, England, doing a final loadout of stores and waving the flag with the Royal Navy as part of NATO. The Brits were excellent hosts, and any American sailor can tell you how much fun it is to get Liberty along with the Limeys. Besides, British girls LOVED American sailors almost as much as did the Sheilas in Oz.

A week up in Rosyth and another in Holy Loch proved that the robustness of Scottish girls only surpassed their ability to outdrink most men and their love of sex.

Here, in England, the bawdiness had flown to new heights as it became public knowledge the American sailors had adopted The Argyle pub near the base.

It had been a favorite with the British sailors for over a hundred years; the heavy wood and nautical décor were quite historical. As always, all girls were welcome, and a good time was to be had by all.

The Argyle was an ancient drinking establishment adorned in

heavy English Oak and shined brass at every turn. Thick carpeting and heavy double doors opened to an atmosphere perpetually smelling of tobacco and beer.

Tile and marble everywhere in the Heads; plaques and wall décor from every Royal Navy command over the entire history of the place. One could sense the atmosphere of royalty and history that hung about the place; one could almost hear Churchill screaming, "Never! Never! Never!"

Usually, a Fast Attack crew numbers about 130. With people on leave or in school, 105 or so took the boat to sea. Since this particular boat was built to be operated by an Artificial Intelligence system the world had never seen before, far fewer people were required, and fully two-thirds of the original complement would be sent back to the states with orders to new commands.

So, here it was, late January 2020, the DODGE CITY's sailing crew of merely 35 men and one woman would go down in history after an epic evening unparalleled in Argyle's lore.

Tomorrow, with the tide, she would get underway for a final shake-down evolution. They would, for all intents and purposes, "deploy" for parts unknown and prove a sub with virtually no crew can get the job done.

2

Friday night and everyone NOT in Duty Section 3 was excited for the last night in port. It was going to be a big deal at The Argyle tonight as every girl in Portsmouth and probably South sea would be there.

British sailors weren't known as big spenders, but the Americans were. Americans even TIPPED so they enjoyed great service from the bartenders and waitresses.

The fact that they didn't really understand the local money was good, too. Cabbies would take a 5- or ten-pound note as payment for a fare and return the change mixed with Pound notes and Pound coins.

As was their habit, the American sailors would pour the coins into the cabbie's hand with a pleasant "keep the change" thinking it was pin money, but it was dollars instead of cents.

A good-looking English babe, with that accent, flirtingly laughing on the arm of an American, was irresistible to most of the young sailors. The older men were too savvy to get hustled, but then again, most of the older men were married.

Speaking of which…there is an unofficial understanding in the Navy known as the "Hundred Mile Rule" which, with a wink and a nod, allows married men to cavort around with other women as long as the boat's a hundred miles away from home port (the wife).

Of course, this "understanding" was never signed onto by the wives, so anyone partaking was being a very bad boy.

England was WAY outside the Hundred Mile barrier, and there was no limit to who and what went on. Even that douchebag Navigator, Lieutenant Commander Kennedy, was banging one of the local broads.

He was a fat old bastard that very few people liked, but he must be spreading the wealth because she was spreading those legs and he couldn't get enough. She even sucked his dick in front of the whole damn place right under the table closest to the door last Tuesday night just after the XO and COB had left.

The boys even tried to get up a game of "Smiles" with her, but Kennedy had a shit-fit about it. For you non-Navy pukes, "Smiles" is a game where a group of players sits around a table and all bet a certain amount of money.

Some chick gets under that table, out of sight of the players, randomly picks one guy, and starts giving him a blowjob.

The challenge is to NOT smile or give any indication that you're getting the blowjob. The object of the game is that the players try to pick out who's getting blown. If you're wrong, you're out and lose your money. If you're right, the guy getting it is out. After a guess, the girl picks someone else until it's down to the last three; winner take all.

Tonight, though, since it was the last night ashore, the final Boat Race was planned. It's the biggest of all drinking games that sees two teams of 12 on either side of a long table.

The first man has a shot glass, the second a rocks glass, and bigger and bigger get the glasses until the last man is hoisting a large loving cup with two hands. There is more to it, but basically, the team finishing first wins. Tonight, DODGE CITY was up against UPHOLDER, the only Royal Navy sub in port right now.

It was past dinnertime; everyone had eaten aboard and those on duty were stowing everything for sea. Deck Division had broken down all the topside lines except for a short, direct path from the brow to the forward escape trunk hatch. As much as could be done in advance of Stationing the Maneuvering Watch would be done so that the crew could stay out on Liberty as late as possible.

One other key individual had yet to leave the boat and that was the Chief of the Boat, or COB as he was known to a crew. This particular guy was unique in that he was the longest serving Master Chief in the whole fucking Navy. He'd been in 49 years and 10 months as of today; that's 12 hashmarks on his sleeve that touched the bottom of his Crow.

Master Chief Joe Durocher was the kind of guy you didn't forget. He used to be a Torpedoman's Mate back when torpedoes had igniters and ran "Hot, Straight, and Normal."

He had gotten himself a Bachelor's degree, Master's, and a PhD in Management AND the son of a bitch was even in MENSA.

He had been a world class athlete and was a full-on ass kicker when he was young in the Navy. He always got the girl and always told you the truth; whoever YOU were. Five feet seven and about 200; even at 68 years old and bald, you knew better than to try this guy.

In another year, he will have reached the milestone of having been Qualified in Submarines for 50 years! 50 years with Dolphins gets you into the unofficial "Holland Club".

Never done before by an Active-Duty guy. He knew everyone in the Navy who was anyone. Admirals who basically ran everything started their careers getting trained (yelled at) by the COB.

They all either loved him and would do anything for him or they knew he had the goods on them and would do anything for him. One phone call from Durocher and you were either going somewhere good or directly to hell. Now, here he was on the newest prototype submarine ever; maybe or maybe not by choice.

All that aside, tonight the COB had a big ass problem......what was going to be the lineup for the Boat Race? You could never live down losing a Boat Race.

Drinking was just a part of the Navy; listen to the words of Anchors Aweigh, for God's sake. You needed a 12-man team and the first slot was a given: the 2 COBs would each have a full shot glass of something symbolic, chosen for each by the other.

They would toast the other's crew, wrap their drinking arms, and shoot that drink. Once done, the glass would be turned upside down and slammed to the table which was the immediate launch signal for the next man to drink and slam his glass down.

First crew to finish wins. No pouring beer down your face, no puking, and no starting your turn until the man before you slammed his glass down.

The penalty for any violation was for the entire offending team to start over. Remember, glasses got larger and larger the whole way down the table until the final drinker, the Anchor Man, had to hoist a two-handed loving cup, 64 ounces of beer, and put the cap on his team's efforts for the win.

So, the COB sat in the Goat Locker, pondering who would be the 12; beside himself at the front, 11 crew needed to defend DODGE CITY's honor and go head-to-head with the Royal Navy. These boys were home ported here and were proud of their undefeated status in the Boat Race most recently dispatching a Danish destroyer crew.

Oh, and the one overarching thought; that which cannot go unmentioned, was that the losing crew had to present the winners a set of underway colors; YOUR country's flag, that means. The humiliation of such a defeat cannot be described in mere words. This was no bullshit little drinking game; this was a matter of National Honor.

There were a couple of lightweights in the crew who always were willing to support whatever the boys were up to, but they weren't the biggest of drinkers.

A small glass of beer should be in their wheelhouses, so COB penciled in Demzer Michaels and Bugsy Moran from Noo Yawk. Demzer was called that because he would say shit like "Demzer expensive sunglasses," or "demzer nice tits on that broad". I don't think anyone was certain of his real first name.

Some of the usual suspects were put in the batting order and, just like always, the last 3 spots were the toughest ones to fill. We know the Anchor Man has to drink 64 ounces AND KEEP IT DOWN.

Well, the preceding guy is drinking a beer pitcher of 48 ounces which is nothing to sneeze at and the guy before him is drinking a standard 40 ouncer. You needed some hard-core drinkers to get through those without any violations. If we had to start over, then we were pretty much fucked.

About this time, Chief Russel walks into the Chief's quarters.

"Hey, COB. What's up?"

"Putting the batting order together for the Boat Race tonight."

"The drinking thing at The Argyle?"

"Yes."

"Put me in."

"Seriously, where?"

"At the end."

"The end." Joe looked at her incredulously. "The Anchor Man slot. You ever played this game before?"

"COB, I know I just checked aboard 14 days ago and we don't really know each other that well, yet, but I can handle the Anchor."

"Russell, do you know who Cornwalis is?"

"The British General from Yorktown?"

No, the monster Sonarman from UPHOLDER. Six feet nine, 330 pounds give or take, renowned throughout the Royal Navy as "THE" Boat Race Anchor Man.

He's the guy you'd be facing. I don't think he's ever lost one of these things. We have to be well ahead by the time he picks up that cup or we will be handing over our flag."

Theresa Russell had a warm wave of nostalgia wash over her in these passing seconds. She had traveled back in time to her teenage years when she went by Terri and was once again at the last barbecue that she attended at her uncle Johnny's house.

He was her favorite uncle and always treated her like not only his own little girl but like an adult at the same time. He was her mom's brother and was one of the cool kind of guys with the tattoos and the motorcycle.

He had a red cat named Toby that he found on the side of the road during a rainstorm. Toby would actually stand on Johnny's shoulders with his front paws on Johnny's head and enjoy rides on the Harley.

She remembered the events of that day clearly as it was a special one. Only one day left before Johnny was leaving for Boot Camp; it was the day of the going away party his closest friends, the Undertakers Motorcycle Club, were throwing for him.

Johnny started this club about 5 years ago after his dad, Theresa's grandpa, died from a heart attack. He had been a Mortician and, hence, the name of the club. Like most MCs, these people were that family that God wanted you to have.

They would kill for each other and they would die for each other and their camaraderie was something Theresa always wished she would find again one day.

These guys had taught her to ride motorcycles, take no shit, stand with your friends, and to shotgun beers out of the can. Open one end with the church key, put it to your lips, and pull the pop top. All you had to learn was how to open your throat all the way and let that beer shoot down there like nothing. Kind of like being a sword swallower… No gulping, no swallowing, just gravity powered flow.

Johnny signed up for the Marines, served in the Sandbox, and was last seen alive standing atop a HUMVEE blasting away with a 50 Cal before an IED blew him to pieces. The funeral held by the Undertakers, without his body, was the most moving, patriotic, and loving displays a person could imagine.

She enlisted shortly after turning 18 and would hit her ten-year mark next month. That tat on the side of her head was in honor of him.

Back to the moment at hand…

"COB, I want you to look in my eyes right now. I will outdrink that big motherfucker like he's never been outdrank before. I will ass fuck him in front of Queen and country as well as the entirety of the Royal Navy and snatch that flag so cleanly, they will talk about this night for ten thousand years."

She sure had a way of expressing herself and the COB was laughing now. Chief Russell was a pretty intimidating looking bull. She was big herself; she said all the right things, and she carried herself with a lot of power. Dirty blonde hair buzzed on one side and combed back on the other. No makeup usually and no smile usually, either.

"Russell, I've never had a fellow Chief lie to my face before, and most know I've been around too long to be bullshitted. So, if you do this thing, then you best realize that your reputation in this man's Navy will be set from tonight until the end of time.

If you say you're the Anchor, you're the Anchor. But, before any of that, I want to give you a piece of my mind. That whole business about "I'll kill you if you call me Kitty," was a little awkward. I don't know if you were trying to be funny and it didn't go over well or if you were serious, but it was kind of a lead balloon.

"I was trying to do that line from that "Soldiers" movie, can't think of the correct title right now. You know, the Vietnam movie where he tells those guys that if they ever call him Grandpa, he'll kill them," she offered meekly.

"Bad timing, Chief."

She looked at her shoes as the old Master Chief plowed on. "We all knew you were coming. Woman with Dolphins and all that. These boys don't know what to do with you."

"The Navy can't seem to wait until it gets a chance to fuck a guy out of his entire career for saying or doing the wrong thing around a member of the opposite sex. You must know this. Guys want to be among friends. I want a tight crew; YOU must want to be PART of it all rather than be the Jonah. No?"

Before she could answer, he let loose another volley. "You also know very well that the boat's morale comes out of that galley which means YOU, the chief cook. You see each of these guys every day; 3 or even 4 times a day. You can get a gauge on how they're doing,

11

while I see them much less often. Our galley is named "The Long Branch;" just like the bar in that show. Who was the owner of "The Long Branch?" Kitty Russell. Do I actually have to say all these words to you right now?"

"I hear ya, COB."

Chief Petty Officer Russell turned and left the Goat Locker. The COB went back to filling in the two slots before her in the order. Had to be The Tripod and that big kid from Compton…the ICman, Benny, right before him.

Hopefully, they'll give Russell a lead. Even if she was as good as she says, Cornwallis drank beer like a great thirsty beast emptying some farmer's well in one of those fairy tales.

3

While the off-duty crew was getting ready for their last night in port, the rest of the boat was buzzing with activity. Cleanup from the evening meal was done and light Midrats were being heated in the galley. The last of the cardboard boxes from food stores were being taken off the ship and each berthing area deck had been covered in Number ten cans of food for the deployment.

The two escape trunks, useless as designed since the depths at which submarines operated made escape impossible, would be filled with potatoes. Cool and dark, they made excellent "root cellars" as it were. In the old days, one of the 4 torpedo tubes would be filled with cases of eggs, but there were no torpedo tubes internal to DODGE CITY.

The heart of the AI upgrade and star of the show, so to speak, was MATT DILLON himself and he watched everything. From hatch and periscope positioning, to tracking that drone flying over Portsmouth at 37,000 feet, The Marshal, as the crew referred to him, was watching it all.

He knew when the Duty Auxiliaryman was 4 minutes late shifting potable water tanks; he logged each time the head valve cycled; he knew exactly how much Amine was in the CO_2 Scrubbers; and calculated how long until the poop in Number 2 Sanitary had to be blown overboard.

Any crewman within 50 feet of the pressure hull was monitored as well. Heartrate, temperature, BP, Oxygen, everything was within the AI's ability to monitor. Any reading, on any system, any out of spec condition was immediately logged and reported to the chain of command. Nothing was missed.

"The Marshal" as this AI was known, even had a ship-wide camera system to video document everything that happened. By design, the system was similar to a high-end security monitor. When and if it was monitoring, it recorded all the time; kept 30 months on a hard drive, and would be reset as part of monthly PMs for the Data System guys.

In the event of a casualty, video of the event could be relayed via satellite back to COMSUBLANT so the facts of the matter would be known and understood.

The cameras were turned off since there were actual people on board who would be disrobing, peeing, pooping, and so on. The cameras would automatically come on if any of the ship's alarms were initiated or if they were commanded ON by the OOD.

Even the boats in the harbor were tracked to determine if they were a threat or if any maneuver was considered dangerous to DODGE CITY. Weapons control was still under the command of the Captain and would only sparingly be turned over to MATT DILLON when the boat was confirmed On Station.

Only 2 guys were charged with the operation and maintenance of MATT DILLON. Their workspace was the AN-UYK20 computer room which housed 2 UYK20s, or the YUKs. Any and all sensory input from Sonar, Radar, hull arrays, towed arrays, SSXBT launches, anything, went through the YUKs. The AI's inputs and subsequent actions passed through those computers.

2 units, 100 petabytes each, could run three small cities. The room was usually freezing cold from the chill water lines exchanging heat with the air-cooling units to keep those YUKs from overheating.

The amount of data exchanged in this one room was unconscionable as every military satellite, SOSUS array, airplane, SEAL team toting a camera and laser designator, ELF signal transmitted through the Continental shelf, every digital photo shot through every NATO submarine periscope, every sound trace on every Q5 Sonar suite and up, EVERYTHING, went through these two units.

Beyond all the real time data was every piece of historical data including the sound signatures of every ship in the entire fucking world.

If a ship had ever been traced by any other ship or driven through the GIUK Gap so that SOSUS could record it, that recording had been stored, processed, and programmed into every Sonar set and Fire Control System in the US Navy.

A sonar suite that picked up a sound source even a hundred miles away could spit out the EXACT ship, its capabilities, who was in command, his history of turning left or right, when he did a Crazy

Ivan, EVERYTHING.

Weapons would be selected, pre-programmed, and ready for launch once in range. This all took less than a second and was all done automatically without the need for human hands. THAT'S why the AI was developed and MATT DILLON was the first to deploy to the badlands of the under-ice world of the Arctic.

One of those two computer techs was an Amish kid named Adam Hochstetler. He was 24 and had been in the Navy 5 years. He was unlike the stereotypical Amish guy, one would say, as he reveled in technology AND was a practical joker.

Like most guys in a submarine crew, nobody called him by his real name, and he was known as Dusty. The whole time he's been onboard he says things like "Woulds't thou pass the salt?" and "Dost thou haveth a pen I might borrow"?

Well, guys had heard he was Amish and since no one ever met one before, they had no idea how they talked so they just let him go on "Thou-ing" and "Dost-ing" and just started calling him Dusty.

Well, it turned out that he didn't talk like that at all and had just been fucking with them and having the greatest laugh about it. He was probably the only Amish person ever to serve in subs and there had to be a story there….

Anyway, back to the AI… There was only one way to disable MATT DILLON, and that was to simultaneously turn the two arming keys to OFF. These were exact copies of the ICBM launch keys from the days of the underground silos and they were kept under lock and key in separate safes.

Even the two locks were physically far enough apart, that if one man got both keys, his arms were too short to permit operation of both keys at the same instant. Dusty had access to one of those safes and the Captain the other.

There was an hour left before the crew was due to meet up at The Argyle. Theresa Russell had changed out of the Submarine coveralls, or Poopie Suit, as it was known and gotten into her civilian clothes.

The Poopie suit made her look roundish and sexless; just the way she wanted. No makeup and her hair combed in that boyish, parted joke many of the dykes wore, it was just assumed she was gay.

More feminine looking dressed as she was right now in her jeans, cowboy boots and button-down western shirt, Terri Russell was

15

actually a full-on babe and rocked a power body of muscle and sex appeal.

No one had seen her in anything other than that damn poopie suit or her work khakis these last two weeks. She reported in late at night in her dress blues and Pea coat and had been loading store rooms, cooking, and doing Navy shit ever since.

She hadn't even left the boat on Liberty at night, but had managed to get pretty close with a few of the hottie Brit chicks on the pier. Since everyone was sure she was a dyke, it all made sense.

She walked out of the berthing area in the Chief's Quarters out to where the seating area was and saw the COB who had just sat down with a coffee. He looked up, panned his vision from her eyes to her boots and back.

Her hair was pulled forward on the non-buzz cut side a little over one eye. She sported some makeup and smelled more like perfume tonight than the expected onion/garlic combo. She stared right back in that defiant manner she had learned along the way.

"Russell, anybody back there in berthing?" All the chief's bunks were right on the other side of the door to the Chief's Quarters lounge area. He wanted to speak to her privately and didn't want any prying ears.

"No, COB"

He lowered his voice anyway...

"Russell, I've been around. I've seen them all come and go. I've worked with hundreds of dykes and fucked about a thousand women. I take one look at you and now we BOTH know you're no lesbian."

Chief Russell was getting ready to speak, but the COB held up his hand.

"I'm on your side. I'm a fellow Chief, old enough to be your dad, AND your COB. I'm not going to say a God damned word either way. You decide how you want to be perceived and that's how it will be. I've been around too long and I know too many things. I just don't like you thinking that I can be fooled that easily."

"Let's talk about this some other time. OK, COB?"

The wise old Master Chief paused and looked her square in the eye, reading what he could.

"OK. Deal. Got your drinking shoes on?"

"Ha ha, Yep." She said a little nervously. Then, stronger now,

"Remember what I told you," she said, pointing a finger at him. "There's a lot riding on this, Chief, and I'm betting on you."

A half hour to go and Terri Russell, Submarine Qualified Chief Petty Officer, and Undertaker, climbed the ladder through the forward escape trunk, clanged over the brow to the wingwall, and walked the hundred or so yards to exit the base through the guarded gate.

It was a typical English winter evening; humid, sometimes blustery, the salty air heavy with history. The buoys belled out their songs in the harbor and the sound of leather shoes clop-clopping on cobblestones always brought back memories of those Christmas Carol movies she would watch as a kid.

She pulled the hood of her coat up over her head against the wind and rain. She picked her way around the puddles and, head slightly lowered as she walked into the teeth of the wind, she crossed the narrow old street.

Argyle loomed in the darkness just across the street now and she was walking into what would be either one of the best nights of her life or the worst. "Hit the gas" Uncle Johnny would say when there was a moment of doubt.

She actually revved her right hand in her pocket as she leaned into and pushed open the great oak doors that separated the modern-day Royal Navy from those times of the Press Gangs, Captain Bligh, Grog, and Breadfruit.

The great expanse of the place was remarkable. Three wide steps down from the entry to the main floor and out before her lay the great table with 12 places on each side set up with the appropriately sized beer glass filled to the rim.

She entered and bent forward a bit to throw back the hood without getting her hair wet. "Hey, honey! Wanna come hang out with us? How 'bout a beer?" She turned and looked into the now shocked and reddening face of one of her shipmates.

"Chief Russell!! Oh, goddammit, Chief, I didn't know it was you.... thought it was one of the local babes. I'm SO SORRY, Chief!"

"Yeah." She laughed. "Don't recognize me in civvies, huh?"

Demzer was standing there with The Tripod and they both were staring with their mouths open. Hair brushed, makeup, tight jeans and snakeskin cowboy boots made her look hot as hell and these two sailor boys were blown away.

"Wow! Demzer some nice boots! You here by yourself?

"I'm here for the boat race."

"You can sit over here with some of the guys; you'll have a good view."

"Well, thanks, but I'm actually IN the damn thing"

"Me and Tripod, I mean Petty Officer Margeson, too! I'm third, he said proudly." Demzer just realized that unless she was number two, then she was taking a bigger glass than he was. He stared and waited to see if she would tell him....

"Hey, there's the COB," was all she said.

They both watched as Durocher shook hands with the COB from the UPHOLDER. All smiles and niceties, but the underlying emotions were running high. It was then that something gigantic seemed to move through the room and skew the gravitational pull of the Earth.

Had we all been sitting outside enjoying a lazy afternoon, this behemoth of a man might have blocked out the sun. Petty Officer First Class Fergus Lowell Cornwallis walked up to join in the conversation.

All red haired, bearded, and with a toothy grin, Cornwallis was indeed an absolute house of a man. Only a week ago turned 30 years old on his tenth anniversary of joining the sea service, he was over a foot taller than Durocher. Rumored to weigh 330 pounds, he was every bit of it and maybe more.

His mates called him "Wooly Boy" which had less to do with the wild head of hair and full beard and more with how they used to weigh wool back in the 14th century.

As the story goes, to try and establish some consistency in the wool market, the Brits came up with measuring things in "Stones" as one Stone equals 14 pounds.

A proper sack of wool, it was agreed back then, would weigh 26 Stone even so the measurements and pricing could be regulated and fair. Cornwallis wasn't quite 26 Stone, but he was damn close enough.

No gut bouncing around over his belt buckle, no slop between his shirt sleeves and his upper arm, he seemed a gigantic pile of muscle.

He had come to the Royal Navy's Submarine Service by way of

the surface navy. His prior expertise was as a FLASH operator on an anti-submarine helicopter.

As do most Type A people, he looked for something more exciting, so he had become a SAR swimmer, as well. As everyone in the sea services knows, it's easier to make rank serving in subs, so he volunteered at his last reenlistment 3 years ago.

Demzer was non-stop droning on about something or other while Russell was sizing up her competition. One of that big bastard's hands was completely engulfing a pack of English Oval cigarettes while the other was strangling some kind of sandwich.

He had crumbs in his mustache, mustard on one great shoe, and his bellowing laugh seemed to blow back the hair on every head within 5 feet of him. Ten minutes to go.

Kitty could hear him chat with his mates. He had a deep and classic Scottish accent in normal speech, and there was always a hint of Gaelic when he was "pissed." Americans think this means angry, but over here, it means drunk.

He was far from drunk with so much on the line tonight. Another boat race, another win; ho hum. He was also far from comfortable. People would look at his great size and boisterous charm never knowing it was all cover for a shy and cultured young man.

He didn't want to be the center of attention wherever he went, but God had deemed it so. A man six feet nine is never comfortable. No piece of furniture is made for a person of such size.

Cars are hard to get into, beds are impossible to stretch out on, shoes are very expensive, the list goes on and on. Most people think they would love to be that big, but they would not if they really knew what it was like.

"Halo, mate! Kimmer uh ha oo?" he bellowed forth as he nearly knocked a man off his feet with a friendly greeting and slap to the back.

Once again, his brash demeanor was just a mask for a sensitive and somewhat self-conscious guy. He was truly happy to see this fellow, but a hug for his old friend was out of the question, so volume and zeal took its place.

It wasn't easy when you were the solitary type who enjoyed quiet days at home, to be the biggest guy in the room; any room. Everybody wanted to shake your hand and get to know you; probably out of fear you'll crush their little heads if they ran afoul of you.

How are you supposed to act when you're THIS big? The other men around you either felt intimidated and had to act a little tougher OR they felt intimidated and slinked around you for fear you would squash them. Either way, it was tougher to be him than it looked.

His greeting sounded to her strange, but it was clearly a 'hello' and a 'how you doin' kind of phrase. She wondered if he was born and bred Scottish.

His accent was so pure and the very sight of him stuck with everybody, that the Royal Navy used him in their Recruiting commercials that played through Scotland. In fact, he had been allowed to grow out his hair and beard since his last two months were spent trying to qualify for Special Ops.

Those guys were allowed to grow facial hair as part of their 'undercover' tough-guy persona. It was decided by Recruiting Command that a new round of commercials was to be shot with him costumed as an old sailor from the sail-powered days all bearded-up and hairy.

Sadly, he had washed out of Special Boat Service school because he couldn't fit into a device known as a SDV, or Seal Delivery Vehicle. It was a claustrophobic undersea transport device carried on the back of a submarine into which climb U.S. Navy SEALS to get ashore unseen and then back to the sub.

He had performed wonderfully in training overall, but his size worked against him a few times AND he snored horribly. So bad, in fact, he could give away the position of an entire team.

They wanted do a medical procedure on him to alleviate the problem, but he declined to have a permanent implant and was returned back to UPHOLDER. He had been growing his beard for 5 weeks during training, 2 weeks of video shooting before that, and would keep it up for the three weeks Leave he'd be starting. He'd cut the hair and beard and get all shipshape and Bristol fashion just before returning to duty.

He joined the Navy from the town of Inverness, a small town on the very shore of Loch Ness. Truth be told, he was born in Edinburgh to Robert and Edwina who had been killed in a car wreck some twenty years back on their way home from a cat show.

Their red Scottish Fold, Robert the Bruce, had placed second and, although somewhat disappointed, they were happy nonetheless;

they were always happy. They loved each other and thanked God every day for all the gifts He had given them.

In His mercy, God made sure they never saw the drunk driver cross the center lane and plow into them. They had been singing to the radio together and had just a second ago turned to look in each other's eyes; their last sight before the trip to Heaven.

The cat was thought to have been named after Scotland's greatest King from the 1300s, which would have been way too predictable. It was just a combination of his dad's name: "Robert" and "Bruce," which was Edwina's maiden name.

Father and mother had been killed instantly, the cat thrown from the vehicle was found alive and unbroken in his carrier well off the road in the weeds. Their daughter, Elizabeth, had survived as well, but with serious burns and a crushed sternum.

Son Fergus hadn't wanted to attend the show as he always found them boring, so he spent the day at Mixe Bixe garage learning to work on all brands of motorcycles. He had been guilt-ridden ever since with the undeserved feeling that he abandoned his family in their time of need.

The head mechanic and half-owner at Mixe, was a bloke named Waldo Michael Quinlan, a local tough-guy who previously worked odd jobs or drove a truck when he could get hired.

He been a long-time pain-in-the-ass to the local Constabulary drinking and carousing and fighting most nights. All that was about to change the night he ran into the Bobby everyone called "Big Bob."

It was said Quinlan had been dishonorably discharged from the Army after two tours in Afghanistan, but nobody knew the details. In fact, Waldo had been a top sniper for the Royal Marines. He was magic with a rifle and could hit a fly in the ass at 500 meters.

The horrors of war and whatever else drives a man to drink all caught up with him that day in Helmand Province during a joint Operation with the U.S. Marines.

Waldo had been assigned Overwatch covering First Street as the USMC cleared buildings. He had his beloved L115A1 rifle chambered in .338 Lapua with a clear view of the rooftops the whole way down the street.

Sadly, the night before, Waldo had again drunk himself to sleep and was a red-eyed stumbling slob when he came to relieve at 0600.

21

He took the prone position, sighted down the road with the responsibility to clear every rooftop in his area.

With blackest of black hair and mustache, his ice blue eyes melted the defenses of many a lass. "Glacier blue," his mum had called them, but, alas, they were dull, achy, and bloodshot this morning as they tried to scan the dry, war-torn landscape before him.

415 yards out, 3 bad guys with cellphones were lying on their bellies trying to see over the edge of one of the buildings in his zone of responsibility.

They were gesturing excitedly while eyeballing the intersection they had mined for a planned ambush. Their hope was to set off the munitions remotely as the American Marines crossed from one corner to the other. Waldo's spotter nudged him and whispered: "2 o'clock, I've got them at 415 yards, looks like 3."

Unknown to his spotter who was locked in on his own scope looking downrange, Waldo had fallen asleep and only the explosions from the street below snapped him back awake.

He couldn't find the right rooftop even though his spotter was yelling and pointing. Any other day, three heads would have exploded on that rooftop, but today, IEDs and alcohol led to the death of 6 American Marines.

In one of the great coincidences that happen when the Universe decides to play games with us, the last 2 Marines to die that day were in a Humvee racing forward and firing to cover the retreat of their comrades right after the first huge explosion.

One of them was standing in the turret returning 50 caliber fire up at the AK-47s raking them from the rooftop to their right. The belt ran out and he picked up the SAW laying at his feet in the vehicle and poured fire at the roofline while the driver tried to get him a good angle.

The next IED was remote detonated and the Humvee was thrown into the air and flipped before it crashed back to the street in a ball of fire. Both men inside were consumed by the flames and, yes, it was Theresa's Uncle Johnny. No one in their families would ever know that he and Waldo were forever eerily connected.

The Marines pulled back one block East as the A10s poured thirty-millimeter death onto those three on the roof. A second pass and the top third of the building crumbled.

Waldo was placed under arrest, flown back to England, and

dishonorably discharged from the service after spending a year in a military prison. Drunk and disorderly while on duty PARTICULARLY while engaging the enemy could have been a death sentence. Guess he was lucky.

Years of aimless boozing, fighting, carousing, pill-popping, and low paying jobs, all also fueled by guilt no doubt, brought him to another of his life's crossroads.

As the story goes, once upon a time, Waldo Quinlan was being arrested for his one millionth drunk and disorderly THIS TIME by a local Copper named Robert Cornwallis.

Mr. Quinlan, unintimidated by this Bobby's size, offered a wager that if he could whip the Bobby one on one, he goes free. "And if no?" the Bobby replies; "Then I'll come quiet and never take another drink in my life."

"I dunna believe ya"

"Waldo Quinlan may be many things, but oim a man o' me word," he slurred while pounding his chest, "but I get the first punch."

Officer Robert Cornwallis's thoughts drifted back to his academy training. Old Sergeant Mikklejohn, his hand-to-hand combat instructor, had told him:

"A reasonable man would think that most people will be respectful and compliant just because yer wearin' that badge. The harsh reality is that there'll be some who will try to shove that thing straight up yer arse. Let's enjoy the first eventuality, but prepare ourselves for the second, eh?"

The Big Bobby smiled; "Let 'er fly, bucko."

As this was just another 'Go Get Waldo' call to the Police and bound to get out of hand, so there were 3 other Bobbies on scene. Chuckling, each turned his back to an event he may have to deny witnessing at some point.

Now, we know that our British Navy friend, Fergus Cornwallis is a big boy, but his daddy's genes is where all that came from. Standing six six at 23 Stone, Big Bob dug in for the blow.

Waldo Quinlan, no midget at a good six feet himself, was outweighed this night by 40 pounds, but wasn't in the habit of losing a fight. He and his full snoot of Guinness were going to give this Bobby "What For" as the yanks say.

Well, Waldo's initial windup was planted full on the side of Big

Bob's face and the Bobby's head snapped to the right, came to a stop, then turned slowly back. His eyes stared straight and the corners of his mouth turned up in a slight smile at a suddenly clear-headed and shocked adversary.

Not to be caught off guard, Waldo rushed in for a chance to clinch and hip-toss his opponent. Instead, he found himself grabbed up tight by bollocks and throat, held flat about 8 feet in the air, and then thrown straight down to the cobblestones as one would slam down a barbell after the winning lift.

2 hours and 45 minutes later, Waldo woke up seated at Big Bob's kitchen table where a nice lady named Edwina was gently dabbing peroxide on his nose.

"Hello," she said pleasantly.

"Hello," he slurred as his jaw didn't want to move so well.

His eyes slowly focused on a smiling Bob seated across the table.

"I decided not to take you in."

"Why?"

"Has it ever done any good before?"

Long story short, Waldo and Bob became friends and Waldo kept his word about drink.

A year later Waldo started up a motorcycle shop as partner with his financial backer and fellow bike lover, Bob Cornwallis.

They agreed to name it "Mixe Bixe" as neither of their names sounded catchy enough, but Waldo's middle name lent itself to inventing a unique title.

After the horrible news of his parents' death had been broken to young Fergus, he was packed off to live with his paternal grandmother in Inverness. He, Robert the Bruce, and his younger sister, Elizabeth, who showed up after 4 months in hospital.

She was pretty much back together physically, but was now completely deaf and never ever spoke another word. I could have been the bodily damage from the accident, but some said it was emotional.

Being covered with brains and guts from your dead parents' bodies would stick with anyone, especially a seven-year-old girl.

So, here they all were, the last remnants of the family. A loving old lady who both cursed the loss of her son and daughter in law and thanked the Lord her grandchildren would spend the rest of her days under her roof.

The cat was now just called Big Bobby as a memento of Robert, his nickname, and his profession. Nowadays, the huge orange blob just loafed around the house and chased birds in the garden. No more cat shows for him.

He'd curl up in uncle Waldo's lap whenever the big man would ride a new bike out for a Sunday dinner. He'd look into Waldo's face and blink approvingly during the retelling of the fight story and the friendship that blossomed afterward.

The Cornwallis's had left behind a decent savings, life insurance, and the benefit of Bob's Police pension to Grandma and the kids. He'd also allowed for a 25-thousand-pound inheritance to Waldo and a signed document transferring his own half-ownership as a silent partner to his son.

On the day of Fergus' eighteenth birthday, Waldo rode out with another bloke in tow. He pulled up to the front of the house astride a majestic oversized chopper. A fully chromed frame set this one apart as did its kick starter. All the bikes nowadays had electric start "for the sissies," as Waldo would say.

When Fergus heard the rumble of the pipes, he came out the front door and whistled in adoration as his "uncle" got off. The white on red 62 Corvette pulled up behind and Waldo's friend Archie gave a wave.

"Happy Birthday, Lad!" and a hug. Waldo's eyes looked a little weepy.

"What's up, Uncle?"

He swept an arm toward the bike.

"She's yours. I've been putting her together nigh on 5 months now. '53 panhead motor, all tricked out. Look at that frame; swingarm, too! I made her bigger and longer to carry your huge arse; as bigger yet you'll no doubt be."

Fergus was flabbergasted. He looked from Waldo to the bike to Grandma (who knew about Waldo's plan this whole time) back to the bike, and was just about to tell his uncle he couldn't accept.

"Dunna tell me it's too much. Yer my family; all I've got. Yer Da saved me from myself and welcomed me in. He gifted me more than I deserve. I've got no one but youse. My heart to yours, boy, ride safe."

It was the second to last time Fergus Cornwallis cried before he found himself in His Majesty's Navy. The last time was when Big

Bobby crossed the Rainbow Bridge the following Christmas.

Kitty Russell was trying to size up this big Scot without appearing too obvious. She liked a bigger man, given she wasn't far from six feet herself. It had been a while since she had her legs wrapped around something like that. She was too young to abstain as much as she did.

Daydreaming now as it had been 4 months since that "Ratman" dude she met on leave last time. He was a really good kisser and somewhat aggressive in his approach.

She lost interest real fast in a "polite" lover. If you really want me, then take me, don't ask permission like some kind of limpdick. The shriek of a bullhorn brought her back to the matter at hand...

"Attention Lads and Lasses." It was UPHOLDER's Warrant Officer Watson who served as what the Americans called their Chief of the Boat.

Greying but fit, Watson had been around and ran with the Special Boat Service in Afghanistan until he took a 7.62 in the ass. It happened in a hot LZ taking small arms fire from all directions.

He was head down and ass up in a crashed and burning helicopter pulling one of his guys out. A random round from an AK47 somewhere went in one cheek and out the other.

"In a few minutes, we will be starting the great Boat Race between the Royal Navy's UPHOLDER (which drew a loud cheer from the room) and the USS DODGE CITY (less of a cheer due to smaller numbers, but loud nevertheless). It seemed everyone was pounding the tables. Watson held up his hands.

"It has been my pleasure to act as host for our American mates these last weeks as DODGE CITY will be getting underway in the morning for her final simulated deployment before taking her place at the tip of the American Naval spear!

From all of us here at Portsmouth, we wish you God Speed and Good Hunting!" Obligatory cheers rose from both sides.

Watson seemed to be enjoying the spotlight. He had a friendly and confident demeanor as it was, but one could sense he was already relishing the victory. He went over the rules for everyone one last time.

Three quarters of DODGE CITY's crew was here as one of the four duty sections was always on board. No officers tonight, though, as they gathered at some Brit Admiral's house to toast the eve of this noteworthy final preparatory deployment, as it were, of the first Artificial Intelligence system on a Fast Attack Submarine. True, there had always been some kind of automatic systems on the boats, but none designed to run the whole shootin' match.

"Now, if we can take our places. Master Chief Durocher and I will be leading off our teams with a symbolic toast. I have chosen a glass of one of our famous Single malt whiskeys for him as a classic taste of our island to fortify him as a seaman at sea."

It was Durocher's turn, now. "And I have chosen a glass of classic bourbon from America's oldest registered distillery to wash out some of the cobwebs from old Warrant Watson's constitution."

About half the room laughed, and most were lighting cigarettes and pipes in anticipation of the events to come.

The two old sailors stood facing each other. Literally hundreds of years of tradition stood with them; thousands of men had stood in this very room on their last night before going to war. Their last drink, last handshake, and last taste of home had been experienced right here.

The whole of maritime tradition looked down from the heavens as two crews took their places across the great table and prepared to defend their flags and honor.

As Watson and Durocher lifted their glasses and twined their arms, it slowly dawned on Petty Officer First Class Fergus Lowell Cornwallis that, standing across the table from him, was a woman. A woman.

He looked around for whoever it was he would be drinking against, but realized it was going to be her. A woman? Aye, the fucking Americans had dared to match him up with a woman.

He who sank boat crews from all over the bloody world. He who had been known to win after starting two men down, he who had beaten entire teams with little to no effort. He, the Great Cornwallis, faced a woman? Absurd.

They must be trying to cushion the blow of the terrible defeat they are about to experience.

"Well, we did have a woman on the team." He could already hear the excuses.

He then noticed she was looking at him; staring really. He focused his vision and looked her over. Tall she was. A little beefy in a powered up, muscular sort of way, but not at all ugly. He didn't like a skinny girl and preferred a lass who could hold her own.

He saw the slight smile on her full lips as she looked up at him. She gave a small wave and he nodded.

The words: "You haven't got a chance" passed between them, but the Great Cornwallis hadn't been the one to utter them. Then, smiling now: "You're messing with the wrong girl."

He felt the blood rise in his face and thought to himself,

"This wench is trying to mindfuck me," he thought. "She can play all the games she wants, but when the bear shits in the buckwheat, she'll have to hoist and drink.

Good luck with THAT, Lassie. "Right, then, I'll shut yer puss, ya jobby cow." He was pumping himself up.

She was thinking, too. She remembered the night she put on the Undertaker cut with her three-piece patch in full member status. She had been a Prospect, like every other member before her.

Uncle Johnny wouldn't let her take the easy way out. She spent many a night guarding bikes, washing them, running beers at whatever bar they were at, she did pretty much everything the others did. Putting on that vest was one of the highlights of her life.

A secret she had been hanging on to had to do with the fact that bikers have Road Names. If you look at a cut, or vest, there is a name on there like "Road Dog," "Lightning," something other than the person's real name.

This is usually done to keep the cops from figuring out who's who, but it also allows a level of anonymity and playfulness. Uncle Johnny, President of The Undertakers MC, had picked out her Road Name and hand sewed it to the cut himself, BY HAND in advance of presenting it to her.

On that night, the Undertakers rode as a club to a nearby MC's clubhouse where an outdoor party was already in full swing. It was bad form to arrive at an MC's event without an invitation and the Winged Devils did not seem very pleased to see the Undertakers ride up.

Although the clubs weren't exactly enemies, they weren't particularly friendly either. Upon arrival, Johnny went over to the chain link fence surrounding their yard and threw Terri's cut over.

"Want it? Go get it."

So, she walked up to the front door of the Devils' clubhouse. Some of the Winged Devils noticed her standing there. They had pretty much figured out what was going on and although supportive of someone trying to get member status, they weren't going to just let someone walk into their clubhouse and have the run of the place.

She was looking the place over trying to come up with some kind of a strategy when the Winged Devils President, Stanislaus Halko, came over to her.

Unbeknownst to Terri, Stan and Johnny had been high school acquaintances and Stan had already been briefed on the evening's events.

"So, you want that cut, eh? If you can get by me, then you go through them," throwing a thumb over his shoulder. "If you can get through them AND can get out of here in one piece, then you can have the cut."

The invitation to join the party had already been given; you did NOT insult another MC by showing up uninvited. The party had been scheduled as a celebration of their long-time friendship, Johnny's departure for the Corps, and Terri's accomplishment.

Sadly, Stan did not anticipate getting kicked in the balls. No, he didn't see that one coming, nor did he see Terri running over his now bent-over body at light speed and diving on top of the first table of Devils.

Glasses, dishes, pizza, cigarettes, and anything else not nailed down, went flying.

She pushed some guy's Old Lady out of the way and was roaring like a lion as she shouldered one of the Devils backwards and up into the air. He flew at least 8 feet before slamming into the buffet table and knocking all the hamburger buns to the floor.

Another of the Devils had her cut and was holding it above his head, taunting her to come get it. One more ball kick and he let it go as he tried to cover up in a fetal position.

She grabbed her vest off the floor, tucked it under her arm, spun around, and got tackled from behind by Big Mary herself, Stan's wife. Terri's head hit the floor and she was just a little dazed. Mary flipped her face up and spit about half a glass of beer in her face which woke her up real fast.

Now, Mary had the cut and was swinging it over her head like a lasso as she rode Terri like a bronc "Woo-Hoo-ing!!" the whole time.

The place went nuts and Johnny started having his doubts. Then, Terri got mad, bucked her hips up, and threw Mary forward into the air.

Protecting herself from face-planting into the floor, Mary let go of the vest and put her hands out to break her fall. Terri grabbed the cut and fast-crawled under that same first table snarling, kicking, swinging, and hauling ass all the way.

Diving back out the front door of the clubhouse "let's get out of here" was all she could breathlessly say.

Johnny held her back and put his arm around her shoulders.

"Jesus, I'm sorry, Stan."

"That's OK, Johnny. I should have known what I was getting into. She's your kin, after all."

Theresa looked at her uncle, then Stan, then back to her uncle, who then told her all had been planned in advance. Had she wussed at the door and refused to go in, the Undertakers would have left, basically in disgrace.

"In my heart of hearts, I knew you'd get that vest one way or the other. I also want to remind you that, other than your mom, I have two favorite souls in this world: you and my cat, Toby. I want YOU to take care of him while I'm gone, my bike, too, AND I want you to know who you really are to me."

He handed her the cut and she saw her secret name perfectly embroidered in the same exact color red as Johnny's beloved cat; the patch positioned and sewn in its proper place.

"KITTY." Her sacred name, her last gift from her favorite uncle, and she had given none of these Navy fuckers permission to use it.

The sound of the first two glasses hitting the table snapped both Terri's and Cornwallis' skulls toward the two old seadogs who started the race.

The mighty English Oak of the table resonated loudly as the cheering rose and soon nothing could be heard beyond the roar of "Drink, drink, drink!

Demzer's glass hit the table one beat before his opponent and the next in line hoisted and drank. The crowd roar was deafening and Bugsy Moran, number 5, put the American's ahead by a second.

The next two Brits wafted their 16 ouncers way faster than the Yanks and after 8 crew, the Americans were at least a full second behind.

The big ICman, "Rochester" Benny, drained his 40 no problem just like any Friday night in Compton and the Texas Tripod held

30

even with his man each hitting the table at the same instant with their 48-ounce pitchers.

This meant that Cornwallis and Russell would start together and nobody beats Cornwallis even up; nobody. Everybody knew it, everybody except Chief Petty Officer Theresa Russell, one of the first women to wear the Silver Dolphins, whose uncle made her an Undertaker, who taught her how to take no shit, and how to drink beer.

Every eye in the place was on Cornwallis in anticipation of the beat down about to happen and the whole room had become eerily quiet as the two anchors dug in.

The sound of Cornwallis's cow-like gulping of beer was unbelievable. In the great hall's silence, there was only the GA-WUMP, GA-WUMP sound he made filling his cavernous maw with Guinness and swallowing.

He downed beer as would some desperate, thirsty bovine whose head was fully inside of a water trough. His eyes were closed, and he hoisted that 64-ounce flagon almost 7 feet in the air, while GA-WUMPING his Adam's apple up and down.

It was the loud CLANG that caused him to choke for a second and for his baseball-sized eyeballs to fly open. He looked down over the edge of his vessel and saw Terri Russell standing as would a golf pro over a putt. Her back was straight and locked at about a 45-degree angle.

She was taking deep breaths and had both hands on an upside-down loving cup she had just smashed into the table. She had gotten her throat open, hefted that cup, hit the gas, and poured every drop right down her gullet; no swallows, no obstruction, no spills, no penalty, no doubt. Champion.

The entirety of the hallowed hall that was The Argyle momentarily stood in silent, respectful disbelief wondering what might happen next.

The spirit of Uncle Johnny watched in pride as did those of every Yank sailor ever to come before her. Terri Russell stared at Fergus Lowell Cornwallis who slowly lowered his tankard to the table.

In a deferential tone of genuine respect, he burred softly, almost lovingly in that Scottish brogue:

"Well, well, well. Congratulations. I can honestly say I've never been beaten, let alone like that. May I have the honor of your hand the pleasure of your name?"

She held out her hand and, as The Great Cornwallis gave it a shake, she yelled to the ceiling:

"I'M KITTY RUSSELL AND I RUN THE LONG BRANCH ON THE MOTHERFUCKIN' DODGE CITY!"

Every Yank in the place burst out in a bellow of "Kitty, Kitty, Kitty" as 3 A-gangers and 2 ELTs threw her backwards into a chair.

The whole of the American crew carried her aloft around the Argyle amid one of the most deafening roars the old place had heard since V-E Day.

It took ten full minutes for everyone to gather themselves and clear away from the great table. The bearers of Kitty's palanquin had returned her to the floor and all had resumed their places.

Warrant Watson faced Master Chief Durocher and held out the folded White Ensign. A gorgeous linen emblazoned with St. George's cross and the Union.

Strangely silent, Watson either had nothing to say, or couldn't bring himself to speak. The thought of losing the Boat Race never entered his mind. The reality of it was too much to bear.

He was repeating "I, I, I…" now and, sensing the absolute horror of this moment for the Brits, Chief of the Boat Joe Durocher took over.

"I do not have the words to describe how honored we are to carry the White Ensign to sea with DODGE CITY; she will command a place of distinction. Our maritime roots are here, in England. We jumped off together in two World Wars to defend free people everywhere from HERE, in England.

If I may borrow from the Bard, when we return from sea, if we do not go directly home, we hope to spend time with our adopted family HERE, "in this blessed plot, this Earth, this realm, this England." Thank you all for this distinct and invaluable honor."

Warrant Watson's eyes filled with tears, either from the sting of defeat or from listening again to those powerful words of England's greatest author, but he clasped Durocher's hand as he would a long-missed friend.

The Tripod yelled out, "Three cheers for Chief Russell!" HIP HIP HOORAYS, back clappings, and hand shakings all filled the Argyle.

Then one voice was heard above the din; the voice of Chief Petty

Officer Terri Russell standing before the Great Cornwalis began singing one of the great British sea chanteys (the only one she knew): "We have worked the self-same gun. Quarterdeck Division"

Then, after the slightest of pauses, Cornwalis in response: "Sponger I and Loader you. Through the whole Commission"

Both now, an Octave higher and in perfect harmony: "Long we tossed on a bounding main, now we're safe ashore, Jack."

Then, as though in answer to a baton-wielding conductor and in concert, the entirety of the hall joined in solidarity in that great British drinking song: "Don't forget your old shipmate, FALDEE RALDEE RALDEE RALDEE R-EYE EYE DOE."

Within 15 minutes, Chief Petty Officer Russell said her goodbyes and headed back to the boat. "Underway preps" was her excuse. The celebration at The Argyle went on well past midnight.

4

Earlier this morning, all departments had their final meetings to report on readiness to get underway. On a normal sub, the gangs and LPOs met with their Chiefs, the Chiefs briefed the Division Officers and met separately with the COB who was the only enlisted man invited to Officer's Call in the Wardroom. The Division Officers reported to the Department Heads and they reported their status to the Commanding Officer.

On DODGE CITY, she would sail with little more than a quarter of the usual ship's company. Most were senior people since they were standing supervisory watches while The Marshal operated the boat.

Morning colors was at 0800 and Captain Scott expected all officers ready to go at 0815. That meant in their seats, all documents ready, coffee or whatever already in front of them, fully prepared to give a detailed brief.

All Commanding Officers in the Navy are referred to as "Captain" regardless of rank. Most often on Attack Boats, COs are Commanders; O-5s.

Lazarus Scott was a full Captain, O-6, AND he had been the second to last CO of the old ALBUQUERQUE seven years ago. He was hand-picked for this job because of that experience and he was just one of those guys that the Navy called on whenever they absolutely had to be successful in whatever we were getting ready to do.

Lazarus? Fitting actually, because, as the story goes, he was born into a very religious family all blessed with names from the Bible. Well, his birth was a tough one, breach AND with the umbilical cord wrapped around his neck.

Ole Captain Scott comes out pretty much blue and dead, but the doctors brought him back to life guaranteeing his parents would go with Lazarus.

Scott was a shoo-in first-time pick for Rear Admiral and would be wearing two stars right after this deployment. No telling who the next CO of DODGE CITY would be, but that guy had big shoes to fill.

Scott was a rarity in that not only was he one of the smartest sons-of-bitches in the Navy, but he was loved by his crew. It's a rare officer who earns that kind of affection from his men.

It takes a combination of strength coupled with humanity, professional knowledge, and execution so precise that others respected you. It didn't hurt that there was a certainty in the heart of your crew that they were not only important to you, but, no matter what, you would get them back home.

The crew made sure that everything was 100% and that they gave their best effort. The reputation of the old ALBUQUERQUE, for the entire time she served, was that they were they best crew in SUBLANT and that they knew it; they knew the other crews knew it, and they knew the other crews knew they knew the other crews knew it. The worst thing that could happen to THIS crew was that they had managed to disappoint Captain Scott and that was NOT going to happen.

Lots of officers are stuffed shirts. They get nuclear trained and hang around long enough in the service that they get promoted. They look down their noses at enlisted men as though they exist to be personal valets and ass-kissers since they are further down the evolutionary scale from an actual Officer.

Just think about every Navy-type movie you've ever seen...it's all about the officers. Even Star Trek was about the Command people; the enlisted douchebags wore the Red shirts and they were always eaten by some monster down on the planet while some officer was the hero.

Scott was nothing like that. He had a mind like a steel trap and remembered everything. One morning, during a personnel inspection of the crew, he stopped in front of one of the Sonarmen and, after gigging him for a haircut, looked over his rack of awards and remembered from reading the man's service record 5 months before, that he rated the Sea Service Ribbon and one more star on his Good conduct award.

"Petty Officer Avery, weren't you on ARCHERFISH when she made that extended WESTPAC before you transferred to ALBUQUERQUE?"

"Yes, Captain."

"2 more gigs. Avery, your ribbons are wrong" he said smiling. Even Avery had to smile. The COB, who always trails the CO during a Personnel Inspection, leaned into Avery, and whispered "He got Payne for no Pistol Marksman Ribbon, so don't feel bad."

Scott was also some Nuclear Reactor hotshot and a procurement genius since he never forgot any requisition, vendor, billing, what have you. He'd probably wind up on the ORSE board or at the Pentagon Procurement Office spending billions in tax dollars.

Now, though, he was back in his old stateroom on his favorite boat (made better, of course). He was ALSO a fan of Gunsmoke and had all the episodes on DVDs. One more deployment and then Two Stars, a cushy desk, rubbing elbows with the muckety-mucks......he hated the thought of it. Anyway, underway tomorrow at 1330, 29 hours from now. It would be good to get back to sea.

"Engineering?" asked the Captain.

"Ready for sea in all respects, Captain. Tagout log cleared, nothing in the Out of Commission log. In fact, we received that piston seal we were waiting for on the Starboard hydraulics accumulator last night, tested just this morning early, and we are fully good to go."

"OK, Engineer. Auxiliary systems?"

"100%".

"OPS?"

"Ready for sea in all respects, Sir. MATT DILLON on line and interfacing with Navigation systems and COMMS is 100%.

The two Spooks arrived last night along with one maintenance tech and their gear is already integrated with the ECM mast and Radar. We are hosting two CTIs fluent in Russian, Ukrainian, and other such languages as well as the CTM to keep the gear running.

One of the Interpreters is a Senior Chief Lancey looking to add Dolphins to his uniform. He is Air Crew and ESWS qualified already. The other's a First-Class male named Mills and one Third Class CTM is female; Oakes, I think."

"Clearances are good, I imagine the COB has them berthed, and they are all set for Port & Starboard watches for the Interpreters while the maintenance tech is on call 24 hours."

"Supply?"

One of the few people in a Submarine crew without a personalized nickname, Supply Officers were universally known as

"The Chop," for pork chop since they ordered all the repair parts and all the food.

Individual petty officers from each division, held the collateral duty of RPPO or Repair Parts Petty Officer. Anything his division needed he ordered on a hand-written 1250 chit, turned it into Supply for digital rewrite as a 1348 by one of the Storekeepers, and the Chop signed off on it to get ordered.

"Ready for sea, Captain. A full 120-day store of provisions aboard which, for us, will be good for near 9 months on normal rations if God hates us enough to leave us out there that long".

This particular deployment was scheduled for 80 days, longer than average, but smart Chops filled the boat with food whenever they could. The fresh stuff, veggies, fruit, milk, eggs, lasted about 12 days. After that, it was fake eggs, powdered milk, and so on for the duration.

Canned goods were stored everywhere; loaded into racks in the store rooms until full and then they were placed on the deck in the berthing areas. Sub sailors walk on their food and can tell how far into a cruise they are by how much of the floor is visible versus how much is covered with number 10 cans.

The cooks made bread and pastry products every night as called for on the menu and prided themselves in being the best cooks in the Navy. Even in the middle of the night, the smell of sticky buns went everywhere as a sub's ventilation system moves A LOT of air. If you could smell it in the galley, then you could smell it everywhere.

Guys would actually get up out of their racks during their off-watch time to head down to the galley and beg for a taste. The cooks would always make extras but act like they were so put upon.

A Navy cook could not only bake breads and all types of sweets, but also prepare meals for an entire crew FOUR times a day; he could plan menus 4 months in advance, calculate, order, and store foodstuffs, keep everything spotless, and cook very, very well. Any restaurant that had the chance to hire a former Navy cook would be wise to do so. DODGE CITY had 5 cooks now since Chief Russell reported aboard.

She had already made a difference because she convinced the Chop, her Department Head, to get some of those Western-wear bartender vests that Sam wore when tending bar at The Long Branch on the TV show.

The cooks loved them and wore them serving meals…they even used those garter belt looking things on their sleeves. Paul Macdonald, the number 2 man to Russell even started walking around with a stiff leg and, of course, eventually earned himself the name "Chester".

Last month, December, the Christmas spirit got the better of Mac (they didn't call him Chester, yet), and he was inside the freeze box taking inventory and singing Christmas carols at the top of his lungs. Well, the COB opens the freezer door and gives Mac an exaggerated quizzical look.

"I can hear you all the way the fuck out here."

He hands Mac a cup of coffee, tells him to move over, climbs in and they both start singing together. As only Karma can do, Captain Scott walks into the galley sniffing the cinnamon buns and, looking around for the duty cook, hears the singing coming from the freeze box, and opens the door. "What kind of nuts have I got in my crew? Are you both in here singing Christmas Carols?

"Yes, sir".

"Move over".

He squeezes by the COB, after all, room is getting short in there at this point, and the three of them launch into Good King Wenceslaus. That's the kind of CO Scott is. That's why you want to go to war with a guy like this.

"WEPS."

LT Bradley B. House was DODGE CITY's Weapons Officer. Anything to do with Weapons Delivery, which means Firing them NOT sending them somewhere, Fire Control, SONAR, the Data Systems guys who cared for the AI, DECK DIV, which usually the COB oversaw, and all the small arms gear AND the SEAL Teams should one be deployed with the sub.

House was also very well-liked by his men. He was about 6' 3", college volleyball player, and a Mormon which he never spoke of, for some reason. He treated people with respect, spoke softly, and struck people as a kind person who SOME people thought they might be able to push around.

It would be a mistake to do that as Mr. House had one of those lines that, should you push him over it, he would flip into a death-dealing ass kicker who had no problem jacking a guy up really bad. It took a lot, but it was something to see.

The gang-banger who tried to rob him on the way back to the boat in Ft. Lauderdale would attest to this as well. Right after this dipshit gets the knife out of his pocket, House whips a spinning backfist into the guy's head and, as he's falling to the sidewalk, he front-kicks him in the gut for the finisher.

The rush of putrid air from this guy's lungs and the gasps of the 3 chicks sitting outside of The Button pretty much said it all. House takes the guy's knife (which he didn't even have time to open) and throws it into the surf.

One of those 3 chicks comes over and says she and her friends saw the whole thing and how cool it was. They really want to buy him a drink. It seems that asshole had been bothering them just before B.B. House happens by.

Long story short, he goes into The Button with them, has a few drinks, fucks the red head in the bathroom and the taller of the two blondes in her car about an hour later. He never tells anyone about it; he's just that type of guy.

"Weapons Department ready for sea in all respects. All weapons communicating with The Marshal, nothing tagged out, nothing OOC, topside will be unrigged after quarters."

That was pretty much it for Officers. Usually about 13, most of them junior, DODGE CITY had a minimal crew so 4 Department Heads, the XO and CO only this deployment. No time to qualify new officers on this OP.

"Excellent. Medical?"

Now, this is an interesting situation as found on a Fast Attack submarine. There is no doctor. There is a Hospital Corpsman; One Hospital Corpsman. He does it all; for everyone. Submariners had to be completely 100% medically cleared BEFORE the boat went to sea. Dental, too. All wisdom teeth out; all cavities fixed.

The Corpsman, called "Doc" by the crew, gave shots, if necessary, treated the odd case of clap, oversaw the urinalysis program that determined if people were getting irradiated, stuff like that. He reported directly to the Executive Officer, or the XO.

In addition to those duties, Doc Adams also had an interface with MATT DILLON as each crewman had been voluntarily microchipped and, as long as they are within 50 feet or so of the boat, are monitored by The Marshal.

This morning, Doc had a problem that was about to get moved

up the Chain of Command. The Marshal was highlighting 4 guys whose readings were out of spec. Temperature elevated, coughing, BP up, heartrate up.

"Captain, Medical Department ready for sea. The Marshal is flagging 4 men as out of spec in terms of temperature, cough, BP, stuff like that."

"Hangovers, Doc?"

"Possibly, sir. If we didn't have the AI, then I wouldn't give it another thought. It's hard to ignore when the lights are flashing yellow."

"Keep an eye on it. Let the XO know if things get worse."

"Aye, aye, Captain."

"Chief of the Boat?"

"Captain, all hands berthed including the riders. As you heard, one of them, Petty Officer Verona Oakes, is female so, since we have less crew than we were designed for, I put her in lower level to give her a little privacy. It's empty down there except for her; she doesn't mind.

To not blindside her, I told her about the Marshal's video system, and I made sure she was aware that it was off-line. I explained the design and purpose just so she was clear there was no intentional invasion of privacy or any weird shit like that.

I also risked my reputation as a devout sexist and took the liberty to introduce her to Chief Russel already so she had another woman to chat with. Every officer looked to the Captain to see if he would get a chuckle out of that quip and, as he did not, they did not."

"Verona's an odd first name"

"Yes, sir. It's a city in Italy, I think."

"Was she born in Italy?"

"Don't know, Captain."

"Speaking of Chief Russel, I hear there was a disturbance in the Force last night."

Every officer freely chuckled at the Captain's quip, though.

"Captain, I've seen lots of drinkers in my short time in our blessed United States Navy, but NOTHING like the exhibition she put on last night. She walked in, destroyed the Great Cornwalis, and left. She even had the political savvy to engage Cornwalis in a Brit drinking song as a face-saver, I guess. All business; no bullshit. Their flag is in a clear plexiglass case in the forward end of the Crew's

Mess."

"A Case? Where'd you get a case with ZERO days' notice, COB?"

"From UPHOLDER's warrant. He bought it in advance to display OUR flag after our 'inevitable' loss. He couldn't bear to look at it, so he gave it to me."

He said he would have preferred another bullet through the ass than have to surrender that flag. He could tell the Captain had no idea what he was talking about…

The Captain then stood, which means everybody stands, so all present stood, and followed Scott out to the Crew's Mess.

Leaving the wardroom through the After door brought you into the Crew's Mess its forward end. There were three, 6-man tables down the centerline and 4, 4-man tables along the bulkhead, port side of the boat.

All the bulkhead locker doors were covered in wood-grained Formica and the overhead was a mass of cable runs and pipes, all painted white. Chief Russel was standing in the forward end of the mess giving the TV screen a wipe.

"Hello, Captain."

"Hello, Chief. I just wanted to see your prize flag adorning our Mess. Heard you put on quite the show."

"It's OUR flag, Captain. One Team one Fight. After all, there were 12 of us on the team; I just finished it off".

Scott chuckled, rubbed his hands together like the villain in a Dudley Do-Right cartoon, and stood in front of the new case. He noted how beautiful the linen was, the embroidery, the vibrant colors.

He was thrilled; he loved to win, and he loved it even more when winning reflected on the entire command. There's an interesting "winning" story people tell from way back when the boat was still the ALBUQUERQUE.

Every once in a while, The Navy decides to make believe the balloon has gone up. Out of the blue, no notice, phones ring and everybody get your asses down to the ship, get underway, go to "war."

This whole evolution is officially called a TRE, a Tactical Readiness Evaluation, a "TREE" to the crews. It's basically an inspection to see if we can sustain a war response and weed out the fucked-up boats who can't find their asses with both hands.

The phone calls went out around midnight. Pack a bag, get aboard, we'll tell you what's going on later. In case you were wondering, everything about the U.S. Submarine Force is SECRET. What they do, how they do it, where they did it, All SECRET.

Until they're already at sea, the crews don't know for certain where they're going or when they'll return. These guys don't even let their wives in on anything. The Silent Service earned its name for secrecy as well as how quiet they are at sea.

Anyway, ALBUQUERQUE was pretty much ready for sea except she didn't have a full torpedo loadout. In order to load torpedoes, a tremendous number of HEAVY pieces of equipment have to be hoisted by crane from inside the boat, assembled on the pier, rigged back on TOP of the boat, and torpedoes loaded one at a time.

By the book, it should take around 9 hours to rig all the equipment and then it's 15 minutes per torpedo to get them from the pier to the torpedo room.

Well, 6 hours and 20 minutes after the first phone call went out initiating the TRE, ALBUQUERQUE's completely assembled weapons loading skid was lifted and placed on the pier, 12 weapons had been loaded aboard, and she was ready to back out from Pier 32 and head to sea. ALBUQUERQUE's torpedo gang was known up and down the seawall as The Death Squad. Every other boat sought their help when there were problems.

They had been in fistfights with everyone around and had all been arrested together after a particularly big bar fight. These guys were as good as it got and a real throwback to the days of Steam fish and hard-charging Knuckle draggers.

Why were they able to complete the loadout so quickly? From the moment the drill was announced, two of the bigger Torpedoman, Sweetwater and Lemon, carried, on their shoulders, about 2 tons of equipment, 2 pieces at a time, from the Torpedo Room where it was stowed, up 3 levels and onto the pier to construct the giant topside skid.

They RAN up and down, made about 30 trips, and had saved hours doing work normally done with the help of a crane; but there was no crane, yet. Normal people wait for the crane, but The Death Squad waited for nobody, they were definitely Mission Oriented.

All the loading equipment got rigged ungodly fast. Every possible corner was cut, every hour of practice showed in speed, even the Duty Machinist Mates and Sonarmen pitched in and helped carry until the TMs who lived out in town could get to the boat and dig in.

There were 7 Fast Attacks in port that night, all of which got notified of the TRE at the same time. ALL needed a crane for something from topside equipment removal or just pulling the brow. It was all planned by Squadron TWO to make the exercise as challenging as possible.

Public Works sent their ONE crane down to the waterfront where 7 Commanding Officers were each demanding their boat be served first. They were even comparing dates of rank to see who was senior. They called in every favor they could, but, obviously, only one boat could get the crane first.

ALBUQUERQUE's Chief Torpedoman was something of a Softball God shortstop and played not only for the boat team, but also for the classiest strip club out in town.

As luck would have it, a close friend of this Chief Torpedoman played Second Base for that same strip club. When he wasn't playing softball, this man, Paulie Gineros, was a crane driver; THIS crane driver.

This very night, the Dispatcher at Public Works had assigned him to work the waterfront and support the boats getting underway. He may have been assigned the task, but he is in charge of deploying his crane, what he says goes, and he has decided to support ALBUQUERQUE, and his Shortstop, first.

Well, all those other COs were shitting bricks and calling the Commodore to complain as the crane made its way from Pier 2 along the waterfront.

Moving at a blistering 3 miles an hour, it passed by the old Steamfish shop where Ace Parker had installed every torpedo ORDALT all the way back to the MK7's; past the Escape Tower inside which submarine sailors had "Ho-Ho-Ho'd" for years and years, ever northward toward the Floating drydock and Pier 32 where sat his friend's boat.

The Squadron Weapons Officer, acting as a drill monitor, and no fan of the Animal Boat, was having heart palpitations as he inspected ALBUQUERQUE's torpedo handling equipment.

He complained of finding "unapproved tools" and couldn't see anyone following the evolution with the Operating Procedures. He told Scott to stop the load and Scott quietly replied: "Get off my boat."

Captain Scott had his ass chewed and threatened by every senior officer available that night. From the other COs, to the COMMODORE, to SUBLANT himself, but he stood firm and reiterated his faith in his Chief Torpedoman (whose MOST recent selection for SENIOR Chief Torpedoman was in jeopardy over all this shit), Weapons Officer, and crew.

Every opportunity was taken, by any officer in such a position to do so, to make clear to him that, if anything went wrong, OR if anyone got hurt, his career was toast. Enlisted guys, especially Chiefs, help each other at every turn, but it always seems that Officers circle like sharks when one of their own is in jeopardy.

It's also important to note just WHO that Chief Torpedoman was: Motherfucking Joe Durocher. Joe had his own way of doing things and he wasn't very good at playing politics. He had made Chief twice and this was his second time as Senior Chief, too, which is why all his hash marks, all 12, are red instead of gold.

Anyway, after just over six hours, ALBUQUERQUE's massive topside loading skid and all ancillary weapons handling equipment were lifted off the boat by Paulie's crane and placed on the pier.

Twelve torpedoes loaded, backing out of berth 32A, heading to sea FIRST; impossible. The boat had barely passed Race Rock on a Flank bell to the dive point when Chief Durocher found himself in the CO's stateroom at attention.

"Durocher, it has been reported to me BY THE SQUADRON WEAPONS OFFICER, that the weapons shipping equipment was missing bolts, no written procedures were visible anywhere so he presumed them to not be used, and unqualified personnel were handling weapons loading equipment. Is that true"?

"We were missing ONE bolt out of four in the baseplate. Wasn't going to throw my hands up over that. WEPS was up in the Bridge with the Procedures so he could look down and see the entirety of the loadout and anyone NOT a qualified Weapons Handler was NOT handling anything weapons related."

"Just to remind the Captain, 12 men other than Torpedomen are qualified in some aspect of Weapons Handling. Their names are in the Qual Book. Most guys were helping in some way or another, though, Captain."

"Why, Senior Chief. Why would you push the envelope like that?"

"I was told to play it as though we were at war. My division was the only one not ready for sea. Since we were not fully loaded out with torpedoes, we were holding up the underway. I was going to do whatever it took to be the first boat to answer the call; the rest of the crew felt the same way."

"Cooks brought us coffee, Sonarmen helped carry equipment up from the Room along with Sweetwater and Lemon, both of whom I intend to put in for Commendations, by the way."

And, yes, it's the same Sweetwater and Lemon who are on DODGE CITY now that were on ALBUQUERQUE then. Durocher made phone calls and got the two of them TAD'd for an undetermined amount of time to get this boat through the last half of the shipyard and the Simulated Deployment.

Sweetwater had been on two other commands since ALBUQUERQUE and was about to be booted out of the Navy for pushing his LPO during a, shall we say, lively discussion.

Lemon had just made First Class and was thinking about getting out as he was recently married. Both jumped at the chance to sail on their old boat with their old chief and favorite CO.

Luckily, both were 688 class qualified Chiefs of the Watch so that was the excuse Durocher used to get them orders. He not only knew all the Detailers, but the Admiral in charge of BUPERS actually went to boot camp with ole Joe.

"Captain, you know that we've got two nuke weightlifters that can each bench about 450; so, since the crane hadn't arrived yet, they held the sideplates in place while my guys sent the bolts home."

"Even one of the messcooks helped grease the topside skid. If you remember, sir, I had air lines made to plug into 125-pound service air and bought some air wrenches, so we don't waste time with ratchet sets.

Those particular tools are NOT mentioned in the Conventional Weapons Manual, so I can't consider them prohibited if, in fact, those tools were mentioned by the Squadron WEPS."

"Yes, it sounds like a tire shop when we're loading weapons, but it saves hours. The ALBUQUERQUE boys were loading ordnance like a machine and I was damn proud to be one of them. Sorry if I caused you problems, sir."

"God dammit, Durocher. Sometimes I hate the way you do things, but if we ever DO go to war, you are going with me."

THAT was Captain Scott. None better. When he found out he was going to Command DODGE CITY, he made some calls. He needed a Chief of the Boat that would do whatever it took to get the job done. He wanted Durocher, by this time FINALLY a Master Chief, for his COB.

Scott had been warned against Durocher, though. Up and down the ranks over 40 plus years of service. Regarded as a smart-ass and disrespectful to officers, he could be very insubordinate. Not many knew him as well as Scott did.

Durocher did not put up with any bullshit or ass-kissing and felt it his responsibility to bring all the facts to his boss' attention even when others feared being the bearer of bad news. When the shit hits the fan, you want guys like this standing with you.

5

Liberty expired at noon. Quarters were held topside; the Spooks were introduced to the crew and the Maneuvering Watch would be stationed in an hour. Chief Russell eyeballed the men through her sunglasses as Petty Officer Oakes was introduced. Lots of elbows, smiles, and although she couldn't make out the words, the same tired comments about her being able to make a lot of side money at sea....

Russell and the COB had had a nice little chat behind the shore power boxes on the pier this morning. Coffees and a couple of last cigarettes since submarines were smoke-free nowadays. He wanted to wrap up the "lesbian" thing. It wasn't even an uncomfortable talk as he had been very Dad-like the whole time. He was one of those guys that hated the idea of women on subs.

"Russell, I'm a very old-fashioned guy. That's not always a good thing as I tend to initially revolt against change, ANY change until, it sinks in with me a bit."

"I don't think I'll ever get past this new "woman" thing in the military. It's not because I don't think women are capable of doing a man's job; it's because if they were jobs for women, then we wouldn't call them "man's jobs.""

"I think that, psychologically speaking, men fight to protect their homes, mother, apple pie, all that shit. I think that a man will try to protect the woman in the next foxhole rather than do his job. Do ya know what I'm getting at here"?

She knew what he meant. She'd heard all this before. She agreed in a way, but he could never see it from her perspective because you have to LIVE it from her perspective.

"I've also known a number of really great guys whose careers were absolutely destroyed over the mere appearance of untoward conduct. One guy I knew and served with early in my career, had a Tootsie pop in his mouth during a Weapons Handling evolution on the pier in Norfolk.

One of his females, someone he had been working with for 18 months, saw him with the stick hanging out of his mouth said: "EL

TEE, got anything else to suck on?" He pushes his hips forward just the slightest amount and everybody who saw it, including this young lady, laughs.

Well, someone reported it to the Commodore and within 3 months, this Lieutenant, a former enlisted man who worked his way up, is out of the Navy. Had that exact scenario have been played out the exact same way but for a male sailor asking him they very same question, then he would have stuck his hips out the very same way, everyone would have laughed, and the work would have carried on with nary a word said. Put a female in the equation and all hell breaks loose."

As she saw things, though, the macho man thing of the military was always womanizing and hard drinking. Women were secretaries and nurses. Men were heroes and women were there to serve them.

Yeah, things change, and through fiat, women were now eligible to fill combat roles and serve in formerly male-dominated worlds like submarine service. Promotions were faster, career opportunities were more diverse, and women should have an equal opportunity to reap those benefits if they qualified for them.

Part of the problem was that, in order for the new "women friendly" guidelines to appear to be a good thing for the service, the women applying were either held to a lower standard, or were passed through with a wink and a nod, or they just fucked their way up the ladder. That's the reality of it.

It's also not uncommon for some women attached to sea-going commands to just happen to get knocked up right before deployment. They would get taken off the ship, assigned to some shore duty billet to calve, and some poor slob male sailor got yanked OFF shore duty and had to fill her billet so the ship could meet the mission.

Russell was a little different in that she was not one of those weak females that needed accommodation in order to be successful. She was tough and smart and proved that an attractive woman could command respect through performance and earn the respect of her peer group. She learned right away that a girl in the military was fair game and you better be ready.

Boot camp was her first exposure to sexual harassment in the Navy. Horny boys and girls in bathing suits trying to certify as a Class III Navy swimmer as part of their initial training. If you fucked anything up in Boot Camp, even if you got sick, you risked getting an Assignment Memorandum, commonly referred to as being ASMO'd which meant getting left behind as your company moved on. The damn Company Commanders would threaten you with getting ASMO'd all the time. You would stay right at that point in your training cycle until you passed whatever it was that held you up. If it was bad enough, you could even get sent back to the very beginning. Spending one more day in Boot Camp than was absolutely necessary was a horror too nightmarish to bear.

So, if you were a girl struggling to pass swimming, then you either got ASMO'd to work on it and improve, or you had a personal counseling session with one of the swim instructors to see what could be done. What oh what can we ever do to get this little piece of paper signed for you today……. hmmmm?

The instructor offices just happened to be isolated from all the pool noise and there was always an instructor or two willing to give you their undivided attention and work with you as best they could.

They were always willing to listen to suggestions on just how they could help a girl get through this crucial part of her training. After all, if you're gonna be in the Navy you better be able to swim.

Theresa was a good swimmer and didn't have to offer a blowjob or get bent over the desk in order to pass. She knew when it was happening, though, and got a knot in her stomach at the thought of one of these city girls who may have never even seen the ocean before, so afraid to get sent back, that they would give head to get by.

We're all supposed to be in this together and it hurt her heart to know that some of those instructors were like that. Where was this comradery she had heard about?

That's when she started playing the dyke role. She wasn't a lesbian at all. She just knew that if you gave these guys an inkling you could be had, well, they'd try to have you. It wasn't just the sexual assault aspect of it; it was being put in a position by a senior person where they figured you owed them a debt of gratitude.

Being assigned to work directly for the Commander, or the CMC instead of out there in the scullery might be deserving of a little fooling around here and there. C'mon, how bad could it be?

Some girls were ok with it. Like most normal people, they liked sex and it was safer and more pleasant fucking the Commander at his summer home than some enlisted goober from bumfuck Egypt in the barracks.

No way was that an option for Theresa Russell. She wasn't going to be disrespected like that; no way would she disgrace her name and her family acting like that. She was just going to put up this façade of disinterest with which her superiors chalked up as HER problem and not hold it against her for refusing them.

AND, if you think just reporting them, those men who wanted to fuck you, or created a hostile working environment for you, or made comments or pinched your ass was easy, then you don't know what it's like when everyone closes ranks against you. Once you get labeled one of those, "Me Too" pains in the ass, then none of those bullshit movements are going to help you live a peaceful life.

"I get it. I can see how it would work for you professionally, but what do you do in your personal life?" Durocher asked. He was smooth. He couldn't just ask "What do you do for dick?" as he wanted to and inwardly laughed at the thought of actually saying it to her.

He didn't know her well enough, yet. She might laugh; after all, she told him she was a biker chick, they're not little prissy bitches. He'd just keep it professional right now and let her define the relationship.

"Thanks for the chat, COB. I feel better now that someone gets me."

"Don't sweat it, Chief. Goes no further. Keep me cut in if there are any problems in this regard."

"Will do."

He flicked his last Camel into the drink and, as Chief Russell walked away, realized she hadn't settled the "dick" question.........

Everyone was back aboard, all lines had been taken in, Pilot onboard, one tug tied to port, and she's heading to sea. Two hours to the Dive Point and then on to Station. The lights were already off in berthing, clocks set to ZULU time (time at the Prime Meridian), and the typical submarine 18-hour day had begun. 6 hours on watch and twelve off for most watchstations.

Historically, on a fully manned crew, if you were a senior watchstander like Diving Officer or Chief of the Watch, you might be in 4 section, 6 on 18 off, if there were enough qualified guys. These watches made up part of the Ship's Control Party which also

THE WRONG GIRL   MIKE DeROSA

included the 3 junior guys who stood rotations as Helmsman, Planesman, and Messenger while submerged.

When running on the surface, like now, only the inboard station, the Helm, was manned and one of the other two was up in the bridge as Lookout. Every half hour or so, they would rotate to keep from getting stale.

Most of the crew was usually in a pretty good mood early in the run. It was good to get back to sea. When you were at sea, you wanted to be home and when you were home you wanted to be at sea; it's a weird sailor thing. The standard Fast Attack boat took about 105 crew to sea, but DODGE CITY only had 38 souls on board including the Riders.

The Artificial Intelligence was designed to operate everything. This deployment was the last step before a fully autonomous boat would deploy. The crew here were just supervisors of the systems and roving watch standers that would verify that all was in spec.

An interesting aside is that Capt. Scott had been one of the outspoken doubters about integrating AI in a submarine. Oh, he knew the ship's systems could technically be operated and monitored by an AI; his concern was the intuitive call a human would have to make from time to time. Like maybe, oh I don't know, actually firing on a contact.

Yeah, the Marshal could track him and target him and program the torpedo, but do you want a machine to make the decision to sink some other country's ship?

Maybe the AI felt threatened; maybe the contact was making maneuvers as would a ship in attack mode. Even though no formal declaration of war existed at that moment, maybe the other ship had launched a preemptive attack; maybe lots of things whose nuances and subtleties could only be sorted out by a Command-qualified Naval Officer and not a program designed by who-knows-who.

At this same particular meeting when he was airing his concerns, he offered to regale everyone with a "Sea Story" making his first deployment North as a Junior Officer. It's all been documented in the Patrol Report, but USS CORPORAL had been making a high-speed transit all night to get into her operating area.

They slowed for morning traffic and, as they came shallow, they found themselves in between two Soviet subs firing Exercise shots at each other in some kind of training scenario.

As they passed through 150 feet on the way up to Periscope Depth, Sonar shouts "Torpedo In The Water!" over the 27MC. The CORPORAL's OOD yells "SNAP SHOT TUBE ONE" as the appropriate response to a torpedo being shot at you is to shoot one back.

It took seconds before they realized what was actually going on out there and that they were NOT under attack. They secured from SNAP SHOT and snuck away. Would an AI been able to check fire or would a couple of Rooskies been on the bottom as WWIII broke out?

The brass heard him out, but they weren't listening. This was a plum project with the full support of the political elites, the contractors were already lining up to present their bids, and he was asked if he wanted Command of DODGE CITY or not.

Career suicide was not in Lazarus Scott's playbook, so he took the job hoping he could figure a way OUT of this Artificial Intelligence crap. At least he could find a face-saving way for the Navy to incorporate AI, but maintain a Command Structure and minimal crew of experts, just like they were doing now. Time would tell.

The refit didn't address the ship control systems and just left the two steering wheels in place. Modern boats had the "Pilot" position where a single senior enlisted operated an airplane looking joystick to control up, down, and sideways. DODGE CITY still had three sections of Helmsman / Planesman / Messenger, Diving Officer, and Chief of the Watch, so 15 guys that were unnecessary on newer boats.

The Marshal really didn't need anybody as he would detect oceanographic conditions like temperature, pressure, and salinity to adjust the ballasting of the boat automatically as well as move through depth and course without human involvement.

The Navy was just having a hard time completely cutting the cord, hence the token crew. Auxiliary man of the Watch, ICman of the Watch and all levels in the Engine Room were manned with roving watches. Add in the officers, the 4 guys in Maneuvering and you have 35 unnecessary, ultimately irrelevant people.

Probably the only two guys with any real purpose were the Data Systems guys, Hochstetler and Schiano. They existed solely to keep the YUKs on line as they served every technical system on the boat including Matt Dillon.

Most guys were walking around having a coffee and watching others do their jobs. The TVs were on in the Control room so you could see what the periscopes were seeing. State 1 seas, so it was just a gentle roll; ah, the sea.

LT Magness was the OOD up in the bridge with Bugsy Moran as Lookout. The Navigator, our favorite Officer LCDR Kennedy, was looking over the plot and comparing it to the charts. He picked up the 7MC mike, "Bridge, Navigator, recommend coming right to new course two one zero."

Then, Magness replied, "Navigator Bridge, Aye."

"Helm, Bridge, Mark your head."

"Bridge, Helm, Steering One Seven Five"

"Bridge Aye. Right 10 degrees rudder, Steer Two One Zero".

"Right ten degrees rudder, Steer Two One Zero, Helm, aye."

"The rudder is right ten."

"Very well, Helm".

"Bridge, Helm, passing one eight zero coming to two one zero."

"Very well."

"Passing one nine zero coming to two one zero."

"Passing two zero zero coming to two one zero."

"Very well."

"Steady two one zero."

"Very well."

Quite the little dance between the OOD and the Helmsman. Usually the communication choreography goes: "Him, Me, What." If you're Sonar, for instance, and you want to tell the Control room something, say you've got a contact at one eight zero, you would report that by saying "Conn, Sonar, hold a contact bearing one eight zero." It's him first, then you, then what you want to say.

"Maneuvering, Conn, make turns for 12 knots" is something you might hear followed by "Make turns for 12 knots Conn, Maneuvering, aye". See? Simple. It's one thing to pass information, but quite another when an order is given.

Always repeat the order to ensure understanding. Where Sonar was passing information about holding a contact in the previous example, Control, the Officer of the Deck specifically, was ordering Maneuvering to do something. Same with Helm orders.

Forty-five minutes later she slowed to 1/3 and the remainder of the Ship's Control Party, the XO and CO were all assembled in the Control Room getting ready to submerge. The Navigator is on Number 2 scope and the Captain orders the OOD to clear the bridge and lay below.

The bridge suitcase, the box with the communication systems, compass, and rudder position indicator, was disconnected and sent down the trunk.

Moran climbs down, Magness climbs down, pulls the hatch shut and reports Last Man down to the CO. It's approaching 1700 hours; only 30 minutes to watch relief, so Scott retains the deck and the Conn.

"LT. Magness, I relieve you."

"Aye, aye, Captain."

"This is the Captain; I have the Deck and The Conn."

"Straight board" is yelled out from the BCP as all monitored hull openings indicate SHUT.

He turned to the Navigator and told him to enter into the Deck Log that he, the Captain would retain the Deck and the Conn until the first underway section came on watch.

On the 1MC, now: "This is the Captain. We'll maintain the Maneuvering Watch until we set the evening watch at 1800 Zulu. Section 1, eat and relieve".

"Lower all masts and antennas. Diving Officer, submerge the ship and bring her to one five zero feet."

"Submerge the ship, aye, Captain. Chief of the Watch, sound two blasts of the Diving Alarm, announce DIVE DIVE, and sound two more blasts."

The Chief of the Watch, or COW as he was known, was the fifth man of the ship's control party. Where the Helmsman operated the rudder, engine order telegraph, and the fairwater planes, the Planesman the stern planes, the COW operated all the ship's systems from his panel, the BCP. Lots to do, lots to know, and only your best guys qualified as COW.

As you would surmise, Chief Petty Officers usually stood COW, but First-Class Petty Officers were encouraged to qualify as well. The Submarine Force always encouraged its people to learn more and assume more responsibility. The more you knew about your boat, the more respected you were in the community, and the more you could be counted on when the shit hit the fan.

The Diving alarm sounded twice, the COW announced "Dive, Dive!" on the 1MC which was heard everywhere, and the Diving Alarm sounded twice more.

"Open all main vents"

"All main vents open"

Now, as the air is released from the main ballast tanks, the ship descends into the arms of the sea. You better hope all the valves and systems are lined up correctly, the crew has done a proper job Rigging for Dive, because the sea is now all around you, constantly trying to get in and kill you all.

The Diving Officer of the Watch, referred to simply as "Dive," was in charge of the planesmen, messenger, and chief of the watch. His job was to 'Reach and maintain ordered depth.'

He would accomplish this task by adjusting angle on the ship, pumping water out or flooding it into the Trim System tanks as necessary to compensate for fluctuations in the ship's buoyancy.

Buoyancy was affected by oceanographic conditions like temperature, pressure, and salinity. Achieving neutral buoyancy was the hope, but maintaining ordered depth was the goal. Ship's angle could be changed, shaft rotation increased to hold her up, lots of factors affected a boat's ability to stay on depth.

There are two things you never do: The first is Broach, meaning you popped up from your hidden place beneath the waves and you were now flopping and bobbing around on the surface like an overweight and pregnant whale. The second is to operate outside the SOE or Safe Operating Envelope.

This 'envelope' was delineated by a graph of speed versus depth which showed how fast and deep, or slow and shallow, you could go without risking a broach or dropping below Test Depth.

"Pump 4000 from Aux 2 to Sea".

"Aux 2 to sea, 4000".

The Dive and COW worked together to lighten the ship by 4000 pounds. Once the Ship Control Party could hold depth with minimal plane deflection and hull angle, the Dive knew the ship was in satisfactory Trim.

"One Five Zero feet. Trim SAT." The Officer of the Deck, OOD, was now free to order bells and give Helm orders.

"Very well Dive. All Ahead Standard, Make your Depth 500 feet."

The Engine Order Telegraph rang as the Helmsman's arrow and the arrow moved by Maneuvering matched up.

"Answers All Ahead Standard."

"Very well."

"Helm, right 10 degrees rudder, steady two seven zero".

Heading West now, DODGE CITY was making her way toward her operating area. At this point, only the Captain knew the details of the mission. The first evening meal of the underway was being served on the mess decks.

There were 4 meals during a Navy day at sea. Breakfast, Lunch, Dinner, and Midrats. Meal hours were 5 and 11; one hour before the watch was to be relieved and you ALWAYS relieved a half hour early.

The Morning watch began at 0600. Breakfast started at 0500 and your dead ass better be relieving your guy at 0530. Earlier is better as anyone who relieved at the half hour exactly was derided as a "Bell Tapper," and no one liked a guy like that.

"Chokers and Sliders" tonight, known in Civilian Land as Hamburgers and Cheeseburgers, was a favorite meal among the crew. The line down middle level past Doc's office had formed a little early, as everyone was hungry after last night's Liberty and the day's preps to get underway.

Mac had cooked and Russell had spent the day checking menus, making sure everything was clean and ready to go. Just about every other boat in the fleet had a big buffet line, but DODGE CITY still served family-style with bowls of food passed around each table.

The aftermost 6-man was the Chief's Table and the damn messcooks better make sure it was perfect ALL DAY LONG. Right now, Pappy sat there alone as he was the oncoming Diving Officer.

Marty Graves, from somewhere backwoods, Virginia, was his COW, but sat outboard at the neighboring 4 main table as he was a First-Class Petty Officer. "There's no food on the Chief's table, God Dammit!"

Oh, shit, that was McCleary. No matter what he said, the sentence ended with "God dammit." It was actually quite hilarious. Many a time, interactions similar to this one could be heard:

"Gimme a screwdriver, God dammit."

"Plus, or minus?"

"The Phillips, God dammit!"

"What size, Senior?"

"The BIG ONE, God dammit."

"Why the fuck's this screw on so tight, God dammit?"

On and on it would go because his guys would ask more questions than necessary and drag it out and laugh about it later.

They called him Pappy McCleary because he looked about 90, but was really about 15 years younger than the COB. He would talk all gravelly and loud all the time and you'd swear he hated the world and would choke a puppy to death if he had the chance.

Graves, or Gravy as he was called, was another funny sonofabitch as he had a strong Southern accent and always talked like he had marbles in his mouth. He told stories all the time and most of them involved one of his life accomplishments which he would invariably add "and Muh momma cried" whenever he wanted to reinforce just how wonderful this deed was.

The crew loved him, and he was one of the most knowledgeable about the boat and one of the scariest checkouts to get when you were trying to qualify. He was petrified of the 1MC microphone, though, and as Chief of the Watch, he was in charge of using it to make ship wide announcements especially during a casualty.

"Man Battle Stations," "Dive, Dive," "Rig Ship for Ultraquiet" were just some of the important announcements the COW had to make.

You knew when Gravy was on the panel because you would hear the click through the speakers which heralded a 1MC announcement, but there would be silence and another click when Graves took his thumb off the button.

Even during a drill, he would stare at the mike and sweat profusely; just couldn't talk into it until the absolute last second. Then, his southern garble would take over, and you might hear "FAR in the Engine Room." Well, it wasn't FAR; it was FIRE, but he was saying it the best he could.

Pappy and Gravy had the first watch and were half-ass anticipating the secret event that might be happening during their watch. No, nothing to do with the mission, or stealthy ops, or anything to do with saving the Free World. They were wondering if there'd be a Mail Buoy.

"What's that"? You might ask. One tradition of submarining is called "Getting the Mail Buoy" and it's actually a hazing trick played on a new crew member to fuck with him a little while welcoming him to the crew.

"We don't got any new guys, God Dammit."

"Yeah. I memba muh first deployment. They had me runnin' all over the boat trahna get some Relative Bearing Grease for the Torpedomen."

"That's a funny one…mail buoy's a little cruel, though, God dammit."

So, to sum it up, there IS NO MAIL once a submarine goes to sea. The Navy will forward any mail to whatever port they may go to, but there's no guarantee the mail and the boat will be there at the same time since every submarine Op is Top Secret.

A new guy doesn't necessarily know that, so someone will mention that the boat has a chance to get mail at a Mail Buoy …. but we need a volunteer to swim up and get it.

Well, the new guy, already intimidated by the whole newness of just being aboard AND feeling totally useless because he's not qualified to do anything and the crew constantly reminds him how useless he is, just may volunteer to be the hero.

He puts on his bathing suit, a lifejacket, gets coated in grease because the water's cold and we, his good buddies, want to protect him, wears flippers, a dive mask, and sit under the trunk hatch in Control until the Captain can maneuver the boat to right under the Mail Buoy.

Then, our new hero, is supposed to climb up the trunk, open the hatch to the bridge, and SWIM AWAY FROM THE SUB TO GO GET THE MAIL.

Do you see how ridiculous this is? This poor bastard might be sitting in the Control Room for hours, all nervous, shivering, smoking his last cigarette back in the day, waiting for the big moment, and eventually someone will laugh and give it away.

Everyone will laugh at this poor fucker and then clap him on the back, shake his hand, and tell him what a good sport he is. Well, no new guys this run because it's so special and we don't even have half a crew.

Back to Senior Chief McCleary for a second. Pappy's story was a sad one; the kind that could make you cry and spit nails at the same time. The Tripod happened to get it from him in Paulie's Anchor

Bar outside of San Juan.

On his way back to the boat for chow, Tripod passes by the bar's big front window, looks in, and sees Pappy sitting there looking all weepy and shit.

It's well known that Pappy usually spends an entire Liberty drunk and either talking real loud to strangers with a lot of God Dammits or sitting alone in some corner.

Now, Pappy's from the Old Guard, you know, and any good sailor back in Pappy's day left a Liberty port "Blued, Screwed, and Tattooed."

"Blued": A Blow Job; "Screwed," fucked some chick, and "Tattooed" speaks for itself. Why the hell do you think old salts have all those tattoos?

Anyway, the Tripod takes the empty stool next to Pappy and buys him a beer.

"What's going on, Senior Chief?"

"Just another day in paradise, God Dammit," he
says wiping his nose on his sleeve.

"Seven years, today. Always surprised when I see another year."

Pappy is kind of talking to Tripod but not really. He's just looking down and sighing.

"What's seven years?"

"Since she died. Since I killed him. Since my life came to an end."
Pappy looked toward the ceiling for a second revealing teary, red eyes.

Whoa, what the fuck was this all about?

Pappy looked up at Tripod and could see the question in his eyes. "I know you don't know. Nobody knows except Joe and the CO. The Navy sealed the whole record."

Tripod pulled his barstool a little closer to Pappy.

"I'll sit right here with my mouth shut and you can tell me whatever you need to tell me, Senior. I'll take it to my grave, if that's how you want it."

There is a bond between military men. I used to hear it said: "You fight for your country, but you die for your friends." All those dead Marines jumping on hand grenades don't do it for the Constitution; it's to save their friends. This was one of those bonding moments.

"I wasn't always a mean and terrible man, Margeson. I used to be happy and nice to people. I even had me a wife. She was kind and loving and beautiful. Amazingly, she loved me through and through. Back in them days, I was convinced that God actually loved me, too, because He sent such an angel to ME."

He punctuates his story with a fist to his chest and starts actually sobbing. A whole minute or two crawled by. A guy at one of the tables was looking at Pappy with a smirk on his face, but Margeson's death-stare made him look away.

"Seven years ago, tonight, outside of Portsmouth in that Texaco across from the shipyard," he looked at Tripod for an acknowledgement that he knew the one... he nodded.

"We got gas on our way to go camping up in the Blue Ridge for the weekend. Always went to this one place, Peaks of Otter, outside Bedford. Well, the card reader on the gas pump was broken, so after I fills up, I goes in to pay.

I figure that while I'm in there, I'll get her an ice cream cone. We'd always share one when we were riding around in the truck. I pick a cone out of the rack and, before I even start to fill it, I hear screams behind me "COLIN, COLIN!! I can hear it right NOW, God dammit." Pappy calls for a double Jack and shuts his eyes tight like he's afraid to look...

"Some druggie homeless bastard has got in the driver's seat and is holding a knife to her neck wanting money. He sees me start running for the truck, so he puts it in Drive and floors it.

He got about 50 feet toward the other set of pumps and my Sharon grabs the wheel. She slams into the column holding the roof up over the pumps and the truck stops dead."

"I'm running the whole time and, as soon as I get to his window, he yells "Bitch!" and jabs the knife into her neck."

Petty Officer Second Class Robert Margeson sits in stunned silence and shoots Pappy's double Jack.

"One more here, please," he says to the bartender.

"She's looking at me with desperation in her eyes, and I can't get the driver's door open because it's jammed from the crash. The guy is holding his bloody mouth because he slammed his face into the steering wheel when they hit and he sees me."

"Blood is pumping slower and slower from my wife's neck and I see her hands slowly drop down to her lap. Sirens in the background, people running over, and all I can see is this sonofabitch holding his chin and smirking at me.

I punch through the window and happened to get one hand in his mouth, grabbed one of his cheeks and the other ear and pulled him through the broken window. We both fall to the ground and my back is burning in the hot anti-freeze dripping out of the engine.

This bastard is making shrieking sounds and people were yelling at me to stop, stop, but I couldn't stop."

"One of the cops that just got there was holding a gun on me. Later, they told me I was biting chunks out of this fucker's scalp and spitting them onto the ground. Apparently, all I said was 'Not yet.' Not sure what that meant.

"Bottom line is, my Sharon died right there, in our truck. I had ripped off that bastard's ear and tore part of that fucker's face off with my bare hands."

The cops had just rolled up and had no idea what had gone on; no idea who's who. They think I'm the criminal and he's the citizen who was sitting in his truck when I come up on him. They're trying to pull me off him and kept hitting me with their nightsticks.

Well, I've got this motherfucker in a Marine Death Lock; one arm across his throat, one on the back of his fuckin' head, both my legs wrapped around his body holding his arms down, and sent him to hell.

"He died?" The Tripod gasps in disbelief.

"Oh, "died" sounds too calm; too peaceful."

"Your grandma 'died,' your good ole dog 'died.' I killed this motherfucker dead and he went out horrible; all bloody and screaming. Sounds better, more deserved, instead of just "died."

"Makes me feel good knowing he gurgled, and choked, and struggled, and bled everywhere. He twisted and bucked and then went stiff as a board. I felt him giving in to it and going and I only felt rage. Fuck him, and I'll tell you something else, when I get to hell, I'm going to kill him again, and again, and again."

The Texas Tripod had no words. What can you say to a story like that?

"Anyway, I'm celebrating the 3 years of joy I spent with my beloved, darling Sharon. I'm celebrating that she is in Heaven and that he is in Hell. I couldn't save my wife, but I killed that motherfucker; killed him good. I would do it again and the man that says he wouldn't is a god damn liar."

"Well, Pappy, here's to Sharon and here's to you."

They clinked glasses and sat together in silence for a long while; Pappy remembering and The Texas Tripod imagining.

Pappy starts talking to no one in particular… "It's a cancer, memory. So few good ones after a while. The bad ones stay with you, all day, all night, all the time. Can't drink enough, sleep enough, stay busy enough. Can't kill 'em, God Dammit."

Then, things started to get out of hand as the booze and the pain all kicked in. Pappy turned around to that smirking little asshole in the table behind him.

"Been watching you in the mirror, god dammit!"

Margeson, at 6 feet 5, stood and put an arm across Pappy's chest.

"Let's not fuck this guy up, Pappy. He ain't that guy and it ain't his fault."

Pappy looked down at the floor, nodded, and sat back down.

6

Magness turns the Dive over to Pappy and Gravy relieves as COW. Five hundred feet, Ahead Standard, heading dead West for another 5 hours before the turn North. Transiting is always boring as there's nothing to do except cover ground and "punch holes" in the ocean.

The evening watch was also when the movie was shown in the crew's mess and things settled in for the night. Any drills were often run during the day as were the All-Hands training lectures and stuff like that.

At this time of night, the non-quals, if we would have had any, would be studying while the galley was getting prepped for the night baker to make bread and sticky buns. Tonight, though, things were about to take a turn...

About an hour into the watch, a lone figure appeared in the after end of the Control Room just inside the door to the SINS room. Covered in grease, carrying a Kapok lifejacket and flippers, goggles, and a snorkel positioned above her eyes and absolutely rocking a red, two-piece bathing suit, stands Cryptological Technician (Maintenance) Third Class Verona Oakes.

A tense silence descended and you could almost hear the threads of all the submarine poopie suits straining to hold back the boners now growing in Control.

All Petty Officer Graves had to do was look to his left to see Oakes smoothly sliding into Control. His eyes must have been all bugged out and he certainly heard his mama crying somewhere. It was almost as though he also heard the angels in heaven all hitting that harmonious high note as she made her presence known.

Even Pappy couldn't take his eyes off her reflection in the rudder position gauge. He womped Demzer on the head because he kept turning around to see and getting further off depth.

"God dammit! What's a matta witchoo cock suckers? Never seen a girl before?"

Obviously, somebody had gotten this girl to buy into the Mail

Buoy thing. Instead of guys covering their mouths or looking away or giggling, all eyes were riveted on this hard body tentatively making her way into Control.

Every space on a submarine is Air Conditioned and kept COLD because of all the electronics belching out the heat. Most guys wore sweaters on watch, just to show you how chilly it gets.

All that the A/C was doing right now, though, was to help chill Petty Officer Oakes' erect nipples and draw even more attention to her perfect rack. In fact, it almost seemed as though the damn A/C wasn't working at all as suddenly it was getting a little warm in there.

About 18 eyeballs had traveled the length of Oakes' body from the slender neck, to the 36Ds, to the shapely six-pack, and all the way down those athletic legs.

"What are you doing here, Petty Officer?" It was the fucking Navigator getting ready to ruin it for everybody. He was probably the biggest perve on the boat, so you think he'd let us all drink this in a while.

"Aren't we getting the Mail Buoy?"

She looked around the Control Room and turned completely around as she said:

"Don't tell me there's no mail buoy."

Besides having already watched the movie in their brains about ripping this girl's clothes off and having her in every possible sex position, most guys started to feel a little bad.

Even if the joke was played out, she couldn't be welcomed as a crew member; she was a rider and they'd never see her again after this run.

"I heard there were no volunteers, so I thought I..."

She trailed off. Kennedy, in an uncharacteristically soft tone of voice and a surprisingly considerate act, told her there's no mail buoy "This Time," because of the nature of the operation, but he wanted to thank her very much for volunteering. The crew would be very appreciative that she would offer and certainly wouldn't forget it.

"Oh, OK sir. I'll just lay below and get back into unform, then."

Oakes walked all the way from the Radar stack, forward past the 3-inch launcher console, made her way behind Pappy, and out the forward entrance on past the CO and XO staterooms. Every eyeball locked on her.

The crew wouldn't forget it, he says. How in the fuck were they going to forget it? These are all piss and vinegar military guys loaded up on testosterone.

Oakes was one put together chick and they were going to tell all their friends THIS story forever, especially that one kid; there's always one in the group that, when something like this happens, he can't just ogle but has to fall in love.

There's always one guy at the strip club that has to fall in love. He'll hand his paycheck over to one of those bitches and believe every lie she's telling him about spending time together with him and how she thinks of him all the time.

So, who was it this time? The Puppy Love award goes to: Dusty Hochstetler! Mister pure as the driven snow Amish Hochstetler. Most guys thought he probably never even sniffed a glistening pussy before, which wasn't true by the way, but he was deep in love now, and one fine piece of ass she was.

It could have been anybody, but Oakes was about to find out that a more perfect ally could not have been had. To have smitten the very guy that works on that Marshal; just perfect.

Once she had gone down the forward ladder middle level, a new show began.

"Messenger!" The OOD roared.

"Yes, Mr. Kennedy?"

"Lay below and get me that Senior Chief Spook. Get him up here and I don't care if he's sleeping!"

"Aye, aye, sir."

About 5 minutes later, Senior Chief Terry Lancey walks into Control.

"You sent for me, sir?"

Lancey was 22 years a sailor and had had his ass chewed a few hundred times. He knew how to handle himself. Originally an Aviation Machinist Mate, he left the carrier Navy and, as a re-enlistment incentive a while back, he wangled a seat in one of the military language schools in Monterey.

Got himself a rating change to Cryptological Technician Interpreter (CTI), which was much more critical than AM, and started to see parts of the Navy never available to him before.

He had graduated with honors and fluent in Russian. Of course, he had a good start since his original family name was Lankovich and his grandparents only spoke Russian around the house.

The end of the Cold War saw a decline in how crucial Russian speakers were as it became very important to focus of finding and/or developing Arabic and Mandarin speakers. Since DODGE CITY was heading North, Lancey would stay busy monitoring the ECM mast and listening to the Trawlers making believe they were fishing.

"Senior," Kennedy started out slowly, "Your Maintenance Tech was just up here in a red bikini, all greased up, offering to get THE MAIL BUOY!" He was already yelling at that point.

"We can't have half-naked women wandering around the Control Room!"

"You're yelling at me for what reason, Commander?"

Kennedy stood stunned. He was one of those officers that could not fathom the idea that someone, let alone a lowly enlisted man, would question him.

"She reports to YOU. What the fuck was she doing up here all ready for THE MAIL BUOY? You do know what I mean when I say MAIL BUOY, right, Senior Chief?" Kennedy was now bellowing as he felt he had the upper hand.

Terry Lancey had been around. He was not only wearing Surface Warfare and Air Crew pins, but two more sigs, his Qual Board, and he would add Silver Dolphins to his chest. Not many men have 3 warfare pins.

"Of course, I know, but I'm surprised to hear that an officer of your rank and experience would condone performing such a hazing ritual on a U.S. Navy Ship of The Line!" he says with feigned indignation.

"You may not be aware that the Navy frowns on hazing, but it's your boat. Oh, and I didn't tell her about any of this shit and I certainly didn't send her up here. I'm not sure of the point of this discussion." Lancey was piling on the phony outrage.

Well, ole Kennedy looked like he'd seen a ghost. Eyes all bugged out of his fat face and his neck vessels straining against the macaroni and cheese-like clogs blocking the blood flow to his stupefied brain.

He was trying to speak, but rage only allowed him to make noises like "Gack" and that sucking sound one always seems to associate with fava beans and a nice chianti. Or maybe that one a person might make if he'd been underwater too long and came up gasping.

You couldn't disagree or argue with LCDR Kennedy unless you were willing to withstand an assault of personal attacks outside of anything germane to the discussion at hand if that was all the ammo Kennedy had.

"If you think of anything you'd like me to do to rectify this situation, then you just have your messenger come get me again, sir."

Lieutenant Commander, formerly Senior Chief Nuclear Trained Machinist Mate, and current Officer of the Deck Kennedy was apoplectic beyond words. He seethed inside and rifled through his mental file of a hundred time-tested insults that have been hurled from Officer to Enlisted man for over 200 years.

He was so incensed, that he was incapable of cogent speech and rational thought and just stood silently staring as CTCS Lancey walked out of the control room, sauntered past the CO's Stateroom and the XO's Stateroom to slide down the forward ladder handrails to middle level.

Doc Adams was in his office and had been watching the microchip readout all this time and, now knowing what happened with Petty Officer Oakes, understood why so many blood pressure readings were up. He could even trace the beginning and end of the conversation between the OOD and Leading Spook; Kennedy had even gone yellow for a few seconds.

None of the riders had been chipped as they were not crew; just filling a temporary role during the Deployment. Doc would have to check in with them every few days or just wait to get a complaint. After all, if you don't want worms, then don't turn over any rocks. Everybody was green, now, except for Kennedy still showing yellow.

The usual calmness of the evening watch took over the boat. The occasional whoop or cheer from the Mess Decks during the movie was actually comforting to everyone as they represented normalcy.

Petty Officer Oakes had returned to her bunk in Lower Level berthing, which she had all to herself, and collected her soaps and what-have-yous to get in the shower.

She laughed inwardly knowing that none of those dumb swabbies had any idea she was fully aware of that Mail Buoy bullshit and had just decided to give them a show they wouldn't forget. It was a power play bound to conjure up an ally. A woman that held power over men could get anything she wanted and sex sells, so, there ya go.

45 minutes later, she's back in dungarees and getting a cup of coffee before working on her equipment stowed in the Computer Room. Very important that she have access to this space.

Not just because her gear was there, but to have access to Marshal Dillon when her plan would be executed. The truth of it was that she didn't WANT to do any of this shit. She HAD to do it. HAD to save her.

7

She hit the doorbell button outside the computer room and waited for someone to open the door. There were only two DSs on board and it didn't matter to her which one it was; the single one would be easier....

Hochstetler opened the door and smiled outwardly as she smiled inwardly.

"Petty Officer Oakes! I was wondering when you'd get up here. We have to get you an access code."

Doors to sensitive spaces on board had a ten-digit cypher panel that accepted your access code. The record of comings and goings made it easy to narrow down who came and went and when, should something go wrong.

The Cryptological test and maintenance equipment was stowed in here even though there was a Crypto room on the sub right next to the Radio Shack.

All that stuff was predominantly for communications, but all Lancey's gear was in there now, too. It was from this room he would monitor different radar bands to determine what vessels were sweeping the seas out there. He would eavesdrop on communications and lower the ECM mast whenever he felt it might be discovered by enemy radar.

Raising the mast was always at the discretion of the OOD since it would, obviously, expose the boat's position, after it was requested by the on-watch spook.

All of Oakes' gear was in addition as it consisted of test equipment, spare parts, and whatever she need to keep the monitoring and recording gear operational.

Crypto could download a six second burst from the SSISIX satellite when the boat was at periscope depth and then we'd take an hour or so to print everything out once we went back deep. News of the day, routine skid traffic, and the Family-grams were all part of that burst.

Once the Radiomen printed out the Family-grams, they would

usually put them in a fancy envelope and deliver them to whichever crewman got one. It was a big deal to hear from your family, especially when you served on a military command that never got a MAIL BUOY!

Sometimes there were problems, though. If the boat had to go deep quickly as in having been detected, then the Family-grams might get cut off when the mast dipped below the surface. Then, somebody might get a sentence like: "Everything's great except for your brother, Bobby, who....................." Then, the guy would have to wait, probably unable to sleep, until the next Family-gram to see what the hell happened.

"Can I call you Verona?"

"Sure. You go by Dusty?"

"Well, the crew calls me Dusty because they think Amish people use words like 'Dost' and 'haveth' and 'thou' so I've been messing with them and talking like that. I'm Adam."

She chuckled as he would probably expect her to, but she had a bad feeling about using "Adam." It smacked of a familiarity the two of them would share which might set off alarm bells for the crew. But if they all used it....

"I'll call you Dusty, too. I like it."

Oh, she could read it in his eyes that she had hooked this fish deep. There's this twinkle men get when they either really really LIKE a particular girl or they really really want to fuck a particular girl. Hochstetler was doing some serious twinkling.

"Fine. Got a 4-digit code in mind you'd like to use for the door? Don't tell me, just enter it...now."

She watched him activate the code reader and then turn his head so she could enter her code. It was almost like using a PIN at the bank.

"All set."

"OK, you're good to go. Come and go as you please. The Marshal will keep an eye on you", he said with a playful tone.

"Yeah, this Marshal thing is way cool. He's tied into everything? This him over here?"

Yep, you familiar with the TV show, Gunsmoke? You get the whole thing we do because the boat is the DODGE CITY? Yep, she knew perfectly well what the deal was. Dusty was pretty proud of his role integrating the AI into the ship.

He was there from day one, all through the shipyard, and right here on deployment. Could mean a big award or even a promotion once they got back...assuming everything worked the way it was intended.

"Yep, this is the front panel or MMI as we call it. Man – Machine – Interface." Usually, the MMI is the biggest physical part of any technology as we keep making digital circuits smaller, but fingers and eyeballs stay the same, so keyboards and ocular readers never shrink along with the equipment.

For me to talk to the Marshal, I have to use MILSPEC keyboards and they are comparatively huge. When you look at the system in its entirety, there are keyboards in Sonar, Fire Control, even the Doc's got one.

Each department with access is limited to that part of Matt Dillon that they use and can't ever get access to the whole system. Only the Captain and I."

He said this last part with a touch of pride and with a twinge of showing off; trying to impress the girl, I suppose. You also have access to your area once we sign you into him...are you ready for that?"

For the next ten minutes, she went through the 7 screens necessary to verify identity and mission critical equipment and selecting a log in. Smooth sailing and now she was operational. The whole time they were chatting, she could sense his nervousness. Any time she would turn to look at the equipment, she felt him eyeing her. This was the right guy.

"Verona. Interesting name. Named after a distant relative?"

"WAY more boring than that." She laughed as she spoke and her sparkly eyes really had poor Dusty's attention. He had been smitten out in the Control Room and now, her sweet nature and playfulness were just pulling him into the web.

There was this time back in SSET (Shipboard Security Engagement Tactics) school where they taught you to eliminate threats posed by armed personnel or terrorists who had gotten aboard your boat.

There were several paper poster type targets you would shoot at on the range. Some of the pictures were of adult males pointing a pistol at you, or someone being held hostage with the gunman to his rear.

But there was this one poster of a man who was standing next to someone who was holding a gun on him. This someone was depicted as an attractive woman; long brown hair, tank top, and big tits. The instructor said to the class:

"Watch it, don't let your guard down and get

blinded by a hardon, because this is the one that's going to get you".

Dusty had forgotten that day on the range and had no idea that he was, at this very moment, the man in that poster.

"As the story goes, just about 6 months before I was born, my daddy got hired at Case I/H in Fargo. We were driving from our hometown in Montana along Route 94 to our new place.

Well, were about a hundred miles from Fargo as we approach the exit for Route 1 in North Dakota, the big green exit sign reads "Verona and Oakes", one name over the other, which are the names of the two towns you can get to if you take this exit and go South.

Well, our last name's Oakes and, since my parents hadn't picked out a name for me, yet, my daddy has this epiphany seeing the thing and decides his little girl is gonna have her own billboard, so he pulls over, stands next to the sign like he's going "ta-da," and mom takes his picture.

They printed it as one side of the birth announcement for their little Verona that they mailed to everyone when I was born. He blew that photo up into poster size and it's hanging in his house to this day. He still tells people they named Exit 288 after me.

Well, old Dusty heard about half that story as he was just lost in her eyes and the movement of her lips as she told her story. He hadn't felt this way about any girl since Abby and still had that horrible knot of guilt in his belly that was fighting it out with the butterflies he felt in the presence of this girl.

Yeah, Abby, the reason he joined the Navy; the story he never told. Nobody ever asked him, really, they would just say something like "Never heard of an Amish kid joining the service," and just left it at that to see if he wanted to fill in the blanks. He never did. All that "dost-ing" and "thou-ing" and "thee" bullshit really kept the boys at arm's length since they thought he was serious.

It's amazing how so much can go through your head so fast; how much time and how many events can be reviewed in your head in fractions of a second.

72

The whole time Verona was chit-chatting about this being her second trip on a sub and how nice it was to have Lower Level Berthing all to herself; he was remembering Abby. He could see her face; he could still smell her when they made love and then again when they found her body.

His thoughts went to that one spring at the time of Rumspringa in Pennsylvania Dutch country. It was that time of life when Amish kids are "permitted" to sow some wild oats.

There's dancing to the songs they've been secretly listening to anyway, singing, drinking, fucking (even though the elders never actually admit it); it's time to explore and actually get away from being Amish to see if you want to stay Amish.

The strong Amish boys, chiseled physically from lives of hard work and chiseled in their discipline from a lifestyle of abstinence and responsibility, found willing participants in not only their Amish girls, but the "English" girls tired of the wussy, Liberal boys at school.

They were young teens; she 15 and he 17, but Rumspringa for them became much more than a Hall Pass. She wouldn't walk away from her life. She needed no such break from being Amish, but she wouldn't rub her parents' noses in her lustful addiction to Adam.

They fell in love, fell hard; first kiss and all that. Hiding their feelings from everyone all the time while trying to find secretive places to meet.

He was breathless around her; he loved everything about her. His belly ached when they were apart and he couldn't sleep. He would furtively glance her way in church and at meals when they were separated men from women hoping no one would notice.

They would almost collide in their running to embrace each other out beyond the haystacks whenever they could think up some lie to get out there.

He would stare at her face, trace every line, and drink in the taste of her. They were totally determined to be together and felt God's presence in their relationship. They were meant to be joined forever.

Then, she got pregnant.

Every so often, other families experienced the same thing thanks to the constant mating during Rumspringa. When that did happen, they just accelerated their daughter's wedding date so childbirth occurred respectfully during a marriage and the shame of babies out of wedlock did not sully their family name.

Like many kids in this age group, neither Adam nor Abby had ever had sex before, nor did they understand the precautions and certainly never considered pregnancy. How stupid we were! He yelled to his inner self for the millionth time. He remembered them saying to one another:

"My father will kill me."

"Your father will kill ME."

"I'll never tell, Adam, never put any blame on you."

He felt better. After all, she couldn't marry at 15! She wasn't going to get an abortion, for Christ's sake. Her promise of silence meant he wouldn't have to bear the shame of knocking her up, but the shame of watching her quietly bear up to the onslaught, alone, was just as difficult a cross to carry.

"What do we do?"

That unanswered question was just allowed to die in the breeze. Hope upon hope for some miracle; knees in the dirt, praying, begging for the Lord to intervene and make her UN-pregnant. Just a mistake, forgive us, DEAR GOD!

When she started to show, the wrath of the elders fell upon her like lightning over Sodom and Gomorrah. The other girls went back and forth between teasing and trashing her and then asking all the titillating questions pubescent girls really want answered.

She wouldn't tell them who the father was, and he hadn't had the guts to stand with his beloved and absorb his share of the fire and brimstone.

He hid in the shadows, protected by her strength and silence, and cowered while she was ostracized and, eventually, shunned. All backs turned to her, no hand of support or encouragement, no forgiveness from these disciples of a forgiving God.

By the time they found her, wrists slit, she had been missing for 9 days. Only the odor from under their haystack and the evidence left by the ravenous coyotes gave her away.

His own father threw up and sobbed like a woman when, as he helped pull her from the hay, saw the back of her scalp slide off like a rusty, matted bird's nest.

He thought about her pretty green eyes and mouth filled with maggots and he would always wonder if she had damned her own soul to Hell.

A few months after this, he "officially" jumped onto the Rumspringa bandwagon and joined the Navy. What kind of world was he growing up in when your church family and all your friends turn on you in your darkest time? It wasn't her fault, alone and terrified, HE should be the one in hell, and, in many ways, he was.

So, since he hadn't been the bigger man and gone off to hell of his own volition, Hell had decided to come for him. The devil himself had sent a most capable disciple; a demon named Bolin Li to finish the job. Bolin Li had conscripted an unwilling Verona Oakes to do his bidding. She was well equipped, well prepared, and brought all the tools necessary.

There was no limit to which a person wouldn't go to protect a loved one. Nothing as foolish as patriotism or duty would prevent someone from doing anything at all to keep say, their mother, from being hurt. Even money couldn't guarantee actions, but love would motivate anyone to do anything.

There was just a nagging bug in the back of Bolin Li's mind. He didn't like the plan. Too convoluted; too many things had to go just right; too many 'what ifs.'

Well, she was aboard now, at least. Things usually worked out for the best if you let events play out. If adjustments needed to be made, well they'll just be made. "Qu tamade" he muttered. Yeah, fuck it.

8

Doc Adams didn't like what he was seeing. He had mounted the beeper that came with this system in the ceiling of his bunk. It would alarm any time there was a Red reading for any of the monitored personnel.

Designed to manage up to 7000 chips at a time, the system was seriously underutilized on DODGE CITY with about 40 chipped crew. So, here he is, still in his rack, looking up at the beeper beeping and flashing.

Usually, Monday mornings would bring that first hot cup of coffee, first check of the crew's chip status, and an all-Green screen. Once that thing woke him up this morning, he came right down to look at the main console. All Greens except for one Red. Might be a glitch; there was no indication yesterday anybody was getting sick.

He clicked on the HISTORY tab which showed a climbing temperature during the night when he was asleep and not here to watch it. Yesterday, everybody's chip readout was in the Green; all within acceptable parameters for temperature, heart rate, blood pressure, blood oxygen levels, shit like that.

Today, on the second full day at sea, a Red blinker with a beeping beeper. Son of a bitch, this couldn't be good. Kennedy's 2-minute yellow during last night's little spat with Lancey was the only out of Spec he'd seen since the few hangovers in Portsmouth, but this was well into the Red Zone.

He tested everything from a system reset, to highlighting the individual's details and saw that Petty Officer Nichols, the Sonar LPO and one of the only 3 Sonar Supervisors on this run, had a fever of 102.6; up from 101 just two hours ago. He wasn't going to raise any alarms until he took a look at Nichols. Gotta be a glitch.

Doc Adams walks from his office in the 3-inch launcher room through the virtually empty After Berthing and into the middle level head toward Forward Berthing expecting to find Nichols who was off watch.

He steps onto the Terrazzo floor of the stainless-steel Head and there's Nichols, in his underwear, puking into one of the commodes. Doc leans in to look and half expects a gross mixture of stale beer and Navy chow, but Nichols barfing up this black stuff that looks like someone dumped an ashtray down the shitter.

"God damn, boy. What's wrong?"

"Doc, I don't know. Started puking a few hours ago. Dry heaves at first and now rrrrrrooooooommmmmmmmfffffff" another pile of black stuff covers the stainless-steel bowl.

"Bad fucking headache, too. Never had one like it."

"C'mon, back to bed. Right now."

"I got watch in an hour."

"BED!"

STS1(SS) Craig Nichols was one of those Navy Lifer dudes. Loved it; every bit of it. He would even iron military creases into his work shirts by hand, he walked around with a pocket-sized Day Timer to take notes about equipment status, work lists, stuff like that.

He was so efficient, that other Petty Officers got themselves a Day Timer so they wouldn't look like a bent shitcan compared to him at the LPO meetings.

For him to be hunched over a shitter and actually agree to go back to bed instead of to the Sonar Shack, meant that something was terribly wrong. Doc got him a couple of Aleves, which he threw back up in 15 minutes, and tried to trace his movements the last few days in Port. Where did he go, who did he go with, what did he eat, any new girls? Had to have picked this up somewhere. Hope, he was the only one.

"Same shit as always, doc. I'm pretty sure it was just The Argyle and that one fish and chips place everybody else ate at. I was still banging that blonde chick from the shoe store the last 2 weeks. Don't I have watch?"

Nichols wasn't sounding like his old sharp self. He seemed to be having trouble remembering and his eyes were closing as though hurt by the little bit of light coming from the Head.

Doc was running symptoms through his head. Confusion? With sudden high temp (which was now 103), nausea, odd headache....

"Craig, turn your head for me; left then right."

"Neck hurts, doc."

Then, he goes stiff in the bed and throws his head back with a groan loud enough to wake everyone nearby.

"Fuck. It's meningitis," Doc mumbles out loud.

He eases Nichols' head back onto the pillow and pulls the bunk curtain shut before walking over to the Goat Locker to wake up the COB.

It's 0430 and the mid-watch is still on. Breakfast in 30 and, even though it's only about twenty guys, there will be two watch sections up and around at the same time. Had to keep people away from Nichols who is probably contagious.

Adams knocks twice and walks into the Chief's Quarters without waiting for an "Enter" from whoever's sitting at their table. Opens the berthing area door and goes to the COB's rack: middle, outboard. He slowly pulls the curtain back.

"COB, COB…big problems."

"What's up, Doc," Durocher says using his Bugs Bunny voice to ease the tension a little.

"It's Nichols. I think he's got meningitis."

This was no little thing to say; not on a submarine and especially not on a prototype submarine that was at the front end of its shakedown deployment.

This was a whole crew exposure, pull the boat off-station, quarantine nightmare. This was 'leave the homefront undefended;' big, big shit about to go down. A crewman with meningitis needed medical care beyond what a Dicksmith could offer at sea and he needed it right now.

"How bad"?

"If it's viral, it might clear on its own, but if it's bacterial, he could die; he'll definitely spread it to the rest of the crew. He needs a hospital ASAP."

"Doc, how sure are you? We could get pulled off the deployment once we tell COMSUBLANT."

Doc Adams was biting his lip. He was sure, he knew what the implications were of this diagnosis, he was good at his job and he knew he was right. Pretty much.

"Tell the CO, COB, it's for real."

"Let me get my pants on, we'll go up together."

Two knocks, "Enter" from the CO, and the COB leads the boat's Corpsman into the Captain's Stateroom.

Scott turns on his bunk light and is sitting up rubbing one eye.

"Well, I can tell by the look on your faces, this is bad."
COB goes first.

"Sir, we've got a very sick man. Sick enough to risk infecting the crew with serious implications on the Deployment. Doc thinks Meningitis."

The Captain looks from Durocher to Adams and back again.

"What are the indications, Doc?"

"All the classics for meningitis: headaches, short term spike in temperature which is still climbing, he's had one seizure that I'm aware of, and he's puking black vomit. Must be blood."

"Well, who is it, first of all and what's the prognosis?"

"Petty Officer Nichols. If it's bacterial, which he could have contracted from someone in Portsmouth, he needs a hospital ASAP. He'll die without that level of attention."

Scott being Scott, never once asked "Are you sure?" He never expressed any doubt in either of his two men standing before him. Of course, they were sure. They wouldn't have woken up their Commanding Officer and basically told him to pull the ship off patrol if they weren't sure.

Other, less capable COs would have said something like: "Do you know what this means? I want you to double check and make damn sure before I make a report like that to Sublant, blah, blah, blah."

The Captain was dressed and, while he stood peeing, asked where Nichols was right now. Pretty close quarters and closer crews on an Attack Boat, you know.

"He's in his rack, sir"

"Let's go see him."

As they walked out of his Stateroom, Scott yelled into the control room to have LCDR Kennedy come see him. Right now. NOW. The unwritten direction in that final NOW could be interpreted as a considerate way of saying: 'I don't care if he's sleeping or what he's doing or what he's got to say about it. Right Fucking Now.'

"Contagious, you say, Doc?"

"Very, Captain."

"COB, let's get all these guys in Forward Berthing moved into After Berthing. The Oncoming Watch is getting up soon, so let's do it this morning and hold a Field Day right after to try and knock down any infection already spread."

"Aye, aye, sir." Durocher was suddenly thankful they had less than forty guys to wrangle instead of the standard hundred and five.

They flipped on the lights in both berthing areas, went to Nichols' rack, and pulled back the curtain.

"How you feeling, Petty Officer Nichols?" No matter how much your Captain liked you or how close your crew was, he was never going to call you by your first name. There are limits.

"Oh, Captain. I'm sorry, sir. I'll get up right now and go on watch. There's only three of us; I can't dump my load on those guys." Nichols' voice was breathy and weak.

"Negative, Nichols, you're sick and you're staying right here in this bunk. Doc Adams is going to stay with you and you are going to be alright, so don't you worry about anything."

Well, Craig Nichols had been in the Navy long enough to know that when the Captain has come to check on you, things were bad. He also knew that the first thing a Corpsman was supposed to tell you is: "You are OK."

Your arm could be laying on the deck next to you, an alligator could have you by the balls, and you could be pumping blood from both your ears, but the Corpsman would say: "You are OK."

Now, he's got a Commanding Officer, the longest serving Master Chief in the Navy and the Corpsman hand-picked to serve on the DODGE CITY telling him that he was going to be OK, so he must be fully fucked and minutes from death.

He looked over the Captain's shoulder and saw a ponderous blob running down the passageway. Oh shit, now here comes Kennedy.

His chubby cheeked fat head is all red and he's puffing like he ran the PFT instead of just down the middle level passageway.

"Where's the Captain?" he's spewing in a voice between trying to be appropriately quiet in a berthing area while panicking at the thought the Captain sent for him in the middle of the night. 3 men are crouched in front of him, Scott blocked by the other two.

"COB, COB, where's the Captain?"

"I'm right here, NAV. We have a sick man, and I want a message sent to COMSUBLANT outlining the symptoms Doc Adams will write out for you along with the timeline of discovery.

Respectfully request direction as I'm sure Sublant Medical will need a chop on this. Make it clear that we are not yet in our patrol area and free to navigate to a NATO port or rendezvous at sea for

Medevac. Do it now, Priority One."

"Aye, aye, Captain!"

The way the Navy works is through a clear Chain of Command. In this case, the Captain tells the Navigator, the Navigator tells the Leading Radioman, the Leading Radioman has one of his guys write up the message. The message is reviewed by the Leading Radioman who would normally give it to his Division Officer, but with this modified crew there isn't one, so it goes to the Navigator and then the CO. Somewhere along the line, the XO gets a cut at it, the rumor mill fills in the crew, and all is hunky dory.

The god damn beeper in his pocket, now is going off again. Doc knows that a Red Status is alarmed every 10 minutes until it's cleared so this must just be a repeat of Nichols' status. He'll clear the alarm when he gets to his shack next. Guys are out of bed now and going into the head or wandering down to get a coffee.

"Boys, were all moving into After Berthing. Pack your shit and pick out a rack." The COB announced. He would do so on the 1MC little later since they had yet to rig for Patrol quiet. He would ask Graves to do it, but no.

20 sailors were now bitching about having to move. You know how it goes: A bitching sailor is a happy sailor. Wait until they find out they'll be holding Field Day in an hour.

Then they found out about Nichols.

It was a line of about 12 leading from the head to Nichols' rack.

"What's wrong, Craig"? "You OK, man"? "You want a coffee or something"? So many good wishes, so many brothers in your family when times got tough. Any one of these guys would trade places with Petty Officer Nichols. There's nothing closer than a battle buddy.

Nichols' face was all scrunched up like he had the worst headache in history. He was dizzy, his feet were sweating, and he kept throwing up into the bucket Doc left with him.

Russell had wandered in to see what all the commotion was. She had just woken up, walked out of the Chief's Quarters, and was heading Aft to the Galley to help with breakfast.

Doc saw her and gave a quick rundown on what was going on. He also said, "I could use your help, Chief. I don't want him to fall asleep. I know it sounds weird, but I'm afraid he's going to sink too low or even aspirate some puke into his lungs and drown."

"I get it," the Leading cook said and walked into the Chief's quarters to get the step stool kept in the first inboard locker. She placed it next to the head of Nichols' rack and sat on it.

"Nichols, got any favorite books or stories?"

"Got a terrible headache, Chief. Can't think right now."

"Well, Doc wants me to keep you awake. So, I'm going to read you a story, if you'd like."

"No, Chief, I just want to lay here." Nichols was actually quite moved at the thought she would sit here with him and read him a book. He didn't really know how to handle such a tender kindness. It was actually a little embarrassing like not knowing what to say to a compliment. He figured that declining the gesture would be the safest way to deal with it.

"You could TELL me a story, Chief. Tell me YOUR story?"

She looked him over for a second and wondered if he was messing with her or coming on to her in some way. He didn't have that little 'thing' in his eye that guys get when they're trying a line.

"What do you mean, 'My Story'?

"You, just you. I've heard some shit about you, but can't possibly know what's true and what isn't. None of us know you real well and most of us were there when you beat Cornwallis. Guys are gonna talk about that for a long time."

Another spasm wracked Nichols from head to toe. His head flew back and he actually shit himself and screamed at the same time. His eyes rolled back and he was scrunching up the sheets as tight as he could. Terri Russell imagined this boy dying right in front of her eyes and a chill ran the length of her spine.

"Get the Doc!" she yelled to whoever might have been within earshot. In a couple of minutes Adams was there. The readout had Nichols' temp at 103.5. They both pulled a totally limp Craig Nichols out of the rack and got him into the shower. Doc cleaned him off as best as he could and Terri pulled his shitty skivvies off and put them into a trash bag.

Doc made him swallow a couple of Motrin and then ran the cool water all over him.

"He can handle 104 even, but over that and we're in bad territory. You OK staying here with him? I've got to finish putting the message together for the skipper."

"I'm good, Doc, my guys have everything under control."

Doc quick-stepped it out of berthing and down to his office. In a few minutes, the message draft had been written and the XO chopped it before having it smoothed for the Captain.

"Send it."

"Aye, aye Captain."

From this moment forward, the mission became Petty Officer Nichols. They were still 'In Transit;' not yet on station, no targets to track or trail, if something like this was going to happen, then now was the best time.

Scott was turning a scenario around in his head that pulls DODGE CITY completely off patrol and back to Portsmouth. This Deployment was just to prove that the AI can handle it at sea in a potential combat environment.

He, as CO, had been unwilling, on some level, to actually turn the boat over to The Marshal. The submarine was originally designed for about a hundred guys to take her to sea. Three underway watch sections, 6 hours on and 12 off.

This underway, 35 men went to sea, just to act as supervisors and roving watch standers to make sure The Marshal did its job. The 3 Spooks are always added on a deployment of this nature, but they were probably not going to be necessary, either, once they loaded up the new software on its way in Nichol's helicopter.

The real ticking point in the back of Scott's head was if The Marshal was threatened in a combat environment, would it shoot? How sure are we that were not begging for an international incident where this computer decides to sink somebody's brand new Battleship.

Don't even think about The Marshal dialing up a nice juicy Tomahawk and sending a nuke into the front door of some dictator's house.

It may seem pompous to someone who is NOT a Submarine Commander, but he was convinced you needed a Command Qualified Human Being to give the order to Fire and not leave it up to a machine.

It took 45 minutes for Sublant, through the Group and Squadron, to coordinate the next series of events. DODGE CITY would go to a specified rendezvous point and a Royal Marine Blackhawk would pick up Nichols, at sea, and bring him to a hospital. Holy shit, this was a first for everybody on board. Heading for the Irish Sea at a Flank Bell.

The morning watch is in place, and the Captain comes into control and grabs the 1MC mike on the Conn.

"All hands, this is the Captain speaking. One of our shipmates is sick and we are going to take care of him. Petty Officer Nichols needs to get to a hospital ASAP. Doc Adams is doing all that can be done here, aboard DODGE CITY, but he needs a little help."

"The Royal Navy is sending out a Rescue helicopter to hoist Nichols, who will be stretchered, and get him ashore. We will divert from our scheduled mission and head to a rendezvous point for 1300 hours rescue evolution. Plan on The Maneuvering Watch at 1130"

He clicked off the mike and turned to the OOD.

"Officer of the Deck, make your depth 600 feet, all ahead Flank. Come to course zero two zero."

The orders and repeat backs were all given. The angle on the boat increased and she banked into the turn. Nothing can stop a Fast Attack on a mission.

The COB took the 1MC mike and announced:

"This is the Chief of the Boat. I want all hands living in Forward Berthing to pick out a rack in Aft Berthing and move as soon as you can. Wash all your clothes and bedding at first opportunity; we may have a contagious disease among us. We will also commence Field Day right now and do our best to contain things."

The COB grabbed Demzer who was the Messenger for this section and sent him into the fan room to gather up a bunch of life jackets and harnesses.

"Look for that Helo kit, too. Don't really need the helmets and goggles, but, hopefully, we've at least got the grounding rod."

As everyone knows, any time you're involved with a helicopter that is planning to lower their hoist, that big ole' rotor up there is just building up a ton of static electricity.

At the first sniff of a grounding point, the whole charge is going to blast from the helo, down the hoisting cable, and into the ground. If you're touching that cable before it grounds, then YOU are the ground strap and you'll get zapped; badly.

So, there's this wooden grounding rod with a cable running from the metal tip to a spring-loaded clip that you connect to something. You touch the hoist with this grounding rod BEFORE you touch it and it discharges safely to ground. If you're drowning in the water and a helo crew comes to pluck your ass to safety, let that hook hit the water first THEN grab on for dear life.

Amid all the hubbub, Chief Russel is left alone with Nichols who is fading in and out of consciousness. She wasn't sure how to feel about being a girl and having just helped shower, dry, and put a naked male back in bed.

She guessed the Navy, and the crew, weren't looking at her as a SHE right now, but as a CHIEF and a SHIPMATE. Wasn't this how she wanted to be treated?

She returned from daydreaming and noticed Nichols looking at her.

"So?" he says. "What's the story?"

"Well, I joined up a few months after my uncle got killed in Helmand Province. I had been a member of a Motorcycle Club called The Undertakers and he was the President. He was my mom's brother and I loved and respected him and just wanted to do something to honor him."

"So, he was a grunt, then?"

She chuckled a little, "Yep, Marines"

"I never had a dad, really. He kind of disappeared before I was born, and my Uncle Johnny filled that role. My mother kept any boyfriends at a distance and never fell for anyone again."

She handed Nichols a cup of bug juice and he drank a little, but only a sip.

"And do you really have a tattoo on your head?"

"Yep. Right here." She smushed down the hair on that side of her head so he could see.

"That's for him, too."

"He must have been a hell of a guy."

"The best."

"And I heard you're the first female to get her Dolphins?"

"That's actually Not true; I was ONE of the first, though."

"Cool"

85

9

The rest of the night had been filled with people moving all their shit from one berthing area to another, scrubbing everything Petty Officer Nichols might have touched, and preparing for an at-sea helicopter transfer of a stretchered man.

This was no easy feat and it's not done very often, so there was no corporate knowledge in the crew. One thing about your average American military person, they don't think there's ANYTHING they can't do.

DODGE CITY had a rendezvous with a Royal Navy Mark 4 Merlin helicopter about a hundred miles from here and had 6 hours to get there. All the helo ops equipment they could find was staged under the Weapons Shipping Hatch: 3 helmets and a grounding rod.

Two of the helmets were still sealed inside plastic bags; somebody must have unwrapped the other to play with it since actually wearing one was a rarity for a submarine sailor.

Sweetwater and Lemon were in the Goat Locker getting briefed by the COB on how they were going to handle the helo transfer. Other than a couple of the Nukes, these guys were the biggest and probably the best under fire.

You know who your best guys are when the shit hits the fan. They're the ones standing next to you and not running away. These guys were the kind you wanted if you were walking into a bar fight or had a helicopter coming to pluck one of your friends off a pitching submarine in the middle of the Irish Sea in the fucking winter time.

"If we can't find that grounding pole, make sure you don't touch that fucking cable until it hits the deck."

"Got it, COB."

That was about it. Nichols would have to be carried by hand, wrapped in a canvass stretcher, up and out of the boat, along the wet deck to the waiting basket, hooked up to the lifting cable, into the helicopter, and whisked away to a NATO base hospital surrounded by well-meaning strangers.

Sea conditions weren't too bad this morning so it was a light pitch and roll of just a few degrees. It could get way worse in this part of the world at this time of year, but fingers crossed.

They were heading to a point about 90 Nautical miles Southeast of Cork, Ireland maybe halfway to St. Ives, UK. This gave the boat plenty of area to maneuver, enough water depth to navigate without risk of grounding, but they would have to surface transit about a hundred miles to the rendezvous point.

In routine operations, a submarine never dives until it crosses the "Hundred Fathom Curve," meaning there's 600 feet of water beneath the keel. So, DODGE CITY is looking at about 7 hours on the surface in the Irish Sea in the winter. That also means that sea conditions this time of year might be very rough and a round-hull submarine acts more like a cork than a ship on the surface.

98 miles from the rendezvous point, Ahead One-Third at 450 feet. Senior Chief Lancey is standing a UI, or Under Instruction watch as COW in order to get a rare signature on his qualification card: Emergency Surfacing.

Usually, a sub uses the Low-Pressure Blower to expel the water from the Main Ballast Tanks in lieu of the Normal Blow System which introduces 4500psi air into the tanks via two electro-hydraulic switches on the BCP. This saves the air in the air banks which takes a long time to put back in there using the compressors.

When things go bad down deep, say if there's flooding in the Engine Room and the boat is getting very heavy very fast, the Emergency Blow system is used. The EMBT Blow valves are located above the BCP and actuate the air dump into the ballast tanks manually and mechanically without the need for electricity just in case that's another casualty the boat is dealing with.

These valves are lovingly referred to as "The Chicken Switches" and are used so rarely, that guys trying to qualify want to get up there to Control when there's going to be a test. Captain Scott has granted permission to do an Emergency Blow so Lancey can get his sig.

"Diving Officer, Sound 3 blasts of the Diving Alarm and Emergency Surface the ship".

"Sound 3 blasts of the Diving Alarm and Emergency Surface the ship, Dive aye."

Once the Diving Alarm is heard, the crew knows what's about to happen. 2 blasts and they're going down, 3 blasts and they're going up. Up fast. After the third blast, the sound of high-pressure air moving through the pipes can be heard everywhere and the boat lurches up.

The front of the boat is pitching up and the crew knows the planesmen have pulled back their yokes to achieve whatever angle the Diving Officer has ordered.

The ride up from 450 feet isn't as exhilarating as one much deeper, but you can still feel the boat break the surface, momentarily seem to hang in the air, and then crash back into the sea before bobbing back up.

Lancey pulls the blow valves back down to the Shut position. That's it. Grab the T-handle, push in with the palm of your hand, lift to go up, pull down to secure the blow. Emergency Surface qualification complete.

Standing across the Control Room, just aft of Fire Control near the door to Sonar, was Petty Officer Oakes. Most people come up to Control when there's going to be an Emergency Blow just to be part of the action and watch the depth gauge spin backwards on the way up. She was there for a little education on how to operate those valves…

LT. Magness opens the lower hatch to the sail and he and Bugsy head up the trunk.

"Crack the hatch!" The Captain yells up the trunk to them and Magness turns the handle to allow the hatch to break its seal but not fully open as it rests against its spring-loaded dog. The sound of air rushing past the hatch is audible as is the popping in everyone's ears as the pressure in the boat now equalizes with atmosphere.

"Bridge hatch indicates Open," Lancey announces from the BCP as the Green bar indicator goes out and the yellow "O" shaped indicator comes on. As the flow of air slows to almost nothing, the Captain orders the hatch opened and for his two men to proceed to the Bridge.

Number Two scope is already up and the Navigator has swept 360 degrees to make sure they were alone.

"No contacts, Captain"

"Very well, NAV."

Magness gets the hatch and clamshell open and yells down for the suitcase; the box with all the communications devices available to the bridge personnel to talk to the crew and give helm orders.

When the Bridge reports they have the radar mast unpinned, it's ordered raised by the OOD and raised by Lancey. The ETOW mans the console and starts sweeping.

Moran is on the Bridge with the OOD and Demzer climbs the trunk ladder dangling the suitcase behind. He passes it through the upper hatch and Magness removes the connector cover to slide the box on the mount and tests it with the Helm.

"Helm, Bridge."

"Helm, aye."

"Helm, Bridge, mark your head."

"Steady 020."

"Very well, Helm."

"Captain, Bridge, I am ready to relieve you."

"Bridge, Captain, Aye. I am ready to be relieved, steering 020, All ahead 1/3."

"Steering 020, All Ahead 1/3, I relieve you, sir"

"Bridge, Captain, I stand relieved."

"Bridge, Navigator, recommend coming right to 030, All Ahead Full."

Terri was still sitting with Nichols and poking him every time he closed his eyes.

"Gotta stay awake, Nichols."

"Fuck. Okay, Chief. My head is killing me"

"All part of the symptoms, Doc tells me. We're surfaced, so probably pretty close to the rendezvous point. We'll get you to a hospital ASAP. Ever been on a helicopter before?"

"They're gonna put me in a helicopter? How is that supposed to happen?"

"Well, hooked up to their winch and lifted aboard."

Nichols' face went white.

"It's wintertime and we're way the hell North, Chief. I'm going to freeze my ass off out there. What if they drop me?"

Without missing a beat and with a deadpan face, she calmly said "You'll be all wrapped in a nice heavy blanket, so if they drop you, you'll drown really fast and we can all get back to whatever we were doing."

"Don't make me laugh it hurts my head."

She patted his arm and he leaned over to puke in the bucket for the hundredth time.

Doc Adams shows back up with the stretcher and 4 guys.

"Do you know what the plan is, Craig?"

"I've got the basic idea"

"OK, we're gonna stand you up and strap you into this thing so you don't fall out and drown."

Nichols shot a quick look at Russell.

"Then, we're carrying you out the Weapons Shipping Hatch, gonna go aft Topside and hoist you up into a Brit Helo. You're going to a Royal Navy hospital and they're gonna make you better."

"Why can't you take care of me, Doc? I don't want to go to some strange country all by myself."

"You need real doctorin' on this one; I'm just a pecker checker, Craig."

"Yeah, he's useless to me, too." Russell chimed in.

They all had a laugh at that one.

"C'mon, it's ENGLAND, Craig, not some Banana Republic somewhere. They'll probably take you to the Culdrose Air Base at Cornwall. Half the chicks that we meet in The Argyle work over there. I'm sure they'll take GOOD care of you," Doc said with a laugh.

Nichols cracked a little bit of a smile and Terri squeezed his shoulder.

"Ready?"

"Yeah, Chief, thanks for everything and for sitting with me and all."

He was a little sheepish and was looking down.

"Sorry about making a mess in the shower."

"Oh, you can do the same for me, someday."

He seized again and threw his head back hitting the side wall of his bunk. He was getting worse.

Meanwhile, up in Control, the dance was beginning.

"Bridge, Radar, airborne contact bearing Three Two Three relative, range 13,600 yards."

"Radar, Bridge, aye."

Normally, the OOD would contact the CO to report such a contact, but Scott was already up on the bridge, too, so he's hearing everything.

"Bridge, Radar, designating this contact as Romeo 1. Bearing steady, range 12,000, Zero bearing rate."

"Very well, Radar."

12,000 yards is only 6 nautical miles, so a fast-moving helicopter is going to get here quick.

It was a grey sky, cloudy, slight breeze out of the North, freshening. The black dot in the sky could be seen with the naked eye, now. Maybe a hundred feet above the grey, choppy sea, heading straight in. This was Nichols' ride.

Nichols leaned out of his bunk while Doc and one of the other guys helped him out and up. They tied the canvass flaps around him and the word came down they spotted the helicopter on the horizon.

Out the berthing door, quick turn aft and up the ladder. Right under the lower hatch that Senior Chief McCleary was hand cranking open. Dusty had the ladder out of the stowage brackets on the bulkhead and got it mounted right away once the lower hatch was clear.

Lemon had the grounding probe so he went up first with Sweetwater right behind. The 4 guys with Doc went up next and all hooked their harnesses into the safety track ready to maneuver Nichols and make their way to the after deck where the helo would hover away from the sail.

"Can you come up with me, Chief Russell?"

"Sure, Nichols, no need to end this party. You might want to know something else about 'My Story,'" she says with air quotes.

Everybody that was there in upper level was busy doing something to prepare for Nichols MEDEVAC. This is no easy task; especially from a round submarine hull AT SEA.

No one was paying attention to them, So,

Nichols lowered his voice and whispered:

"Well, there is something I'd like to know. I have my suspicions, but it's just too personal to ask."

She knew. It was the whole dyke thing again. Is she or isn't she, you know.

"Well, you just keep this to yourself, I'm not."

In what could only be described as an exasperated tone, Nichols says "Chief, everybody already knows that. It's OK. You've got your reason for acting the way you do, I guess."

"You're also part of a submarine crew that will hunt down and beat the holy fuck out of any man that's mean to you. You can be yourself around us."

She was really taken by this little interaction.

What made him think it had something to do with men being mean to her?

She could tell he was being sincere and she was surprised she was so easy to read. Maybe it was time to drop the façade. She'd have to think about it.

Captain Scott was in the bridge, now, and had the helo pilot on radio. They coordinated a 90-degree approach from the Lee side into the wind. The Westland WS-61 Sea King creeped over the after deck and hovered right above the Aft Escape trunk.

All personnel had gone Topside and the two big weightlifter nukes pulled Nichols' stretcher through the hatch and headed aft with him. The hoist and basket were coming down and Lemon kneeled directly below reaching to touch it with the grounding rod.

The COB was screaming at Lemon trying to be heard above the noise of the rotor blades "DON'T TOUCH IT!" GROUND IT! GROUND IT!"

Lemon nodded his head wildly as in "I know, I know." The basket hit the deck and Terri looked up into the helicopter.

Just aft of the open side door she sees a gigantic orange orb wearing a green flight suit looking thing and tan-ish helicopter helmet. The orb is a human head covered in hair that is blowing in the rotor wash and ocean-driven wind.

With head hair and beard flopping around and waving like a field of orange wheat… he raises his goggles.

"Oh, my God, it's that Cornwallis dude!" goes through her head.

He sees her and raises one hand to the side of his head in a backward-looking Brit hand salute. THEN he puts two fists together, raises one finger and rotates that fist toward her.

"Son of a bitch," she thinks aloud, "he's Signing. That was "hello" and "how are you?"

Could have been dumb luck, so she signs back:

"You can sign?"

"Sister deaf, took a chance – you?"

"School project"

"Drinks when you get back?"

"Why?"

He holds his hands in front of his chest with fingers bent at 90 degrees and raises both in the sign for "Promotion" and grabs his collar. He must have made Chief.

"OK, on me"

"Huh," she thinks to herself.

"Of all the people on planet Earth, THAT big fucker is hovering in a helicopter over MY boat in the middle of the Irish Sea. What are the odds?"

"We'll take good care of your lad."

The helo is cross-ships to the boat and sends a rope down with an olive-green seabag dangling from it.

"CO EYES ONLY" is stenciled on the side and it's brought below into Scott's stateroom.

Next, the lifting hook comes down, Stokes stretcher bearing Nichols goes up, helo flies away, no sweat.

Everybody watches it go and wonders if Nichols will make it. Gear gets gathered up and 9 guys head for the Weapons Shipping Hatch to head below. The swells are rolling up onto the deck and everybody's pantlegs are wet. A few more minutes and a bigger swell takes the feet out from under the COB. He falls onto his back and is heading over the side.

The safety harness rope goes taught and he's hanging between the safety track and the deep blue sea until Sweetwater pulls him back aboard. Some of the others head back to help, but Durocher waves them off and gestures to go below.

"Let's go, Sweets!"

The two of them regain their footing and make their way forward dragging their safety lines along the track. The next swell is even bigger knocking both men off their feet and a shitload of seawater gets down the hatch.

Kennedy starts to panic and starts screaming like a little girl to close the hatch. He would have left those guys topside to drown had Lemon not taken advantage of a roll of the ship to "accidently" crash into him and get him the hell out of the way.

This is the kind of officer they would have fragged in The Nam. The COB slides headfirst through the hatch and into Lemon's arms followed by Sweetwater who jumps all the way from the main deck into upper level and yells "Last man down!"

The upper hatch is pulled shut but not before another couple of hundred gallons of seawater finds its way into the boat. The three, soaking wet Torpedomen are all laying on the Upper Level deck laughing; something that fat fucking Kennedy just cannot understand.

10

All the activity provided perfect cover for Oakes to get further along on her plan. It was a lot easier to get here than they had thought. "They" were her handlers and the inside man they had at Portsmouth.

You would think that in the most Top Secret of worlds, the Submarine Force, you would get a microscope shoved up your ass anytime you got near one, let alone wanted to go aboard. Oakes had flown out of NAS Norfolk on a C-130 one day before Lancey and the other interpreter, CT1(AC) Mills left Pensacola.

None of them had met before, but Oakes was a known quantity in the small world of Spooks. There are women everywhere in the military, but the super-hot ones are usually known by reputation and Oakes was one of them.

No one checked her bags before she boarded the plane; no one checked her bags or gear when she walked aboard DODGE CITY at the pier in Portsmouth. In fact, a couple of the duty section guys helped carry her equipment and personal bags stuff into the crew's mess and then into berthing after the COB assigned her a rack.

She came onboard carrying an olive drab canvas duffle, which was actually a GI parachute bag. It was just the right size for uniforms and stuff as well as girly shit like make up and whatever.

No one sniffed her perfume bottles or powders; no one went through her skivvies and she made sure to keep the Tampon box right on top to scare off prying eyes and hands.

After all, no one tasted the Listerine bottles ole Pappy brought aboard. You would have thought him a fanatic about oral hygiene given the amount of mouthwash he had, but these bottles were all empty of Listerine and now full of Bourbon. It should have been a giveaway to watch him brush, take a mouthful of Listerine, swish, and SWALLOW.

If anyone had opened the plastic seal and sniffed Oakes' body powder, the cyanide mixed in would have killed him immediately. She had special plans for that stuff. It was her idea, too, and her people loved it.

She had watched this documentary show about the Iceman; this gigantic dude who was actually a real Mob killer named Kulinski, Boblinksi, or something like that. He used to get pure cyanide and mix it with water in a spray bottle.

One spray of this mix into a guy's face and that guy was dead. Real dead, real fast. No traces and almost impossible to detect even in an autopsy.

Introducing this shit into the ultra-high-volume air flow of a submarine ventilation system would spread it through the entire boat. The kill rate would be fantastic. All she had to do was keep herself from being exposed and figure a way to dispose of any stragglers.

Once the crew was dead, the plan was to emergency surface, open a hatch, and let her people in to take control of the boat. Just had to do it at the right place and time. Their inside man at British MOD already let them know the operational plan for the deployment; where the boat was going, and when. It would be followed, tracked, and they would be ready when Oakes emergency surfaced through the ice.

Oakes punched her code into the cyber lock and walked into the Computer Room. She was hoping to spend a little time grooming Hochstetler, but the other guy, DS1 Schiano, was in there.

"Hi, Petty Officer Oakes," she said introducing herself and stuck out her hand and gave that phony 'Real Estate' agent grip women use to try and be perceived as an equal when meeting a man for the first time.

"Nice to meet you. I'm Petty Officer Schiano, Paul Schiano. Adam told me a lot about you, there, Oakes."

"Oh, hope it was good"

"Definitely. Sorry I missed the whole Mail Buoy show you put on."

Now, what did he mean by that, she wondered.

"What do you mean by that?"

"C'mon. Everybody knows the Mail Buoy is bullshit. Are you trying to tell me that no one briefed you about the games we play on Subs? You're a Spook Rider on Subs and you don't know anything about "Get me 10 feet of Waterline" or the "Pain Club?"

She just laughed and said "Sorry."

"OK, then. Maybe a private showing one of these days?"

Schiano had a creepy grin on his face. It wasn't anything she and a million other good-lookers haven't seen during their time in the military. Besides, the whole point of her mail buoy deception was to hook one of these fish, and she did. Another crotch sniffer like this douchebag would only be a hinderance.

"In your dreams, and if you keep this up, we're going to have a nice talk with your CO."

Schiano was no dope. In his 12 years of service, he had seen plenty of guys stand before The Man for saying or doing the wrong thing around a female. Truth be told, the "wrong" thing was whatever the offended female said it was.

The Sexual Harassment guidelines were pretty clear. Quid Pro Quo, Hostile Working Environment, all that crap was at the discretion of She Who Has Been Made to Feel Uncomfortable.

Christ, couldn't even keep a naked picture to beat off to anymore. If one of these bitches saw it, down you go. Besides, he'd been married long enough that his wife could get half his retirement if they got divorced, so…

"OK, Oakes, no need to start off on the wrong foot. We've got 80 days or so together, so let's try to be friends. Jesus, I'm just fuckin' with ya," he threw out there behind an obviously fake smile.

She wasn't buying it. She let on that all was ok, no hard feelings, all that shit, but she would have to keep an eye on this guy.

"So, were you one of the original crew?" she asked to be perceived as conversational.

"No, I got here a couple of months ago. Hochstetler, you know, Adam, was here the whole time in the yard. The civilian Tech Reps did 90% of the install and the Yardbirds did the rest; Dusty just qualified on the system and helped with testing."

"That Dusty shit is pretty funny," she said testing out her well-practiced smile.

"What Dusty shit?"

"You do know that he doesn't really talk like that? Dost thou, wouldst though, you know."

Schiano felt his face reddening. No, he didn't know and he didn't like it. How was he supposed to know how Amish people talked? He didn't know any god damn Amish motherfuckers. This bitch knew something about his own co-worker that he did not?

97

"Oh, yeah, yeah. I didn't think YOU knew."

She knew he was full of shit. She surprised him and he was trying to pass it off. Why, though? He must be one of those people that had to know something you didn't. The messenger, the rat, the gossiper. He was probably passive-aggressive, too, and would dig and dig until he had something on her. This guy had to go; he was a threat now.

"So, what've you got going on in here, today, Oakes?"

"I'm just going through my gear and making sure everything is SAT." A believable enough response...she had been hoping to work on Dusty, but...

Well, speak of the devil and up he jumps. They hear the cypher lock keys clicking and the door opens. Hochstetler is pushing his way backwards through the spring-loaded hinged door with two cups of coffee. He says "Howdy!" to Oakes and hands Schiano a cup.

"Thought you might want some coffee, Paul. Didn't know you'd be here, Oakes, or I'da brought you one, too."

"No sweat."

"We were just getting to know each other better," says Schiano as he gave a sideways look at Oakes. She silently smiled and never looked back at Schiano.

"Well," she says, "I'm going to go through my gear real quick and then I'll get out of your hair."

She reached down to the outside of her left pants pocket to make sure the thumb drive was still there. She took to carrying it all the time now hoping for any opportunity to get at The Marshal. It held the entirety of the virus she needed to upload into the AI.

Her people would be able to access the system by satellite once the program was in there. MATT DILLON could not be accessed from off-ship. Only onboard personnel could do that. He could not even be turned off unless it was done locally by two men, simultaneously turning keys.

She needed about 40 uninterrupted seconds to stick that thumb drive into Matt Dillon and let it work. Only one way she could figure to do that and it involved taking complete advantage of an immature, horny sailor. One other problem was that damn cypher lock...

A well-practiced hand could punch in 4 numbers and be through that door in seconds. Luckily, you could hear the clicking when it all started which might give someone enough time to jump up or pull up her pants or whatever had to be done to avoid discovery.

Yanking the drive out of the machine might be more difficult as you couldn't do it without everyone around seeing it. The USB drive slot was right above the keyboard and there wasn't anything blocking it from view.

Even if you just ignored it and tried to distract someone from looking in that direction, the damn thing was right in front of your face. If you were used to seeing the panel every day, then you would see that thing immediately.

Beyond that, doing it in the daytime was out of the question with drills, training, field days, or whatever, there was always someone up and around. It would have to be done after the midwatch came on. The whole boat was either asleep or on watch and the chance that someone would walk in at that time of night was slim.

If it was quiet enough, then you could actually hear someone approaching before they got to the cypher lock. If they were heading aft out of Control, then they had to walk on the upper level deckplates which were bolted down to allow access to middle and lower levels if necessary.

Back in the time of ALBUQUERQUE, weapons loading and unloading came through the Weapons Shipping Hatch, right past the computer room, through middle level and down to the torpedo room below. The new "Wheel Gun" setup made all that obsolete, but there was neither time nor money wasted on backfitting the walking decks, so they just left them the way they were.

She looked around the computer room a little and thought, "This place is small; really small. 5 by ten tops." The YUKs were at the After end with the workbench, keyboard, and all support equipment on the inboard bulkhead.

Chill water piping in the overhead along with miles of cable, and ventilation ducts dumping freezing air into the space and exhaust filters sucking it out. Nowhere to hide, nowhere to remain unseen, this was going to be a problem.

If she laid some of the equipment boxes on the deck when the time was right, if someone entered his code and pushed the door open, the boxes would block it from opening all the way and she'd have a few seconds to recover.

It would still be a few days before they were on station. The time would come soon after.

11

Bolin Li expected news every day. He knew the submarine had left port 3 days ago and, as yet, he heard nothing. That bastard he had in the MOD would die a horrible death if he thought following instructions was optional.

Recently, they had recruited a key candidate in Planning; the department that coordinates the major waypoints of Royal Navy ship deployment. Everything from stores loadouts to operational assignments went through these guys.

A Mr. Lawrence Rothington was in charge of this group and had been an employee of the Ministry of Defence for almost 25 years at a cool 100,000 Pounds Sterling per annum. He had remained single his entire life, loved golf, and had a penchant for little boys. Oh yes, the littler the better.

Information like this was very valuable to Bolin Li. He had learned just how disgusting human beings were way back when he was little himself. "The Street," as it were, knew just whom to convey such a tidbit of information and Mr. Rothington's tastes were made known to Xiansheng Li Bolin, "Mr. Li" in English, and a handsome reward was paid in cash.

Oddly, the gentlemen who provided such intelligence was found floating in the Thames just a fortnight ago; no cash on him at all. The coroner reported ultra-high levels of fentanyl in his liver. Terrible, just terrible. Anyone who knew Bolin Li, knew that he never allowed loose ends. He may be old, but he was thorough.

Anyhow, Mr. Rothington's overall demeanor was one of superiority over his fellow man. He gave the appearance of a pasty, inverted lightbulb. He walked duck-like to such an extent that images of Baby Huey came to mind. His perfectly trimmed mustache and beard became ridiculous when he plugged his oversized Calabash pipe into his fetid mouth.

He would laugh in great guffaws at things few men found amusing and his wildly open maw revealed greenish teeth that never experienced the joy of flossing. Women abhorred him and men felt revulsion at having to look at him even during the briefest conversations at the office.

His favorite pub was The Dog and Cat in Carnaby Street. He liked it because it seemed to be a rallying point for others who shared his abhorrent tastes. The clandestine meetings in small groups held there were coordinated exclusively on the Dark Web.

It was at these Dog and Cat meetings these perverts would schedule play nights with some kid they had purchased or kidnapped. The international pervert club reached far and wide and many an innocent was available for sex and murder. About 460 thousand kids disappeared every year from the U.S. alone; where do people think they went?

There were rumors that it was in some of the private residences of the wealthy all over the world that these kids were brutalized, tortured, ripped apart, and even eaten. Can such an abhorrence be true? Surely, that's just tabloid fodder...people can't be that satanic. Oh, yes, they can. The world can be a horrible place filled with horrible people and Larry Rothington was one of the worst.

He sure came across as an upstanding example to all. A government employee of well over two decades; he had even played golf with Andrew; an acquaintance many respected and few were willing to anger. He was also quite well-off financially thanks to a comfortable salary and making the most of investment tips shared by his equally well-connected friends.

A man like Rothington thought he was hidden on the Dark Web pursuing his disgusting interests. But, a Bolin Li, through his infinite contacts, pretty much commanded the Dark Web.

He employed a cadre of experts to keep him abreast of the types of goings on and the people involved. He had no problem targeting someone whom he thought would be useful to him. He would then use money, favor, blackmail, or any other "incentive" to get what he wanted.

Once identified, he would direct his people to commence their digital assault on that person and that fucker was dead meat. It took but a few moments for them to lock in on Rothington's IP address, screen names, and avatars.

Less than 3 minutes more and they had hacked into his personal computer and copied all his documents and video records of his little boy interludes.

They had all his passwords and, with one click of the mouse, were ready to transfer ownership of all his worldly possessions and every Pound Sterling he owned to the All-Powerful Wizard, Bolin Li.

They knew the plans for the next meeting he would be attending and, although they had airtight proof of his penchants and hobbies, Li wanted to seal the deal with some added motivation. Rothington was about to learn that his dear old dad had been invited to a different sort of small gathering.

At this particular meeting, which consisted of two men very reliable and very close to Xiansheng Li, the senior Rothington had been beaten unconscious, stripped naked, and had been trussed up like a Christmas goose into a tight fetal position.

A half inch thick glass rod had been inserted just into his rectum, and the accompanying photographs, which could easily find their way onto the internet, made this poor man's predicament crystal clear.

This very afternoon, a very dapper Zhang Wei had followed our friend Larry into a tobacconist. Zhang was well into his fifties and was one of the grandsons of the revered Qing Shan who saved little Bolin Li all those years ago. His obedience was complete and beyond question.

Larry placed his reorder for the pipe tobacco mixture he believed Albert Einstein preferred; something along the lines of a House of Windsor Revelation. Zhang walked up next to him and spoke once the clerk walked toward the back:

"Pardon me, Mr. Rothington, I wonder if you would look at this photograph?"

"I beg your pardon" Rothington spewed in his haughtiest tone, annoyed that some lowly commoner would dare speak to him directly. He looked down and, as he began to understand what he was seeing, his eyes opened wider and wider.

"Someone of great importance wants to speak with you, Mr. Rothington. The intent of this discussion is to ensure that your father will be permitted to return home completely unharmed. If you refuse or if you even hesitate, that glass rod will be rammed as far as it will go, and then broken. Your answer, sir?"

"Who in the bloody hell are you?"

Pervert Larry tried to manage indignance and strength as he searched the shop for any form of assistance, but Wei just held the photo higher and motioned to the door where two burly men stood silently.

The Great and Powerful Lawrence Rothington almost pissed himself, but held it together and tried to puff out a "Good Lord! Very well, let's go." Sadly, he barely managed a mewling agreement and walked toward the door resignedly through tears and snurfelling.

As he drifted slowly toward the door, Rothington was forcibly ushered and hurried from the shop. A confused clerk returned to a now empty counter with a tobacco tin, hand written invoice, but no customer.

The Mercedes Maybach S650 waited at the curb as Mr. Larry Rothington was thrust into the backseat. An IPAD was handed to him and he looked upon the smiling face of Bolin Li. A very rare event indeed, as Bolin usually never got within one or two buffers of a target.

"Thank you for joining us today, Mr. Rothington."

Rothington sat in silence; listening and watching as one of his large new friends handed him a packet of documents. Some were printed papers detailing places and times where he and his more prurient friends met for an evening's festivities.

Some of these photographs had been lifted from his very computer. One particular photograph captured Larry's interest as it showed the gentleman currently seated at Mr. Rothington's left standing over him while he slept.

He read through the papers that transferred his two homes and three cars to Bolin Li along with all his money. They were processed, stamped, and all very legal looking.

All he had to do was refuse to play ball and he would be dumped out onto the street in total destitution. Dear dad would bleed out through his rectum and some other slob would take his place tomorrow.

"There is a small service you can perform for me. If you agree, then it would be my pleasure to present you with all these documents for you to do with as you please. Your father will be allowed to return home, call you, and say that he is free and in good health."

Rothington was starting to feel a little better. What the hell could this Chink possibly want that wasn't worth getting all his shit back and his father released? Hope it wasn't killing someone I really like, he mused.

"Mr. Zhang will convey the details and you can decide if you would like to work with us or......well, the OR should be pretty clear at this point."

"If I agree then all my property is returned to me, I get my documents, and my father is freed?

"Since you dare question me, you get all I promised when you have completed your service to me. You seem to be hesitating and I sense you are considering to try and negotiate with me."

Bolin Li wasn't the kind of man you fucked with. Larry Rothington wasn't completely sure of that until Mr. Sitting on Your Left grabbed his left hand and cut half his pinky off with a set of Lineman's pliers.

"AH, YOU FUCKING BASTARD!" Rothington screamed until the pliers were around his left ring finger.

"Stop! Stop!"

Always the planner, Bolin Li had arranged for a red tea towel to be ready in the car for just such an eventuality. Rothington had about a 4-minute presentation to listen to from Mr. Zhang and then he was dropped at the Chemist.

One phone call a day on the cell they gave him for maybe a week? Yeah, I can do that.

He crossed the street from the Chemist to the ER at Lambeth Hospital. Hell, at least he could still grip a golf club.

12

Verona's inability to sleep was getting worse. She would climb into her rack, pull the curtain, turn off the bunk light and slowly sing "Ave Maria" to herself in an attempt to calm down and sleep.

She might get a half hour, but beyond that, it was impossible. She kept reliving THAT day in Disney World when she and her mom were enjoying their last vacation day together before Verona went off on deployment.

They had met in Orlando two days before. Her mother had driven down from her home in Pensacola and Verona had flown in from Virginia Beach. Verona's command was actually on the Naval Operating Base in Norfolk, but she had a little condo in Virginia Beach up in the Thalia section about 7 miles from the beach.

She had been lucky to get it as she had been transferred from her first command at the Submarine Base in Groton, CT to Norfolk, VA and had to take a 3-month "Dead Horse" in pay to cover expenses. She rented an apartment for a year and then ran into a realtor, Mr. Pugh, who was also a retired sailor.

He fixed her up with a deal to rent the condo for 3 months at $500 a month and then he gave her back the money which she could use as a down payment to buy it. He even threw in a refrigerator. It's great when veterans take care of other vets.

So, now she's a homeowner and well on her way toward a good career in the Navy. She's respected in her work and, because of her specialty, she gets to go on assignments all over the Navy instead of being locked on one boat or branch of the service.

She wasn't dreaming of condos and beaches; she was reliving the moments she watched her mother's hair get set on fire as she struggled against the bindings and screamed. The chair bucked back and forth, but the big oriental-looking looking guy standing behind her just pushed down on her shoulders and smiled into the camera.

It was always at this point that she woke, covered in sweat. They had just come off the Pirates ride and were being ushered off the car and into the throng heading for the exit.

One second her mom was walking next to her and the next, she wasn't. Verona searched everywhere without luck and eventually asked one of the Disney employees for directions to security.

It was just at that moment that her cell phone sounded that little noise heralding the arrival of a text. Certain it must be her mother looking for her; she opened the text dialogue and saw only a hyperlink. It had been sent by her mother's phone, so she clicked.

The link took her directly into the proprietary Disney World security video system. The security video showed them getting of the ride, walking about 20 feet and then her mom had been bumped in to by that same big guy in the video who sprayed her in the face with something.

She slowly collapsed and he guided her to the seat of a waiting wheelchair pushed by a second man. All this happened within seconds. It was really smooth and none of the other people in the group seemed to notice anything out of the ordinary.

Then, the video switched to her mother, still sitting in the wheelchair, but now she appeared to be inside of some kind of vehicle like a van. The voiceover began and she had to hold the phone close to her face to hear over the din of the crowd.

"In one hour, you will be contacted again with instructions. Prepare yourself to follow these instructions to the letter or…" it was then that the hair burning and the screaming began.

Who could have done this? How could they get into Disney security video? What the hell was she going to do?

She was lying there, staring off into the dark of her bunk, covered in sweat; the desperate sweat of the helpless. The instructions had been clear. They, whoever they were, wanted her to help steal an American submarine; THIS one. They wanted her to choose between her country and her mother.

How in the fuck was she, one person, supposed to do this? How did these people even know she would be on this boat? What made them think she wouldn't spill her guts to her superiors?

They knew everything. They were tied into everything. That pasty, disgusting bastard who met her outside the Billeting Office the day she checked in knew all about her. He said he represented the people who had her mom and he was to give her the powder.

A little tin of "Woods of Winthrop" Lavender Body Powder was handed to her.

Larry Rothington had said: "You know what to do with this, I assume?"

"Yes."

"Good luck, then."

He ambled off and she watched him duck-walk his way down the sidewalk to a waiting taxi. The cab drove off and she put the tin in her parachute bag.

Originally, they had wanted her to shoot as many people as she could and then Emergency Surface the boat. A surprisingly stupid plan, since she would have to kill them all. Just one survivor would certainly kill her before she could get that sub to the surface.

It would have to be done so secretly that none would see it coming. That's when she thought about The Iceman and his trick of spraying cyanide. She could spray it into the sealed atmosphere and get them all at once. As long as she could get an Emergency Breathing Mask on first, then she would be spared.

Now, here in her bunk, crying, sweating, and shaking in fear, she was unaware of two more problems. First, her mother was already dead as Bolin Li never left survivors or any loose ends.

Second, that seabag lowered from the helicopter during the EVAC of the very sick Petty Officer Nichols, the one that read "CO EYES ONLY," had been opened and read by Captain Scott.

Since he had had no official notification that this thing was coming, and the helicopter captain didn't tell him about it, he just put it aside in his stateroom until he finished up some housekeeping.

When he first saw the bag, he had figured one of his opposite numbers in the Royal Navy sent him a bottle of brandy or cigars. Once he got into it, though, he wished he had opened the damn thing sooner.

The Red folder was sealed inside a red see-through document protector. He pulled the top open and opened the folder:

TOP SECRET
From: COMSUBLANT
To: COMMANDING OFFICER USS DODGE CITY
Subj: SUSPECTED CORONAVIRUS PANDEMIC

1. Find enclosed one sealed container of 30 vials of the vaccine Hydroxychloroquine and 100 hypodermics.
2. Find enclosed one thumb drive of Universal Translation Program Alpha One.
3. Department of State, Health, and Human Services, COMSUBLANT and BRITISH ADMIRALTY have concurred with the WORLD HEALTH ORGANIZATION determination that a Virus has been released from a Laboratory in Wuhan, China and is spreading around the world. Numerous deaths in all countries have been reported.
4. The vaccine Hydroxychloroquine has been reported successful in combatting said virus and you are authorized to immunize your crew immediately. One injection, 100mg IM.
5. Universal Translation Program Alpha One is authorized for upload into the Operational Artificial Intelligence System. Universal Translation Program Alpha One will interface with Electronics Countermeasure Mast Monitoring Systems, provide real-time translation of all signals in all Bands, and record both raw data and translated data on the AI drive designated for Monitoring, Surveillance, and Countermeasures.
6. Upon successful upload of Universal Translation Program Alpha One, Commanding Officer's discretion as to whether Special Onboard Riders be retained as backup or transferred off. At-Sea transfer will be arranged with tug if so desired.
7. SITREP expected by 2400 today.

At the same moment, Doc Adams had finally remembered to check his beeper. The chaos of getting Nichols stabilized and off onto that freaking helicopter had pushed it from his mind.

He had taken a shower, put on a clean uniform, grabbed a sticky bun in the Crew's Mess and a coffee, and was now seated in his little space in the 3-inch launcher space. The beeper was soaked through, so he took out the batteries and fired up his other beeper.

He looked up at the main Status screen and almost spit out his coffee. 13 Yellows. All temperature elevations. How the fuck can this be? Everything was Green two hours ago, and now 13 yellows out of 35?

The Dialex phone rang next to him.

"Doc Adams."

"Doc, this is the Captain. Come to my Stateroom, please."

"Aye, aye, sir."

4 seconds later, he's at Scott's open door and sees the XO standing next to the CO's desk. 2 quick knocks.

"Enter. Doc, what do you know about Coronavirus."

"Never heard of it, Captain."

At the very same moment, in what some would describe as Coincidence, while others would invoke Jungian Synchronicity, Bolin Li was watching CNN a half a world away. He found it amusing how the West was so caught up in markets and prices while people were starting to succumb to this new phenomenon called Coronavirus.

His dear China was being unfairly blamed. His beloved land which held the bones of his parents and the joy that was his youth. He thought fondly of his childhood visits to Wuhan's Dong Hu, or East Lake to fish with his little cousins.

He was a mere teenager when the Chinese Academy of Sciences started up the place in oh, 1956, or so and he was aware of its development since their work was brought to his attention in the 80s.

After he devastated Chernobyl, it was easy to install the same type of malware into the systems at Wuhan, drop the containment protocols and release all that Coronavirus on an unsuspecting world. It took surprisingly few people to do such a thing. You had to find the "Right" people and "Properly" motivate them.

He supposed that was the reason that a country's Special Forces troops were always so few. Motivation and a deep desire to be successful is a rare combination. Bolin Li's long life taught him that either money, pain, or love were the best tools for motivation.

Pay enough, torture enough, or threaten to grind up a loved one into cat food could get pretty much anybody to do anything.

Bolin Li targeted people. He wanted the ONE person who could get him what he wanted. His extensive payroll of experts in every field always came through to either get the job done or get him the guy who could get the job done.

A mid-level programmer in Wuhan, whose mother was sick and dying, would do anything to see her healthy again. Sadly, once the job was done, both the programmer and mommy would die in a housefire, car crash, something awful. No loose ends, ever.

Yes, the release of Coronavirus from the lab would cause China to lose a few million, but a small price to pay for global retribution. Besides, we had too many people as it was.

What the world didn't know, was that the Coronavirus wasn't the be all and end all of this sad, accidental leak of the virus. Some have had the audacity to accuse China of starting a Bio War by intentionally releasing Coronavirus, but that wasn't true. China, the country and the government, had NO IDEA what Bolin Li had been up to.

It was so much worse than anyone on Earth could imagine. The release of Coronavirus was merely the first step in Bolin Li's ingenious three-part plan. Thanks to the greed of key figures in the West, all those politicians desperate to keep sucking at the teats of a wealthy China, eager to avoid any suggestion of incompetence or, heaven forbid, intentionality, parts two and three were imminent.

"Vaccine, vaccine," they would shout and their billion-dollar drug companies would find a way to profit at a rate of a thousand dollars a second. They would, stupidly, buy their useless masks and raw material from China, further enriching the nation they were accusing of starting a Bio War, but they never knew it was Bolin Li all along.

Coronavirus was constructed in such a way, that only one particular chemical compound would lessen its effects. Once an infected patient was injected with the "vaccine," then the original Coronavirus would be altered making it ready to accept one more chemical that would cause it to evolve into its final form.

It's just like making gunpowder: Charcoal, Saltpeter, and Sulfur…alone, each is harmless, but together? Coronavirus, Vaccine, and finally the third piece of the puzzle, The Booster, and everybody exposed to all three, well, they die from a 3-part poison for which there is no vaccine, no treatment, no salvation.

The lapdogs who have risen to power across the western world who MANDATE vaccines, are unknowingly sentencing their people to death. If you don't have all 3 pieces, then you live. Yes, he wouldn't be able to get everybody, but 5 or 6 billion should be restitution enough for his parents, his friends, his country, and his youth.

He would call it Ai Li, "Lovely" in Chinese, after his mother.

He closed his eyes, rolled the Zippo in his fingers as his mind's eye watched his mother be raped for the ten thousandth time.

"The XO and I never heard of it, either."

Scott went on to brief his Corpsman on the information in his message and the package he was holding.

"Captain, within the last 15 minutes, my status board is showing 11 men developing a temperature."

"Doc, go do a search on this Coronavirus through the Marshal and let me know what you find."

"Aye, aye, sir."

A half hour later, Doc knew all about Wuhan, bats, the amount of sick, dying, and dead people around the world. He knew that high temperature was a sure sign of being infected and there was no cure as of yet.

The President himself took some of this Hydroxychloroquine and swore it made him better.

One shot, Intramuscular, bang, all better. He let the Captain and XO know what he learned and said he could immunize the whole crew in probably 90 minutes if they were all in the same place. If they took their shots around their watch schedules, he could get one section coming on and the off-going section right after; 6 hours later the last section. Stragglers, officers, cooks, everyone else within 7 hours. With such a small crew, he could just wander around and give them all shots in an hour or so.

The beeper went off as he was standing there talking to the Captain. He reached in his pocket and silenced it.

"You better look at it," the Captain said.

He pulled out the beeper and muttered, "Fuck. Oh, sorry, sir."

"What's up."

"I've got 3 in the Red, now."

"For what condition?"

"Temperature."

The Captain had read the supporting documents sent along in

the seabag that outlined some of the suspected symptoms and high temperature was one. Difficulty breathing and coughing were symptoms as well, and older folks were most at risk.

The average age of a Nuclear Attack Submarine crew is about 23 so that's a non-issue, but DODGE CITY did have an old guy onboard: Master Chief Durocher.

"XO, have the COB and that Senior Chief Spook, Lancey, come see me, please."

"Aye, aye, sir."

It was 2340 hours, so he yelled out after the XO to not wake them if they had turned in. He re-read the orders and then started to consider the translator upload for The Marshal.

"Why hadn't this been thought of before?" he wondered aloud. The YUKs could handle so much data, that this should have been part of the suite from the beginning.

You can buy a hand-held language translator to take on vacation with you, but the Navy's primo AI can't ask for a cup of coffee in Mexico?

We must have brought a half ton of equipment aboard to support the Interpreters, but the info on this thumb drive is all we ever needed? This is bullshit.

He had heard all about the Red Bikini and the Navigator blowing a gasket over it to Lancey. Getting Oakes off the boat isn't THAT bad of an idea. Yeah, it's not her fault, but it's not THAT bad of an idea under the circumstances.

Two knocks at the door.

"Enter. Oh, hi Senior Chief."

"Hello, Captain. You sent for me?"

When the messenger came into the Chief's Quarters and told him the Captain wanted to see him, he was convinced he was getting an ass-chewing over his little chat with Kennedy.

I can't imagine that fat bastard brought their little encounter all the way to the CO's attention. Fucking pussy. He had slowly walked toward the CO's Stateroom and ran a bunch of comments he might use through his head in case Scott was pissed.

"Senior Chief, I'm sorry to tell you this, but your services may not be needed this trip."

Hmm, didn't sound like this was leading up to an ass-chewing, but was he kicking him off the boat over Kennedy? He might have been written up and facing a Mast over this crap. He was only a few months from pulling the plug.

"Captain?"

"Are you familiar with the AI system we have on board, MATT DILLON?"

"Somewhat. I know it's tapped into all the other ship's systems and that the ultimate plan is for it to take the boat to sea without any people on board. I don't know all the details."

"Close enough. If it's tapped into all the systems, then why are you and your team here?"

Lancey took a second to think this one through; a second too long for Scott.

"Because it seems to only speak one language. You, for example, are expert in Russian?"

"A couple of others, too."

"See this thumb drive? It's going to turn The Marshal into a universal translator. We capture voice messages, in any language, and he translates, records, compares, all that stuff."

"I'm going to upload this in the morning and you are going to help us test the Marshal's capabilities. If he passes, then you get to transfer off the boat, spend a week of Liberty in England, and then fly home. If not, then you make the trip with the rest of us. Clear?"

"Clear. When would the transfer take place?"

"Got a hot date, there Senior?" Scott said smiling.

"No, sir. I'm retiring a month after this deployment and I wanted to finish my Submarine Quals this trip. I'm already ESWS and AC. It would be a nice capper to my career."

"What are you lacking?"

"The Emergency Blow was the last Practical Factor. All that's left is the Final Board."

"If we find that we don't need you this trip, we'll get your board done. How about if I assign Commander Kennedy?"

Lancey looked at Scott in that Oh, Fuck kind of way and Scott burst out laughing. The bastard DID know.

"OK, Senior, meet me in the Computer Room at 0800."

"Aye, aye, Captain."

Meanwhile, in the Lower-Level Head, Verona Oakes was trying not to puke. No, it wasn't meningitis, it was worry and guilt. Was she really going to murder 30 or 40 some people? NAVY people like her? Innocent people just to save her mother? Did she actually think she could help steal a nuclear submarine? It sounded like a story in some shitty comic book.

This was only her second time on a sub. She knew almost nothing about the boat. She wasn't here to operate the damn thing, just do her job WHEN and IF a piece of her equipment went FUBAR.

She had had a few short briefings at SUB SCHOOL about EABs and the basics of how a submarine works, but STAY OUT OF THE WAY was the main message.

She had been given two hours of classroom instruction and knew the main compartments, the whole "Time-Distance-Shielding" crap about guarding against getting too much radiation, where the Mess Hall was, the Heads, the Command Structure, all the basic stuff.

She also went through the Escape Trainer where they put a Steinke Hood on you and let you shoot up from a depth of 50 feet AFTER they've ensured you're not claustrophobic.

Now, she was supposed to commit the worst act of treason in the history of America. I don't think they'll care about her saving her mommy once she's offed an entire crew and handed a couple of nuclear weapons to...whom?

She didn't even know who the fuck had put her up to this. She had only seen that big, fat guy in person and that one oriental dude in the video. The instructions were given to her by a faceless voice once the video of her mother's hair being lit on fire had gone to gray.

No, no, yep, she was going to puke. She whipped back the bunk curtain and bolted to the Head...just in time.

13

The rest of the midwatch was uneventful. Doc Adams had researched Coronavirus through The Marshal's archives and had made a list of people to check on in the morning. He had put all the vaccine vials in the chill box inside of a locked, shoe box sized safe, with MEDICAL DEPARTMENT stenciled on it. He had let the Night Baker know it was in there.

One last check of the status board and he would turn in. Same 8 Yellows and 3 Reds; no change in temperature. As he was getting into his bunk, he heard coughing somewhere out in the dark of Middle Level berthing. It was 0115. He could get maybe 4 hours before the rustling of the Messenger making Wake-ups would unintentionally wake him, too.

It was exactly one hour and one minute later when the pocket beeper started chirping. 11 Yellows and 9 Reds now. The beeper went off when certain parameters were exceeded; one of which was body temperature because that was an indicator of infection.

He had silenced it earlier this evening when the first 3 Reds showed up, but they were barely 100 degrees. Now, he had 11 crew at 99, and all other alarms over 100.5. He bolted out of his bunk and got dressed. He headed to Control to check out the first guy on the Red list, LCDR Kennedy Himself.

Brandon Nix was the Quartermaster of the Watch and greeted Doc as he walked into Control from the NAV Space.

"Hey, Doc. You're either up late or early."

"I've got to check on a few guys...."

He looked over at Fire Control and saw the OOD sitting on one of the benches with his head down.

"Sir, I'd like to check your temp. I'm showing high on you."

"Now? I'm on watch" in his haughtiest tone.

"Just takes a second. You feel OK?"

"I feel like shit. Headache and all congested and shit, too."

Doc aimed the laser at Kennedy's forehead. 102.

"Commander, you're running a fever. Can you get a relief"?

"Doc, I'm on watch until 0530. I won't die before then. Gimme an aspirin."

"I think it's worse than that, sir."

Doc Adams wasn't sure what to do. Headaches, a little temperature, some coughing. They could all be coming down with colds. He wouldn't have given it much thought had he not found out about this Coronavirus bullshit and how it's spreading around the world.

He wouldn't dare suggest Kennedy take a shot of that Hydroxy stuff; Kennedy would put up a big fuss and basically shit a brick because he's scared of needles. They had to carry him from his stateroom (where they found him crying) into the crew's mess to get his Shot Card topped off for the deployment.

It was pathetic and hilarious at the same time seeing this fat fucker hanging between two big Auxiliarymen holding him up by the armpits and weaving their way to where Doc was giving out shots. Can you imagine if the enemy had this guy? They could wave a hypo at him and he'd spill his guts.

Anyway, the only way the Great Kennedy would agree to a shot was if the CO gave him a direct order. It was probably best if the Captain would make a 1MC announcement so the whole crew knew they were getting vaccinated. They would all be worried about their families once they found out the severity of this Coronavirus crap.

It was almost 0300, so he'd better get his equipment together to be ready to dose everyone. The boat will go up for the morning Skid around 0500 and, if it's rough up there, shit will be flying all over the boat. Periscope Depth in this part of the world, at this time of year, was always sketchy.

He had to get down to Middle Level berthing before Schiano woke up. Doc had been cutting little pieces off the end of his web belt to make Paul think he was getting fat. Today he should really take notice if he sliced off a half inch more and readjusted the belt buckle.

The whole last deployment, Adams was cutting out the last few pages of whatever paperback book Schiano was reading and would leave ransom notes for him to find. Either you give up on the story OR you pay the ransom and get directions to the spot where your NEXT page was hidden. The hardest part was keeping a straight face when Schiano would complain about it.

It was so easy for Doc to do this kind of shit to people since they all had scheduled watches and Doc did not. He was always free to take advantage of their unattended bunk and mess with their shit.

He even put condoms and phone numbers written in lipstick into a guy's bags when they were getting back from sea. Their old ladies would find this stuff when they did the laundry and go apeshit. The whole time the poor bastard was innocent. Hilarious.

In fact, it was just a commonality of submarine crews to fuck with each other. Many a guy got off watch with only one thought: hit the rack for 12 hours of sleep. He pees, goes to his bunk, pulls back the curtain, and hops in to find his pillow is a solid block of ice!

Somebody wet it down in the shower right after he'd gotten up 6 hours ago and threw it in the freeze box until just a few minutes before he got here. Entire mattresses have been frozen with the bedding made as though nothing was amiss. A guy would roll in and find himself on a frozen lake.

For a while, subs carried a shitload of instant coffee which everyone hated. So, it was only right that several jars of the stuff would get dumped onto a guy's sheets and covered with the blanket. 3 inches deep of instant coffee would be waiting for the poor, tired bastard. Hooray for Camaraderie.

Schiano, though, was a pompous asshole and always thought of himself as some kind of handsome devil women craved. He worked out all the time and always bought himself fashionable clothes.

The whole time the boat was in England, he'd hit on the best-looking girls but barely one in ten were ever interested. Each time he got shot down; he'd make the same comment when he got back where his friends were sitting: "she must be a dyke."

He said it so much that everybody would say it all at once whenever he'd approach a girl and get shot down; which was pretty much always. He'd get up, walk over, and talk to some girl, ask to dance, or buy her a drink.

The boys would watch him turn around, head back to the table, and just as he got there, "She must be a dyke!" rang out from the group along with snide, derisive laughter.

He was such a cocky bastard that he never saw it as a slam on him, but that his shipmates really thought that of her since that lezzy bitch turned HIM down.

As he was turning to leave his space with a pair of surgical scissors, the COB walked by on his way to the coffee pot.

"COB! Am I glad to see you? Do you know what's going on with the vaccine and all?"

"Yeah, I saw the CO a little after midnight."

"AND the possibility the Spooks will leave?"

"Yeah. He met with Lancey right before I saw him. Something wrong, Doc.?"

"I've got temperatures going up all over the boat. 20 Yellows and Reds. I'm hearing coughing in Middle Level Berthing. We must have the virus onboard."

"Everybody still upright and functioning?"

"I think so. Most guys are asleep. Kennedy's the OD and he seems sick."

"Keep me updated if the number goes up. We'll probably vaccinate everyone this morning."

Joe Durocher took out a hanky and blew his nose. Green gooey-looking stuff. He looked at it oddly.

"I never have shit like that in my snot locker." He mumbles to no one in particular, but the Doc heard him.

He pulled out his pocket beeper just as the thing went off. 2 more yellows and the COB was one.

"COB, your temp's going up. McCleary, too."

"He's on watch, Doc, go tell him."

Three minutes later: "God Dammit" rings out in Control and 5 or 6 guys start laughing.

The COB went into the Crew's Mess and got a cup of coffee. He noticed Petty Officer Oakes sitting in one of the outboard tables looking at her phone. He hadn't had much of a chance to talk with her since assigning her a bunk, so he walked over and sat down across from her.

"How's the reception at 400 feet?"

She looked up, red eyed, and gave a short, forced laugh. "Just looking at pictures, Master Chief."

"I'm the Chief of the Boat, so you can call me by my real name which is COB."

Obviously, something was bothering this girl, so he was trying to lighten the mood. Must be tough going aboard different ships and only staying for the deployment. Never really get to know anyone other than the fact that they all want to be balls deep in you.

"This isn't your first time on a submarine deployment, is it?"

He already knew the answer, but he needed something to get a conversation started.

"I did a Northern Run on the North Dakota last year."

"And?"

"Well, all my equipment worked fine, so it was pretty boring. I don't mean to sound stuck up or anything, but it seemed like a good idea to keep my distance from the crew and not get too chummy."

"I understand."

This is when he wanted to ask why she thought displaying the goods in a red bikini could even remotely be a good idea, but he bit his tongue. He had a sense that something else was in play here.

"Everything been OK while you've been here? Senior Chief Lancey seems pretty good to work with."

"I only worked with him once before when we took a COD onto the Abe Lincoln and set up some ECM gear for them. He's nice."

"Who's the lady?" Joe asked when he saw the picture on the phone.

Well, this got Verona Oakes to crying a little more and wiping her nose with a bare hand. Joe handed her a napkin out of the dispenser. She wiped her nose, one eye, and whispered "my mom."

"Well, I see where you got your good looks from" is what he WANTED to say, but the little bit of a filter 49 years in the Navy left him, cut in just in time.

"It's normal to miss people we love when we're at sea. That's WHY we're at sea...keeping the bad guys away from hearth and home."

The Bad Guys she repeated inside her head. SHE was the Bad Guy now. She was the enemy. Other than the dangers of operating a nuke sub, she was the closest thing to death these guys had ever had, and they didn't even know it. How could she?

If her mother knew what she was going to do, she would die a thousand deaths. She would sacrifice herself before she would ever ask another to give his life for her. She raised her daughter better; she didn't raise a traitor. How do you make that decision?

"I have a little bit of interesting news for you, Oakes, if you promise you'll keep a secret."

"Yeah, sure."

"There's an outside chance you won't be making the trip with us."

Lightning bolts flashed across her brain and she couldn't believe what she was hearing.

"What do you mean?"

"It's not definite, yet, in fact it may not happen, but you may get to go home in a couple of days. We may not need any riders if things go as hoped."

She sat back on the bench and took a deep breath. If she gets sent back, they'll kill her mother for sure. Shit, they'll just kill the both of us. They'll be afraid that she'll rat out the whole plan. What would she say? She didn't know anything, really.

She didn't know who was behind it; so, what exactly was she going to say? There was no proof. The only hard evidence she had was that tin of cyanide powder and the thumb drive. It could be said she thought the whole thing up all by herself.

It was at this moment that one of the many lessons one learns as they age came to pass. Oakes' posture, the way she held her face down a little but raised her eyes to his own, gave Joe Durocher the sense that this girl as about to reveal something sensitive.

In this second, she reminded him of a little girl that had done something wrong and was about to come clean to grandpa even though she would get a spanking.

He turned his head a little and was just about to ask what was up when she sat forward again and seemed to try and compose herself.

Listening to her own thoughts, she made up her mind that she wasn't going to go through with any of this. If she had the chance to get off this boat, then she was going to throw that shit in the sea and lay as low as she could.

They couldn't just kill her mother, could they? It wasn't her fault or mine if the Navy yanked me off of here. She had zoned out and didn't realize the COB was talking again.

"You OK? Is there something you want to talk about?"

"No, no thanks. I'm just processing what you told me. Thinking about packing up and all that."

The boat pitched up a little and Durocher looked over to the depth gauge repeater under the bug juice machine.

"We're going to PD for the morning traffic. I'm going up to Control... if there's anything you'd like to chat about, you just let me know, OK, Oakes?"

She could tell he was being sincere and she just wanted to totally break down and get some help. What the hell was she supposed to do?

"OK, COB, will do."

"Oakes, I'm fucking serious. You're in MY tribe now. Whatever it is, you hear me?"

She looked down and nodded.

Durocher slid out from the table with his coffee cup and headed forward. He never went up the ladder leading to the NAV Space. Too vertical and narrow through the hatch. Hard to maneuver a cup of coffee through there, too, unless you'd put it on the floor over your head and then climb up to get it. They had that stupid chain across the hatchway, too.

He just went forward past Doc's space and up the ladder to Upper Level and then Aft to Control. He noticed the CO's and XO's stateroom doors were shut and just kept going into Control.

He passed Demzer seated at the inboard station and said "Pappy" to acknowledge McCleary on the Dive. He took a quick turn left and stuck his head into Sonar, said good morning, and then sat in front of Fire Control to let his eyes adjust to the dark. He wanted to observe Kennedy since Doc mentioned he was sick.

0510 and Pappy had the boat trimmed at 150 feet ready to go up.

The QM of the Watch announced: "The Captain's in the Control Room" since we were rigged for black and no one else saw him come in.

Kennedy informed the CO that the ship was trimmed SAT at One Five Zero feet and he intended to come to Periscope Depth.

"Dive make your depth Six Two feet."

"Six Two feet, aye, sir." 7 degree up angle, boys, full rise fairwater planes. Make your depth Six Two feet."

The Helmsman and Planesman knew it was going to be tough to stay at PD. They were still at 150 feet and the boat was already taking 5-degree rolls. Depending on which way the seas were going, they might get sucked up and broach.

"Chief of the Watch, Flood Auxiliaries."

"Flooding Aux 2…2 thousand….4 thousand."

"Secure flooding. Pump two thousand to After Trim."

"Two thousand to After Trim, aye" Gravy belted out.

Best to come up a little heavy with an up angle so the surface action of the waves wouldn't get a hold of that big deck aft of the sail and pull the boat up.

Besides, the floating antenna was out and you didn't want to stick the ass end of the boat up so the prop would cut the damn thing. All they needed was a few minutes to get messages and then back down.

"Conn, Radio, message traffic onboard. Ready to go deep."

"Radio, Conn, aye."

"Diving Officer, make your depth 400 feet".

"400 feet, aye. 5 down."

Both Ship Control watchstanders acknowledged.

"Helm, All Ahead Full."

"All Ahead Full, aye. Answers Ahead Full."

"Very well. Rig Control for White."

All the regular lights were turned on and everyone would squint and blink for the next few minutes.

"Well, if it ain't my favorite person, my Relief. 'Bout time you got here, God Dammit."

14

The entire Midwatch got relieved and just about everyone went to eat breakfast. Kennedy, who was known for never missing a meal, went straight to his stateroom. The few officers who sat in the Wardroom at 0600 breakfast were astonished that the Navigator was absent.

"He must be dying," LT. House quipped.

The XO even chuckled at that one ESPECIALLY since Chief Russell was cooking breakfast today and had made Biscuits and Gravy. Of course, the biscuits had been made fresh that night by Mac, who was, hands down, the best baker on board. To make the meal even MORE inviting, Russell had made "Sawmill" gravy which had cornmeal in it, and it was Kennedy's favorite.

"Somebody checks on him so he doesn't sleep through his favorite breakfast," said the XO to no one in particular. At that exact moment, Doc Adams was staring at the black square next to Kennedy's name on his screen.

"What the fuck?"

Adams ran out of his little shack and across the passageway into Officer's country. He crashed into House who had just stuck his head into Kennedy's stateroom.

"Commander Kennedy?" They both called out in unison.

House pulled back Kennedy's bunk curtain.

"Jack. JACK. Biscuits and gravy."

Quiet.

House reached in and flipped on the bunk light. Kennedy was lying there, eyes open, staring.

"Doc!"

Adams pushed by him and reached for Kennedy's throat. He turned to look at the Weapons Officer.

"Jesus fucking Christ. He's dead."

House went white and left the stateroom headed to the Wardroom and stuck in his head.

"XO, come with me, please."

Lieutenant Commander Berns had 14 years in the Navy and had been around the block a few times. He had never had a man die at sea and, other than calling the Captain, had no idea what to do next.

Third Degree Berns, as he was called by his friends, cleared his head immediately.

"House, get the CO. Doc stay here and keep everyone out."

Two "Aye, aye, sirs" and two minutes later, Captain Lazarus Scott slowly entered the stateroom and looked at his Navigator.

"Doc, check him over."

Other than eyes open and having peed himself, Kennedy looked as though he was deep in thought. No injuries, no bleeding, nothing.

"XO, document everything. Get statements from anyone who interacted with the Nav in the last 24 hours. Log his death, time of discovery, ship's position. Doc, take photographs of the body and the condition of the stateroom. Get the COB."

"Doc, I want you to take a vial of his blood and document a chain of custody. I think NCIS will want to analyze it."

When the CO entered the Wardroom, only the Engineer and Chief Russell were there. He could tell they were reading his face which must have shown some grave level of concern.

"Coffee, Captain?"

"Not right now, Chief. I'm afraid we have serious trouble on our hands."

Both were looking at him and then at each other when he told them of Kennedy's death. Kitty Russell had to sit down and took off her chef's hat.

"How, Captain?

"No idea, yet. He wasn't feeling well last night."

"Doc!" the Captain yelled.

"Sir?"

"Take his temp and give me your best idea for time of death."

"Captain, he just got relieved 45 minutes ago. It couldn't be very long. I just noticed his Med Status had changed to Black and came running in here. The Marshal will have it recorded. Must've just happened."

"And nobody heard anything?"

"No, sir. He had the stateroom all to himself since we're so few and he's senior" added House.

The COB knocked on the Wardroom door even though it was

open.

"I already heard."

"It just happened."

"Word travels fast on a submarine, XO."

"We need statements from anyone who saw him last night. Document any conversation and observations of his condition."

"I saw him, too," Durocher said. "Doc even tried to get him to get an early relief because his temp was in the Yellow and he was sweating and having difficulty breathing."

'Well, what do we do with him, now? The XO seemed to be thinking out loud. "COB?"

"We had a guy croak on the NARWHAL back in the 70s. Put him in a body bag and then into the freeze box. We had been in trail under the ice and couldn't leave station, so we just put him in the aftermost part of the freezer and left him."

"Jesus, sounds so cruel."

"Nothing else to do. Can't let him decompose and stink everything up. He has to be autopsied and all that when the boat gets back. Full inquiry, investigation, statements, photos, the whole nightmare."

"How long was he in there?"

"We did 63 days deployed. He went out on day 30."

Everyone shivered and thought about how their own families would be notified and when.

"House!"

"Aye, Captain?"

"You're the Navigator, now."

"Yes, sir."

See if there's any message protocol. Draft a message to COMSUBLANT and give it to me ASAP."

"Aye, aye, sir."

By this time, there had been enough commotion that everyone eating breakfast out in the crew's mess knew of Kennedy's demise. 4 seconds later, the rest of the boat knew. 5 seconds later, Verona Oakes was throwing up in the lower-level Head with the horrible feeling that, somehow, she was to blame.

About 1200 miles East, back in Portsmouth at the Royal Navy HQ, Larry Rothington was shitting bricks. This whole Coronavirus bullshit had resulted in forced quarantine for essential staff ever since the afternoon of DODGE CITY's departure from the base.

If you remember, the elder Rothington was being held captive and only his dear son's daily updates regarding the whereabouts and condition of the DODGE CITY would keep him alive.

Unable to make any calls on his special new SAT phone while in lockdown, Larry was certain his father was dead by now. He was right, of course, but the lockdown had nothing to do with it. Bolin Li NEVER let anyone live and Larry's daddy had been dead ever since that photo had been taken.

Today, after 5 days, staff were being permitted to go home as long as they went DIRECTLY home and then DIRECTLY back to the office next morning. Larry burst from his building and "ran," inasmuch as a fat, disgusting, ball of blubber could run, toward his car.

He drove out the gate and stopped at the first open parking spot out of sight of the gate guards. He made his first call.

"Mr. Rothington, you are either out of your mind or you have other relatives you care for more than your father."

"It's this pandemic! I have been quarantined in my office by The Admiralty and have been unable to call! Is my father alright?"

He asked out of concern, certainly, but also because if his dad had been killed, then he, Larry the Great, could deliver this Satellite phone to base Security and report an attempted extortion on himself. He could easily feign dignified patriotism as he sacrificed the life of his own father for the good of the Empire. Good lord, he might be knighted!

He spent the next few minutes spilling his guts to his dear friend from the tobacconist's, Mr. Zhang. He told him of the vaccine sent aboard to help stave off the infection and that it was being tossed about to send a Royal Navy Doctor aboard for the remainder of the deployment.

Zhang was unaware that Attack boats didn't already have a Doctor...When he heard Rothington speak of the tentative plan to remove the technicians if the translator worked, he thought he might have an idea.

Larry wracked his brain to sound as informative as possible so that they would not only keep his dad alive, but not put a half-powered .22 in his head like the rumors of Mossad hitmen.

Zhang clicked off and turned to Bolin Li to fill him in. They were both seated on the same Poul Kjaerholm sofa, so Bolin only had to turn his head once Zhang was ready to report. He had spent the last few minutes regretting buying this ugly, uncomfortable couch. It was the last remaining one from the 50's and had cost him around forty thousand dollars.

Zhang filled him in on the difficulties of late.

"We have the girl on board already, but another ally would well work to our advantage. I seem to remember that your dear "nephew," Li Wei, served 4 years in the People's Liberation Navy; aboard submarines, no less. Wasn't he also a doctor?"

Bolin Li already had the same idea.

"He did not complete medical school. We had to get him out of Boston when that Harvard co-ed's body was discovered. He is a Chinese citizen, so removing him from school and getting him safely to China was easy."

"It was after pre-Med school that he volunteered to do his sacred duty to the Party. Because of his short education in America, he was trained as a medic, as it were, and served 2 years aboard The Peace Ark, China's only hospital ship."

His last 2 years were spent aboard one of those new Shang class subs. He certainly knows enough about the submarines and the medical aspect to be useful in this effort."

Zhang went on: "IF we can get him aboard that submarine, and IF he can administer the cyanide, then everyone will die immediately. Hopefully, he won't be discovered and killed."

Even if he is discovered, the blame can never be traced to us. At the very least the Chinese government will take the blame and that pig Brockington will be arrested, but we will stay in the clear. There will be other opportunities."

Bolin Li was thinking out loud: "It's Rothington," he corrected.

"He will be watched, of course. He will have to inject the vaccine and he will have to disperse the cyanide in the way we originally intended. Our Angel of Death will have to show him what to do before she leaves that ship.

He'll have to contact her immediately, get the powder from her. And she'll have to show him where to release it. Bring him here and tell him what must be done."

"We can have Rothington tell him all that. He just has to get the cyanide and her mask. All he needs to find out is where to operate the levers that surface the boat."

"Your nephew is taking an enormous risk. Are you sure he is up to it? Are you sure he can actually do this? His motivations are not the same as ours."

Firstly, he is technically NOT my nephew. My beloved Qing Shan, who saved me all those years ago in childhood, is his Grandmother. He wouldn't do this out of love, he knows he owes me for that whole Boston thing. He would STILL be in a US Supermax prison had I not used my influence.

Besides, I'll tell him that, once successful, he can run the entire Thailand Operation. Complete with house and boat. He loves it over there on Pattaya Beach; lots of foreigners to sell to and all those perversions to enjoy."

Zhang said nothing; just slowly nodded.

"Get that English pig to show him photos of the levers and teach him as much as he can. Dear nephew probably knows more about that sub than we give him credit for. Remind our dear Mr. Rothington that his father is hoping his little boy does well."

They both laughed.

15

"The odds of this plan working are astronomically low," Larry mumbled to himself as soon as he clicked off his conversation with Zhang. He did find out that the kid had submarine experience in the Chinese Navy.

He also knew that those Shang boats were very similar to the Soviet Victor class attack boats, so he would have a surprising amount of knowledge going in. The Pre-Med school would be a help too, since he had to convince the Americans that he was a doctor…

He FIRST had to get with Li Wei, or Wei Li, or whatever the hell his name was, and brief him, THEN he had to get him on whatever ship was scheduled to meet the DODGE CITY, and SOMEHOW get the real doctor out of the picture.

It might be better to send a helo out there since there would be less people in the entourage to fuck things up. THAT'S what he'll do. Recommend to the Admiralty they send a Helo instead of some tugboat or something. The seas will be rough out there this time of year and transit time for a helicopter will be much less.

One doctor lowered in a harness and two riders brought up wouldn't be so hard to do. He looked at his watch; had to meet Li Wei at the same tobacconist he had met Zhang in one hour.

The only saving grace to this entire debacle, would be that Rothington would be the coordinator for the personnel transfer. He opened his computer and got into the staff roster for the entire Royal Navy. There had to be ONE doctor that was Oriental. There had to be someone he could assign to the operation and then secretly replace him with Li Wei.

Of course, by "replace" he meant kill the guy. There wasn't time and certainly no motivation to do anything else. He arrowed down through the Medical department thumbnail photos as he tried to formulate some kind of a plan.

There! Lieutenant Commander Robert Kellogg, Royal Navy Medical Service. What the fuck kind of Chinese name is that? Must be adopted or something. He clicked on the photo to blow it up and get a better look at him. Black hair, check. Almond shaped eyes, check. Five feet five, check. General Practitioner.

He was 34 years old, though, and Wei was maybe 26ish. He was thinking it might be a tough sell, but his racist brain told him that Orientals always look younger than they are….

He just then realized he had no idea what Li Wei looked like. Most Anglos couldn't distinguish between one Oriental or another, so as long as they were close, he just might get away with it. The doctor's home address was listed in Perranporth; not very far from the base.

The best bet, he thought, was to just go to Kellogg's flat, kill him, take his ID and medical bag, give all that shit to Wei, and get HIM on the helo. If he faked some kind of air sickness, no one would talk to him and would be none the wiser that he wasn't the real doctor. Once on board, he gets the cyanide and mask from Oakes, does the deed, and Bob's your uncle.

He'd try to call Zhang. Maybe he'll kill Kellogg for him. He's the expert on that kind of stuff, not me, Larry mused.

Now, he had to find pictures, or a You Tube Video on Emergency surfacing a sub. There must be some easy way to get out of this. Larry Rothington was just following his natural urges to be as lazy as possible, always have someone else to blame, and to take credit for anything that went well.

It was closing in on the cocktail hour and Larry really needed at least a quick shower since his meeting was in 40 minutes. He might as well get some more tobacco while he was there…he didn't get any the last time, thanks to Zhang. He rubbed his hand as he thought about that big fucker with the pliers.

Larry waited outside a small clothing store just down the block from the Tobacconist. He saw an Oriental-looking man enter and he headed over. The little bell over the door rang and both the clerk and the man he assumed was Li Wei looked in his direction.

"Ah, Mr. Rothington," the clerk called out pleasantly. "Excuse me, sir," he said to Wei as he moved toward his old customer.

"So sorry about last time, Al. Got an emergency text from the Admiralty; had to go. Time and Tide."

"Completely understand. I have your usual order calmly sleeping in the humidor, if you're ready for it this evening."

"Yes, please, Al. Bag it up, if you would."

Al pushed his way through the curtain that separates the front from the back of the house and returned a moment latter with Larry's parcel.

"On the book, sir?"

"If you please."

Turning to the new face in the shop, Al asked how he could help.

"I am quite new to pipe smoking. Still learning the different types of tobacco and so on. Any advice for a novice?"

Larry thought it a perfect time to speak up and begin to engage with this future mass-murderer.

"If I may. A mild cavendish like this one would be an excellent jumping-off point. It's particularly well suited to a Briar pipe for a smooth and cool smoke."

He was pointing at one of the retail "Captain" blends since it was sitting right in front of him and Al wouldn't suspect anything underhanded going on.

"Excellent. I'd like to give that a try. I'll take one of the 2-ounce packages, please. Perhaps you would join me in a brandy as a token of thanks."

Well, this guy was pretty smooth, Larry thought to himself. Great suggestion to get away from the shop together without arousing suspicion. They could chat at will unobserved.

As they walked out of the shop and down the street, Larry sized this guy as best he could. Physically, he was just about Kellogg's size so the uniforms might just fit. His accent was terribly thick, though, and, as he had never heard Kellogg speak, he wasn't sure if this was good or bad.

A hundred yards or so from the tobacconist's, Larry stopped and spoke closely and directly to Li Wei.

"I don't want to spend any more time on this than necessary. We needn't be seen in some pub together, so listen closely…"

He spent the next 6 minutes going over the plan as he saw it. Kellogg would be eliminated, his papers and equipment brought to Wei, he would use Kellogg's ID to get on the helo and make his way about the DODGE CITY. The main sticking point, the one of a hundred things that could go wrong, was that Larry had no way to reach Oakes and fill her in. Wei would have to do that as soon as he got below.

Wei eyed this pasty faced, bulbous, and smelly man the whole while he spoke. His uncle's friend, Zhang, had made most of this clear, but he was to take any information or guidance Mr. Rothington could offer and use it where he could.

He couldn't help but think it a foolish plan; smuggling poison, trying to spray the entirety of a submarine interior, surfacing a nuclear submarine in the middle of the ocean, and actually thinking this would work? Uncle Li was certainly smarter than that.

He knew he had enough medical knowledge from med school to probably pull this off. He only had to act like he was examining people and give them a shot. In fact, if he acted in a commanding manner and stayed sharp enough, he could get the sub's Corpsman to do the shots while he prepared himself for his part in this whole plan.

He had a pretty fair idea about the inside of a submarine. Part of his submarine training was to learn as much about the American boats as could be learned. Rothington assured him that the real doctor wouldn't have any knowledge at all, so he was actually way ahead of the game.

He was expected to appear lost and unsure, so it actually added to his cover. Since everyone assumed he was Dr. Kellogg, he would most likely never be asked for any identification, anyway, so that was one more point in his favor.

After all, he was handpicked by the British Admiralty to come aboard and save the crew from this new virus. No one would dare question him, would they? He would certainly be treated with consummate respect by the enlisted people, he just couldn't waste a lot of time interacting.

Medical people weren't particularly all that military, so to speak, he would just have to be careful not to give himself away until the job was done.

He had to know more about this whole "Artificial Intelligence" thing. Less crewmembers than usual, first Deployment of the operational system, there had to be a way to exploit this.

Then there was the issue of several of the technicians being transferred off the boat? A dead body, too…he needed more info on what he was getting into. He wanted to hear it from Zhang and not this perverted Englishman.

This wasn't going to be easy and he was certainly taking a tremendous risk trying to pull this off, but he would do anything for his uncle Bolin. It had nothing to do with love…he was just sick of having his past misdemeanors held over his head and his future would be ideal once he pulled this caper off.

He owed Bolin Li, after all, and success in this endeavor would bring untold rewards from one of the richest men to ever live and only a handful of people knew he even existed.

Across the entirety of the planet, virtually every shipment of fentanyl, marijuana, meth, poppy, whatever was in some way authorized, owned, profited from, directed, scheduled, arranged, and/or financed by Bolin Li.

He even owned stock in most of the legal pharma companies and was very nearly planet Earth's first Trillionaire. When he commanded something to happen, it did. When he wanted someone dead, they died. Regimes rose and fell on his word.

A petty tyrant whose residential compound was located outside of Manila had been skimming off the top. He called himself Blackbeard as though the name would instill fear in his competitors. He probably just thought himself a badass and needed a fitting name.

Having never actually met Bolin Li in person, he must have had some crazy notion that such a man was a folk tale and the stories about his anger were meant to keep the underlings in line; mere exaggerations.

He ran his business however he saw fit, exacted reprisals on whoever crossed him, and withheld Uncle Li's cut. That happened for almost 6 months right up until the moment that Malaysia Air Flight 370, yes, THAT missing flight 370, nosedived from 39,000 feet and slammed into his house and killed him, his whole family, and over half the thugs that worked for him.

One stewardess, one thumb drive, and the promise of a loved one's release from political prison, and whammo. If you could motivate the right person, with the right finger on the button, so to speak, then anything was possible. Bolin Li knew how to get what he wanted and nobody, nobody crossed him.

Senators, magistrates, celebrities, famous and influential people the world over, fawned, prayed, and drank from the fountain of Bolin Li. Willing or no, they drank; if they were useful, then they lived and were lavishly rewarded. It was Bolin Li's way or it was the end for you.

The word "Ruthless" didn't go far enough to describe the dark nature of his dear uncle. To make a play to steal an American nuclear attack submarine would be insane for the normal man, but the reach of his uncle's organization, the tools at his disposal, and his natural force of will made it a fair bet.

Besides, Li Wei LOVED Thailand, and if his uncle was going to set him up as the new drug king in that part of the world, even Caligula wouldn't have had a better time.

Images of Hawaiian shirts and lavish parties danced in his head. Just had to stay calm, find the girl, get the shit, and kill off, what, 40 guys? If he could get them all in one place....

As is usually the case when a plan is being thrown together, even though people claim to understand Occum's Razor, no one actually thought about the simplest way to approach this.

After all, there had been an epidemic of some kind on board. Why not order the submarine to make port and take the crew to hospital? No, that wouldn't work. If that boat were sitting at a pier, how the hell would they get the sub started up and moving? Does Uncle have people who can operate a sub?

I suppose so; he seems able to get anyone to do anything. No, best to try and take the boat at sea while it's already operating. Get our people below deck and hang onto it until the next phase of the plan went into action......Li Wei looked off into the distance and wondered just what the next phase would be.

Anyway, what if that girl had gotten rid of the stuff? What if she had already chickened out and spilled her guts? Rothington would have heard if such a thing had happened. There was no way to know what was going on aboard that submarine. He'd put his Colt in his kit bag and tell Rothington to get him a new cyanide supply of his own. Can't have too much poison, eh!

He realized that Rothington had finally stopped talking. He grunted something about making arrangements from his office tomorrow morning. Kellogg had to be removed and Zhang was just going to have to do it.

16

Rothington's last conversation with Zhang had made it clear that the ONLY way this plan would work was to get rid of Kellogg and have Wei assume his identity. Rothington, the Head of Planning for the Admiralty, would draw up the plan to get the "Doctor" out to the DODGE CITY.

He would advise to stay away from an ocean-going tug and schedule helicopter transport. He had yet to find out that Captain Scott was about to help his plans if that Translator worked.

Captain Lazarus Scott, Senior Chief Lancey, and Petty Officer Hochstetler were gathering in the computer room to upload the translation software.

Once they let the software install and run it's programmed self-test, then they would give it a few real-world tests. It would be at that point the CO would decide if the Spooks were leaving.

He was a big Team Player, ole Captain Scott, and he looked upon the Intel Riders as outsiders who, although professionals in their work, did not have as their priority, allegiance to his ship. He always wanted the First String in the game.

After announcing: "FORMAT RECOGNIZED." It took seven minutes for the Marshal to suck all the data out of the thumb drive. He was ready.

Scott looked at Lancey and asked if he knew any Russian phraseology that was more street talk (he actually said 'colloquialistic') rather than the kind of speech right out of the textbook.

The Senior Chief told the Marshal a few jokes he had heard Grandpa tell around the Vodka glasses once Terry's Babushka went to bed.

The Marshal translated and spit them out almost perfectly. Lancey threw some Icelandic at him including several of the many words they use for The Sea.

All came back good. Even the little Mandarin Lancey knew was no match for the upload.

"Looks like I'm spending the rest of the week in Jolly Ole England, eh Captain?"

"Not until you finish your Qual Board, Senior," Scott said with a smile. "I suppose you heard about the Navigator"?

In the black humored manner with which military people seem to tinge all their commentary, Lancey gives a quick p'shaw of breath and says: "Well, don't look at me."

They all smirk and the Captain and Hochstetler remove and retain their keys from the console. The Marshal now speaks a hundred and some languages, and the CTs need to pack their shit.

The CO wandered down to the Chief's Quarters, gave a quick respectful knock on the door, and stuck in his head.

"COB, are you in here"?

"At the table, Captain, please come in."

Durocher took one look at his CO and could tell something was about to happen.

"COB, we have uploaded a new language program into the Marshal that the Navy previously overlooked. He's now able to receive and translate pretty much every language on earth. That means…"

"We don't need the riders," Durocher finished Scott's thought.

"Correct. Since we've got to take the Navigator off the ship, I'd like to send them, too. I plan to request a helo for them that can bring us any mail or other goodies the Admiralty may want to send."

Have Senior Chief Lancey report to me at his earliest opportunity."

The COB sensed there was more.

"We have had so much bullshit happen to us since we left port, I want to go all in on this deployment and also reduce the crew to absolute minimum. What's your feeling"?

The old Master Chief had to think about this a second. 'Absolute minimum' meant one roving watchstander per section Fore and Aft instead of one guy on each of the 3 levels. Geez, it could even mean Port and Starboard roving watches.

That means a total of 4 or 6 where there had been at least 18. The ship's control party could drop from 9 planesmen to 3.

"You thinking Port and Starboard or one rover per section, Captain"?

"One per section. Port and Starboard for 3 months is exhausting.

136

We'll need a replacement for Nichols, though. I want 3 qualified Sonar Supervisors; one per section. Offload all the other Sonarmen."

"Well, sir, if we go 12-hour Port and Starboard for the rovers it should be ok. The ICman of the Watch and Auxilaryman of the Watch are pretty used to 12-hour watches. It would save 2 more guys."

"I can see 3 Sonarmen but we've only got 2 Supervisors on board. There are none of 'em left in England. All our guys flew back to the States."

"Well, then it's a good time for some diplomatic good will."

"What's that mean, Captain"?

Scott's idea was priceless and the CO and COB had a pretty good laugh about it. The crew would shit a brick.

Within the hour, DODGE CITY had messaged COMSUBLANT and the Admiralty the results of the language program upload and the CO's request to modify the crew.

So, guess who gets the tasking to make all this shit happen? Larry fucking Rothington.

When a Commanding Officer sends a massage requesting something, he usually gets it. Particularly in the case of a Prototype Nuclear Fast Attack Submarine pushing all the envelopes on the way to accomplishing a virtual deployment.

About 20 "Yes, Admirals" later and the Royal Navy's Director of Ship's Scheduling was on his way to his office to get a helo rendezvous orchestrated and a tug rendezvous scheduled as well. He was practically skipping as this just solved his problems.

The crew heard the 1MC click and: "This is the Captain. Change of plans. Tomorrow at 0900, we will again rendezvous with a Royal Navy helicopter who will carry the body of Lieutenant Commander Kennedy ashore."

"Two of our riders will also depart as we have uploaded new software into the Marshal to translate all languages. A universal translator, if you will."

In 3 days, we will rendezvous with a tug and transfer off the majority of the crew. As this boat was designed to deploy with ONLY an autonomous AI, we are going to get as close to that level of manning as reasonable and see how good of an idea it is. The Chief of the Boat will inform everyone of who's staying and who's leaving. That is all."

As the CO clicked off the mike, he saw Senior Chief Lancey standing in the forward end of Control.

"Let's talk, Senior."

The Captain led the way to his stateroom and it was agreed that Oakes and Mills would depart on the helo. Lancey would stay and finish his Enlisted Submarine quals and then depart on the tug with their equipment.

As the Senior Chief was leaving, Scott asked him to have Mr. House report to him.

Scott leaned back in his chair and looked at the photo of his wife and daughter. Barbara was a smoldering beauty with eyes that looked right THROUGH a man.

It wasn't easy being a Navy wife. The service came first and she knew it. Even if a monster hurricane was heading right for their house, the Navy husband had to take his ship to sea in order to ride out the storm. His family would have to fend for themselves.

The Captain's wife was the Grand Dame to all the other wives of the crew. There was none better than Barbara Scott and the crew and their wives loved her.

"Sir"?

"Come in, Brad, since you don't have anything else to do;" they both chuckled, "I'd like you to set up a final qual board for Senior Chief Lancey. He's gotten all the signatures; he just needs the final qual board and a certificate.

Pick a Forward Chief and a Nuke, do it tomorrow, and get it done. Tell the Yeoman you need a certificate, have it dated 3 days from now and we'll give it to him before he boards the tug."

"Tug"?

"Shit. XO!!"

17

In half an hour, the XO had gathered all the officers and CPOs around the Wardroom table so the CO could to brief them on what's happening.

Being a submarine crew, the news had already traveled completely through the boat, and some guys were packing already.

Russell and Mac had already put out the coffee and were slow to leave hoping to get the straight skinny from Scott.

"Gentlemen….and lady" Scott nodded to Terri, "Circumstances have forced us to alter course. As though not enough out of the ordinary stuff has happened so far this deployment, we have suffered the Medevac of one shipmate and the death of another. It appears there's also some kind of pandemic making its way around the world."

"We may be insulated from that pandemic as we are safe in our boat, but we may already have brought it aboard during our time in England. Nichols may have contracted it, even though Doc Adams is pretty sure he's got Meningitis."

"The Navigator may have gotten this thing that people, SOME people are calling the China Flu, while the name COVID, for Coronavirus Disease, is more politically correct."

"Either way, in order for us to operate as safely as possible, The British Admiralty are sending us a Doctor to supervise administering the vaccine we need to keep clear of this thing.

Tomorrow at 1300, ANOTHER helicopter will rendezvous with us and drop him off along with the vaccine. They will also take LCRD Kennedy's body AND two of our crypto riders off."

Everybody we send ashore is going to the Culdrose Air Base at Cornwall as they have the Naval Hospital there. I want everyone checked out for this virus, or whatever it is.

I'm pretty sure that's where Petty Officer Nichols is, too, and it will be good for him to see a few friendly faces while he's recovering.

"Now, for some unknown reason, MATT DILLON, who allegedly can do anything, was unable to translate languages. Hence the Spooks. Senior Chief Lancey, Petty Officer Hochstetler, and I have uploaded a program into the Marshal which makes him able to translate any known language."

"Petty Officers Mills and Oakes will leave with the helo and the Senior Chief will depart the ship, with his equipment 4 days from today on an ocean-going tug. Here's the major point we all have to be ready for: we will also transfer off even more of the crew."

Everyone at the table looked at everyone else and a few murmurs and 'holy shits' were exchanged.

"DODGE CITY was designed to deploy with an autonomous AI and we are going to get as close to that condition as reasonable. Roving watchstander only, 4 officers total, I want 3 sonar supervisors and 3 Maneuvering watchstander qualified to operate the Reactor, Electric Plant, and Throttles. The Marshal will operate all ship's systems with our few people there to keep an eye and jump in if something goes terribly wrong. Questions so far?"

Doc Adams, the only non-khaki in the group asked "Is the doctor staying aboard through the deployment, sir?"

"No, but you are," giggles….

"He leaves with the tug and everybody else."

House spoke up; "Which officers, Captain?"

"I, of course, stay along with the Engineer. The XO and you, Brad. You both are qualified multiple jobs, the XO is also Command Qualified in case I go down, AND I do not intend to turn weapons employment over to the Marshal."

"You will retain your duties as WEPS, and assume Mr. Mowrer's duties as Comms Officer, and Navigator. The XO will back you up as well as Mr. Hartman in engineering who will also act as MPA."

"So, 4 officers, 3 Watchstanders in Maneuvering, 2 engine room rovers, 2 Forward rovers, 3 Sonar supervisors, 3 Diving Officers who are also qualified Chief of the Watch and Helmsman/Planesman. That's 17 men total."

Terri Russell raised her hand and before the CO pointed, she smiled and asked, "Do you guys want to eat anything?" More giggles.

"Chop. You'll be leaving, but how many cooks do you recommend.?"

He looked at Russell, "I'm thinking 3 cooks and 2 messcooks?"

"Sir, I recommend sending the Messcooks ashore and leaving my whole Division. We'll take care of everything."

Well, that seemed like a good idea to the Chop and he nodded to the Captain. "We'll go with that plan, Captain."

"Don't forget me," Doc Adams volunteered.

"We have to keep Hochstetler, too," said Homes. "Any Weaponeers, Captain?"

The COB spoke up and said he'd cover that slot.

Scott said "OK, that's 24 total crew remaining and 14 to transfer to the tug." He turned to the COB, "Do we have anybody qualified all those three ship control stations?"

"Yes, sir. Do you want to know who?"

"No, you pick them, make up a watchbill and show it to me by evening meal."

"Aye, aye, Captain."

"Dismissed, shipmates, let's get everything ready."

At the same time this meeting was going on, Rothington was sitting in a Mercedes Benz with Zhang on a Zoom call trying to explain all the problems he was having with the changes that were going on.

"I HAVE to be in my office making arrangements for a helicopter and a tug to get your man on board and all those crew off! I need some help or this whole thing is going to flop! You have got to take care of the real doctor; I can't do it! You've got people for that sort of thing, don't you?"

Zhang was watching the beads of sweat drip down the pasty white face on the screen before him. He was disgusted by this man not just because he knew what he was all about, but the blubbering and begging made him even more detestable.

When the time came to get rid of this guy, he wanted to do it himself, but England was just too far away for that.

"Calm down. I'll take care of it. What time tomorrow does the helicopter leave?"

"Ten AM. It's a 4-hour flight out."

"You just pick up Li Wei in an official vehicle and take him to the copter. I don't want him to spend much time around anyone who may engage him in conversation. Have him arrive JUST before takeoff and put him in his flight gear. I will instruct him to act airsick to avoid interacting with anyone on the flight."

"They'll all be wearing headgear and a headset, anyway; it'll be too noisy to chat."

"Good. Good. See? Getting easier already. All loose ends will be tied up on our end by the morning. You just have him at Kellogg's house at by 10 tonight. I want you to help him with uniforms and whatever else he can use of the doctor's then get him to the helicopter in the morning."

Rothington audibly exhaled in relief. "My father?"

"You have this far conducted yourself admirably, Mr. Rothington. Tomorrow, you will be instructed where to meet him. Goodbye."

Feeling better now, Rothington got out of the car and crossed the street to the pub he noticed. A quick nip should calm his nerves.

Zhang called the driver, Mr. Lineman's Pliers, on the satellite phone and gave him his instructions. He nodded, said "Dui," put the Benz in drive, and left.

One more interaction with Mr. Rothington, Zhang thought to himself, and he would make the world a little better place. Time to brief Bolin Li.

18

When Verona Oakes got the news from Lancey, she almost peed herself. She had not been able to upload the zip drive into the Marshal, yet. She was panicking that her mother's death was just about sealed.

It was obvious to Lancey that something was wrong. "What's the matter? Don't you want an extra week's Liberty in merry ole England."

She had to come up with something, "I was looking forward to getting my dolphins on this run. Like you."

"Well, I don't have them, yet. Are you sure that's it?"

She wondered what he meant.

"I saw the way that one kid was looking at you. You sure it's not him." Lancey was smiling.

She thought she'd go with that. "Well…."

"I thought so. Go get all our shit gathered up and then spend some time with him if you want. If you guys hit it off, well, he'll be back after deployment."

"Thanks, Senior."

Lancey walked away and Oakes ran to the Head just in time to puke. It took her a few minutes to gather herself and head up to Radio to disconnect everything and load it into the cases.

It only took about 45 minutes to get everything situated and the 3 cases stacked in the fan room out of everybody's way. There wasn't enough floorspace in the SINS room to pile up the boxes anyway, and they were leaving tomorrow on the helo.

There was about a box worth of cables and small stuff in the computer room she would need to gather up, so she headed over that way.

Hoping Dusty was in there, she punched in her code and shouldered the spring-loaded door open. Oh crap, it was Schiano…

"Oakes! I hear you're getting out of here tomorrow," he said with unusual charm and good humor. If there was ever a time for him to make one last 'suggestion,' now was it.

"Yep, I guess that universal translator is going to put us out of business. I'm a maintenance tech, so I'll still have shit to fix on some ship somewhere."

"Got a new assignment, yet? There's always some boat headed into the badlands."

"Not that I've heard. That's a Senior Chief and higher-level conversation. I just wait until I'm voluntold where I'm going."

They both chuckled at that invented word combining Volunteered with Told; something everyone in the military understands. It's almost as popular as Hurry Up and Wait.

As she chatted, she kept trying to figure a way to load that thumb drive into the Marshal. She had 3 coaxial cables plugged in right above the USB connector.

If she could reach up and stick it in there while undoing the cables, this dipshit might not notice. They told her it would load in 40 seconds; no more than a minute...maybe there was another way.

He had turned his back for a second to put some paperwork into a folder. She was observing his body language and kept checking to see how far that connection in The Marshal's MMI was from her hand.

She unplugged one of the cables to see if the sound would cause him to turn around. He did not. She pulled the thumb drive out of her pocket and reached up. He turned and looked up at her hand as she pulled the other two cables.

He grabbed the clipboard hanging on the station and put it down on his workbench to scan the news.

"I'm glad to see there's no hard feelings between us since we got off to a little rough start," she said as she was loading some of her gear into the first storage box. She didn't look at him but wondered in which direction he would take this.

"Maybe, if you hadn't come on so strong…" her voice trailed off and she saw his head come up from his reading. He slowly turned around.

She went on, "it's tough for a girl in the Navy when she sees an attractive guy. I mean what are you supposed to do, ya know. Geez, especially on a submarine, for Chrissakes, not a lot of privacy."

Schiano just knew that every girl on planet Earth had the hots for him, remember. He just kept running into the dykes. She could tell from his face that his hamster was in the wheel wondering if she was

144

saying what he thought she was saying.

She had the thumb drive in her right hand as she undid the first two buttons on her chambray shirt with her left. She backed away from the workbench maybe an inch to see if he would take the bait. The thought of fooling around with this pig was tightening up her gag reflex.

He turned the rest of the way to face her and moved the slightest bit closer. She noticed him licking his lips, not in a lecherous way, but as in a scared to death sort of way. She was certain that he wasn't very experienced in this kind of thing.

Her left hand went to the back of his neck and she pushed his back against the workbench. He was maybe 3 or 4 inches taller than she, and she looked up at him with her best puppy-dog eyes to make him feel powerful.

Schiano's face was completely red and he was burning up with desire for this hot piece of ass. She slowly pushed her hips into him as her right hand went to the back of his head.

He was fully hard and he unbuttoned her shirt with both his shaking hands. His fingers roughly worked their way under her bra and he had both perfect tits in his hands as he kissed her neck.

With his eyes closed, she had no problem slipping that drive into the USB slot. Her brain kept repeating "One minute, one minute, God dammit, hurry up, hurry up…" She half-heartedly returned his kisses and he fumbled for her belt.

"Oh my God, you feel great," he said over and over. "I've wanted to fuck you from the first moment I saw you." His hand was inside her panties now and he fingered her clit awkwardly as he French kissed her hard.

He was so unskilled and inexperienced in the way he touched her. Nothing romantic or sexy about this guy. It was as though he were a 12-year-old who was trying to get his first kiss from the farmgirl next door.

She really thought she would choke as her disgust for him got worse and worse. Her took her left hand from around his neck and placed it on his cock. She rubbed the outside of his pants and opened one eye to see if there was any status on the screen.

"What would the damn thing say when the program was loaded?" She had no idea what to look for to know to remove the drive. She opened the other eye and scanned the whole face of the status board.

Nothing.

"God damn this was the longest minute ever," her brain screamed out.

"I want to get behind you" he whispered. She couldn't let him turn around or he might see the thumb drive. What now?

She acted scared and antsy. "We can't fuck in here. What if somebody comes in?" He pulled his hand out of her pants and licked his finger. THAT one almost had her puking…

"Suck my cock, Oakes…please" he was breathless and sounded like a little boy begging. As if the Lord himself had seen enough at this point, a loud metallic voice made them both jump:

"FORMAT UNRECOGNIZED." Schiano whipped around and looked at the screen.

"What is THAT?" He asked her sternly as he pointed at the thumb drive stuck into the MMI console. She took it out of the slot and held it up. "Music. I thought you might like some music. I'm sorry."

"This equipment doesn't play music. Give me that and I'll plug it my player."

Knowing the program was not going to load into The Marshal and that it certainly was NOT music, she just couldn't give the damn thing to him. She tried to figure a way out of this. It was going to be pretty dangerous leaving this dude with a hardon.

She acted panicky and afraid, "I can't do this. If we get caught…" she let her voice trail off as she buttoned up.

AGAIN, as though God were intervening, they heard the unmistakable sound of the cypher lock. She just got tucked and belted in time.

"Hey, you two!" it was Dusty. "I heard you were leaving, Oakes. Getting your shit packed and stowed?"

"Yep, leaving on tomorrow's helo. Wanted everything boxed and ready to offload. Can you grab the big one and help me put these in the Fan Room?"

Schiano was glaring at her and then to Dusty. She didn't look his way again and bent over to lift the smaller of the two boxes. Dusty pulled open the door and followed her out.

Schiano had turned away from Dusty once he entered to hide his obvious bulge. He looked over his right shoulder at the USB port and wondered what made her think she could play music through there.

That thought lasted another 15 seconds in his brain and it was pushed aside at the memory of those perfect tits and fluffy little muff.

He grabbed a few tissues out of the Kleenex box and jerked himself off in about 10 seconds. It was either that or he was going to come in his pants.

He had never been that close to a girl THAT hot and this was a memory that would never leave him. He wondered if the guys would believe him if he told them about it.

The Command would probably fuck him over if the story ever got out, so he just resigned himself to keeping it a secret. The music thing crept back into his mind again.

Couldn't be anything else to it, could there? Well, it wasn't like he was going to bounce it off anyone else. Even the COB wouldn't ignore what happened if he found out.

He should have been thinking about Doc's chip reader down in the launcher space. Bright yellow it had been for him these last few minutes. Temperature. Temperature. Temperature.

Dusty and Oakes made their way aft down middle level and hoisted the boxes through the hatchway into the NAV space. They climbed the ladder and opened the Fan Room door, placing the last two boxes with the others.

"Are you staying aboard or going ashore, Dusty?"

"Staying aboard. They need me to stay with the Marshal," he said with a little puffery in his voice.

"Where to next for you?"

"No idea. I guess we're getting the rest of the week ashore while they come up with orders. I hope I just get sent back home for a while. Got some shit going on I need to work through."

"Oh? Anything you want to talk about?"

Yeah, there was a lot she wanted to talk about, but just couldn't. She was tearing up and Dusty asked her if there was anything he could do. She could tell from the concerned look on his face that he was being sincere and really appreciated it.

"Well, if it's a Navy problem, no one better to talk to than the COB. He knows everybody and he'll help you all he can."

No, not a Navy problem; but a problem. She was filled with fear and guilt that her mom would be killed. She hadn't been able to load the program; she had no idea who it was that had her mother, and she didn't know what to do next. Shit, she had a whole bag of cyanide in her bunk pan. What was she going to do with that now?

Then she realized all she had to do was throw that bag of poison into the very fan room she just left. The airflow in there was like a hurricane and the powder would be carried throughout the entire boat in seconds killing everyone.

"Everyone" meant her, too, and then who would operate the blow valves and surface the boat? How would the bad guys know that the boat had been surfaced since the thumb drive program had not been loaded? Either way, her mom would be killed.

She looked at Dusty. He had been so nice to her and even HE would be killed. Her mother's soul would not be able to rest if she did this terrible thing. Not only would her legacy be one of a murderer, but as a traitor and THAT was something with which she could not live.

She thought of Senior Chief Lancey. She had met his wife and kids; would they ever forgive her for killing their dad? How in the fuck did she ever get into this situation?

No one knew anything about it and she was going to keep it that way. She'd leave tomorrow and throw that cyanide out of the helicopter somewhere at sea. She would wait for those assholes to contact her and she'd explain how the AI wouldn't accept the program and that it wasn't her fault. She had done ALL SHE COULD, please let my mother go.

What then? Threaten them with telling the authorities? She didn't know who they were, where they were, or why they wanted to do this. No one would believe her and a bag of poison wasn't going to convince any investigator.

She could always tell them about that big English guy that approached her? But who the hell was he? Maybe he was known to the authorities somehow. Then again, all he had to do was deny everything and she couldn't prove a thing.

Better to keep quiet, get off this boat, get back to the States and try to beg for her mother's life. She would do anything. When a girl this good-looking says she will do 'anything,' she usually got her way. We'll see.

"Oakes? You up there?" It was Lancey yelling up from the messdecks.

148

"Yes, Senior."

"Come down here a second, please."

She climbed down the ladder from Navigation and stopped next to the Scuttlebutt outside Doc's office facing Lancey.

"Bad news, Oakes. They're sending you back out." She looked at him inquisitively.

Two Spooks out of Norfolk have come down with this bug and you and Mills are taking their place on the ABRAHAM LINCOLN. That means a Med Run, so you're tied up for the next 4 months."

Goddammit. She won't be able to contact her mother. They'll kill her for sure.

"You two will go by helo to the hospital and get checked out. If you're clear of this virus thing, they'll fly you by COD out to the LINCOLN and then you deploy. At least you'll get a few days ashore, IF you're not contagious."

"You know Chief Markey, out of our Charleston office?"

She looked down and shook her head.

"He's the lead Spook on this one; you both work for him. He and I go way back. Good man."

Nothing to do now but pack and get ready to fly out of here. Her heart sank.

19

Dr. Kellogg was just leaving the front gate at the end of a busy day in the Culdrose Air Base hospital in Cornwall. It had been his turn for the Emergency Room and a hundred people suffering from whatever this virus was, this China Flu, had crawled in gasping.

He had heard the reports that London had already experienced over a thousand deaths. That HAD to be a hyped-up story from the newspapers; couldn't be that many in so short a time, could it?

The truth of it was people were dropping all over the world and the social and economic impact of this was going to be biblical. He stopped to put on his overcoat and shift the briefcase to his other hand.

Good Christ, it just HAD to have come from China, he thought. The world would hold it against every Asian, no doubt. He had gotten many an angry glare from random white people as though he was one of "those people" somehow personally responsible.

He was in a bit of a hurry as he had only an hour ago found out he'd been ordered to attend to an American submarine crew who had been infected with the virus. The Admiralty was flying him out to the DODGE CITY to administer the vaccine.

Very rare to get a personal phonecall from the MOD Planning Department head about any assignment let alone one as sensitive as this. "Written orders to follow," the Director said ending the conversation.

So, he had been informed by Strategic Planning that he must be ready for a 0800 pickup for transport to the helicopter taking him out to the sub. A little exciting this whole thing. He had neither ever been aboard a submarine before nor had he ridden in a helicopter.

Of all the available Medical Officers, the Admiralty had picked him to perform this assignment. Quite the compliment, he thought, but a little odd, nonetheless.

He had been a researcher this last year in Cornwall. He spent his days in a lab trying to invent antidotes and vaccines. Perhaps this is the very reason they called him for this assignment.

Like all the other doctors, he took his turn in the ER about every 8 days. Last night was his turn. He should have been sleepy, but the excitement of this upcoming assignment had him wide awake.

He was running everything he needed to do in the next 14 hours: get home, eat, pack, and arrange for his girlfriend to take his cat. He should call her now and ask her to meet him at his place.

"Hello, Jill?" his call began and he spent the next few minutes telling her of the goings on. She agreed to meet him at home and assured him that his darling Natalie would be well-cared for until he returned home to both his favorite girls.

He clicked off and walked a few more steps down the sidewalk toward his usual London Transport bus stop when a Mercedes pulled up next to him.

The driver's window rolled down and he saw the obviously Chinese face of the driver. He stopped to see if he recognized the man who spoke to him now.

"Hello, Naval Surgeon Kellogg? I have been assigned to drive you home and help you get ready for tomorrow's evolution" the driver sang out in excellent English, although thickly accented.

Although now an English subject, Kellogg had actually been born in America. His family moved to England when Kellogg was still in grade school as father had been offered a position with an investment firm.

He sported a bit of an English accent himself after almost 2 decades, but still spoke noticeably like a Yank. He would often fool around with his girlfriend with quips like "me likey" and stuff like that.

He was keen on accents and took an interest in the way people spoke. He was especially sensitive about fellow Asians who were trying to master a language their mouths just didn't have an affinity for.

"Naval Surgeon?" he thought to himself. He didn't think that term had been popular in the Royal Navy since the sailing ships.

"It's Medical Officer, nowadays," he said with a slight smile and a wave as he tried to figure out if he knew who this guy was.

"Time is of the essence doctor. The Admiralty wish for me to collect you and take you home. I am to assist you in any way to prepare for your 8am pickup."

Well, this was nice. He had rarely felt so important before. He never considered that this fellow might be a fake. After all, he knew of the assignment, the timeline, knew his name, and a Mercedes!

Our Mr. Lineman's Pliers, actual name Haoyu Wang, was one of Zhang's most loyal and reliable people. Formerly a national-level weightlifting competitor in the heavyweight division, he had been injured during the Olympic Trials in 1984 and, at only 20 years old, a torn biceps tendon brought his weightlifting career to an end.

Zhang had always been a fan of the sport and was well-known to the team as an enthusiastic and generous supporter. Once Wang's injuries disqualified him from competition, Zhang offered him a job as bodyguard and driver; a position he has held ever since.

Never one to ask frivolous questions and trusted to keep secrets at any cost, Wang had been a part of much of Zhang's, and Bolin Li's by extension, global pharmaceutical enterprise.

Whenever someone had to be positively killed overnight, it was going to positively be Wang who got the assignment. Not only was he still a powerful man, but at 58 years old he was mature, calm, and very experienced in his work.

Dr. Kellogg was just the next assignment and Wang would do the job quickly, quietly, and completely without remorse. This is not to say he didn't enjoy his work. Tonight, he would have an unexpected extra treat as the luscious Jill was, at this moment, dripping from a shower and preparing herself for a sweet goodbye with her lover doctor.

It was only about a 15-minute drive to the Doctor's house in Perranporth, a beachy community where surfers would gather. Wang had never been here before and he found the place quiet and pleasant.

Little conversation between driver and passenger as Wang thought it best to avoid the risk of spilling any secrets. Kellogg went through his phone catching up with emails and answering a few comments on Social Media.

He was thinking random thoughts like where was his suitcase, what should they have for dinner, and what good luck it was for him to have met the well-known Jill Bartley.

She also worked in the medical field but as an Administrator in the same hospital. She oversaw ordering and maintained the inventory of all hospital supplies from paper and pens to penicillin and laptops.

He knew her as a wonderful person, soft in her demeanor when it came to helping others, but very direct and professional in her work. When presented with a purchase request, she would scrutinize the dot on every "i," re-compute every column of numbers, and would return any document that had the smallest error.

"Bitch Face Jill" and "Bad News Bartley" were two of the unfortunate names the staff had for her because she took everything so seriously. Well, she wasn't just going to let everyone order whatever the heck they wanted! She had a budget to manage and requests she deemed frivolous were returned without any pleasantries but with a very matter-of-fact "Sorry, no room in the budget for this."

Jill finished dressing, sprayed on a little of that perfume her "Bobby" liked so much, picked up her overnight bag, and headed out to her car. Little did either of them realize, tonight would be their last and a foul ending it would be.

20

Li Wei had been preparing, too. Shaving kit and a couple of pair of underwear were pretty much all he needed. According to Rothington, the uniforms and medical gear he was taking would all be supplied at the real doctor's house.

It was almost 9pm and he got a little worried at the thought he'd be boarding a Royal Navy helicopter in about 12 hours. Never would he have ever thought he would be asked to commit murder, but here we are. Besides, it wasn't the first time he killed anyone and, probably, not going to be his last.

The only potential problem was if the gate guards looked too closely at his ID card. Of course, he wouldn't look EXACTLY like this doctor, but with them sitting in a staff car and enough "hurry ups" from the Planning Director, they should get through just fine. If not, then there was going to be hell to pay as Bolin Li did not tolerate failure.

Wang parked the Mercedes in front of Kellogg's townhouse, got out to open the doctor's door, and followed him to the front door. Kellogg was really enjoying the royal treatment, so much so, that his guard was completely down.

Key in the lock, door open, lights turned on, and he walked in leading Wang who held the doctor's coat and briefcase. His little cat, Natalie, walked over to her dad and rubbed against his leg.

"Please put those there, on the couch." Wang complied and complimented the doctor's home. "Very large place, doctor, every get lonely?"

Wang couldn't care less about Kellogg's feelings; he was trying to figure if there might be anyone else here.

"I have Natalie," Kellogg said pleasantly as he held his kitty up to his face and kissed her before putting her back down.

"I'm surprised a man of your stature isn't married," again Wang trying to get some intel on his mark.

Kellogg liked that word 'stature.' He was really having his ego fed and remarked that his girlfriend often stayed over and was on her way right now.

Well, THAT was good to know. His pistol was loaded with 22 shorts that he had taken half the gunpowder from. Pretty quiet in and of themselves, but the homemade silencer would ensure his activities wouldn't be detected by the neighbors.

Just then, the doorbell rang and Kellogg sang out with "here she is now!" Wang pulled the pistol and pointed it at Kellogg's head. The doctor stood shocked into silence.

In a predictable second or two more, the doorbell chimed again and Wang simultaneously put one round through Kellogg's right eye. He fell dead in front of the couch and Wang walked to the door.

"Hello!" he said pleasantly, "You must be Jill!"

She stood silently trying to figure out who this large man might be.

"Bobby is in the kitchen and asked me to bring you in. I'm his friend, Wang," he half bowed and grandly waved his hand toward the living room as would an usher in a theater.

She took a step or two and, just cleared the door before he quickly shut and locked it. Her gaze shifted from his hand on the lock to his face and realized there was trouble. As her mouth opened to scream, Wang backhanded her on the chin and everything went dark.

He looked down on her crumpled body and a thousand tortures and sexual degradations flitted through his mind. He wasn't picked for this kind of work because he was prone to giving in to tawdry desires. There would be no biological evidence left at the scene by him.

He picked her off the floor and carried her to the guest bathroom. He placed her in the full-sized tub and executed her with two to the head.

After going through the man's pockets to retrieve his wallet, MOD ID card, and cash, he plunked Kellogg on top of her, pulled the shower curtain and, as instructed, waited for Li Wei.

He sat on the couch petting Natalie, then got up and went through the kitchen cabinets to find her some food. The cold-blooded killer who just ended the lives of two human beings was concerned that a little cat might be hungry; people are so strange.

It was closer to eleven by the time Wei and Rothington knocked on the door. Luckily, it was dark and rainy, so there were no prying eyes in the road out front. Wang opened the door and laughed out loud as Rothington's "YOU!" announced he recognized the guy with the Lineman's Pliers.

Wang did his best to assuage Larry's fear and congratulated him for being thought of so highly that they were now on the same team! Rothington held his damaged hand away from Wang and tried to keep from showing his terror.

For the next three hours, they had Wei try on every uniform the doctor owned. At only an inch or so taller than Kellogg and with a slightly smaller waist, the clothes went on easy.

"I'm not worried about the clothes as much as talking with the crew," Wei offered. It was true that the biggest problem they had was Wei's thick Chinese accent; thicker even than Wang's.

"Nothing we can do about it, now." Rothington said. "You seem to speak English pretty well"

"Perfectly, you asshole. It's the technical submarine and Navy stuff I'm concerned about."

"OK, take it easy. Just say as little as possible, but, hey, you're Chinese. They're going to expect that English is not your first language. Just don't make a big deal about it. AND you're a medic, so you're not expected to know much about the boat. Besides, you've got Navy experience. Hell, you're only going to be there less than 2 days. You can bullshit your way for 2 days"

"What if one of them knows the real doctor?"

"Well, then you're fucked, but I think the chance of that happening is zero."

Other than the accent, if the uniforms were a problem, he could always ask for a poopy suit or two to wear once he got to the boat; they are customary wear for submariners at sea. This was going great, so far.

The Identification Card photograph was black and white and grainy, so it should probably work if the gate guards even checked it. Ever the sneaky bastard, Rothington had brought a Royal Navy Admiralty flag they could attach to the Mercedes bumper which should guarantee them safe passage through the gate and right onto the flightline.

Just then, the satellite phone went off and Rothington stood up as though an electric shock hit him in the ass. This call only could come from one place.

Fully scrambled and untraceable, the SAT phone had been the perfect tool to get information from the boss.

"Zhang here."

"Oh fuck. What now?" Rothington looked like he was going to faint.

How many men will be on the ocean-going tug you are sending?"

"8 for a run like this"

"Change of plans."

Rothington exhaled as though he was punched in the gut and rolled his head all the way back on the couch. Zhang laid out the new plan, but it had to get started right now.

In the new plan, there was no cyanide, no girl, and no mass assassination by Wei. The old plan they had come up with was deemed too intricate with too many ways it could fail.

Wei was to get aboard with a weapon, get that poison away from the girl so she wouldn't kill the both of them, and then commandeer the boat when the software kicked in.

Wang was to board a boat this morning in Perranporth Beach and, with a handful of trusted allies, motor out to a spot where they would intercept the tug on its way to DODGE CITY, overpower the crew, overpower the submarine personnel, board the sub, and hold it until it could be given over or emptied of enemy and crewed with friends.

The Perranporth Beach area, as for much of Cornwall, was populated with surfers and people who liked to party. That meant drugs and, ultimately, meant Bolin Li and all who worked for him.

Of course, the local dealers had no idea who Bolin Li was. When speaking on the phone or, in the rare case, actually met with someone, it was always Zhang. Bolin Li never risked exposure.

It took one phone call to a local distributor to get a crucial asset to the new plan in place: a boat. A boat large enough to hold 4 grown men and their gear, but small enough to not draw too much attention.

Wang and three others, with proper equipment, were going to take that boat out to sea and wait in an area through which the Royal Navy tug would transit to get to the DODGE CITY.

The men on the boat would fire a red flare as though they were stranded at sea in a broken-down boat and needed to be rescued. There were usually fairly rough seas this time of year, especially being winter. The Navy crew couldn't just leave them foundering; they'd be obligated to rescue them.

21

"So, Chief Russell, it's just going to be us and a few other guys? No messcooks or nothin'"?

"That's right, Mac. We'll do the same things we always do, except for smaller meals. We can keep our own galley clean with so few preps to do and plates to wash."

"Hey, let's do lots of omelets and frittatas for morning meal since we'll have three times the number of eggs as usual." Mac was joyfully rubbing his hands together.

"Knock yourselves out," she said smiling. "You can make all different kinds of quiche, too. It would help use up the vegetables before they go bad."

The cooks were getting a little excited at the freedom they were going to have. It was normally a menu planned a month out and everything by the Navy cookbook, as it were.

Submarine cooks were known to be the best in the Navy and they were looking forward to really stepping it up, now.

The crew was just sitting down to evening meal and were wondering about what the Navy had in store for them. How long would they stay in England; when would they get new orders; those types of conversations.

Many had already packed their stuff which, for some, was more involved than for others. Some of the married guys (and those with serious girlfriends) usually went to sea with cards and small gifts they were to open on designated days during the deployment.

This type of thing was universal if a boat was to be at sea over a major holiday; whether it was a birthday, anniversary, or even Christmas. The sailor would open his 'surprise' on a designated day.

Simultaneously, the beloved would open their gifts and he and his people could feel somewhat connected even for a moment; even at such a distance.

Now, all their little packages had to get put back in the seabags or whatever carry-on the guys had for further transfer to the tug.

While all this planning and chatting was taking place on the sub,

Wang had met with the Howard brothers, Joey and Jake, who ran the underworld in the Cornwall area.

The Howards, formerly of His Majesty's Navy, had been long time associates of the Bolin Li enterprise in this part of England, although never having met him. They had seen enough proof of his existence and were well acquainted with his savagery if he was not obeyed.

Most drug dealers across the world never knew of the man Bolin Li; he was at the apex of the food chain and too smart to be known to the lower level entrepreneurs. Zhang did all the communicating and threatening and just a few of the executions.

Wang's was usually the last face you saw, but the world is a big place, and there were a small army of 'Wangs' all loyal to the death. They went anywhere and would do anything to ensure the commands of their Zufu, or grandfather, were obeyed.

The rewards for success were great and failure was not tolerated at all. Oh, they may not kill YOU, but say goodbye to someone you gave a shit about.

The Howards thought they knew the 'Big Guy' in this part of the world because they were installed by him two years ago when the previous guy was caught skimming from the take.

Joey Howard still had nightmares of a naked, limbless, and screaming Roger Echelson hanging by a meat hook from the gap in the Tintagel Castle Bridge.

There was a one-month period when Roger had seemingly disappeared. No one had any idea where he had gotten off to. As it turned out, the word had gotten back to Bolin Li that the take had been way off for a couple of months in the Cornwall area.

Since there could only be one possible reason for a shortfall in this normally profitable district, Zhang was assigned to restructure their organization. Any hands-on work needing to be done anywhere in Great Britain came under the direct supervision of the vaunted Mr. Wang.

Wang coordinated the details of what was about to come, hired the right people, commandeered the right places, paid the correct sums of money, or terminated the correct complainer. He began the reorganization of their operation in the Southwest Peninsula.

Unbeknownst to any of the locals except for the trigger man, Poor Roger had been shot with a tranquilizer gun and kidnapped.

During the 30-odd days of what some thought a vacation, he was kept in a coma and his arms and legs were surgically removed and allowed to heal.

Easter morning found Roger hanging below the bridge screaming his lungs out for almost 3 hours before he died. That very day, the Howard brothers accepted the favor of their promotion and took over the entirety of the drug trade in the touristy and lucrative Land's End area.

Now, Zhang came calling and asked for a favor in return. As it was always assumed that Zhang was the Big Guy, the Howards discussed the details with him over the SAT phone.

His requests were clear and simple. Yes, they were easily able to get a boat, weapons, ammo, and that Wang would accompany them AND provide the one other guy they would need. Refusal was impossible and failure would mean only the worst possible outcome for the Howards.

The tug was leaving in 14 hours, so they wanted to be well at sea and away from prying eyes to make their rendezvous. By 6pm, they were all aboard, gear loaded, underway and headed straight into the teeth of a 20 knot wind as it pushed a heavy rain eastward.

At the time the Howards' boat left Perranporth, the DODGE CITY was beginning to clear away the evening meal. Since so much was happening and even more of the crew would be leaving, the CHOP and Terri Russell decided to serve, what would have been, the meal for "Halfway Night;" a big event on a submarine deployment. Every day on the other side of Halfway Night was on the downhill slope of getting back home.

Since they had loaded stores for way more people than were actually aboard, they could serve steak and lobster and STILL have steak and lobster when the actual Halfway Night was achieved in about 40 days.

"Oh man, demzer good-lookin' lobstahs!" and everyone clapped for the cooks.

Senior Chief Lancey walked into the forward end of the Crew's mess and announced that he had passed the "Forward" portion of his qual board!

Nobody really knew Lancey, but they knew that getting your dolphins was a huge deal and getting signed off by Graves was just as big. That son-of-a-bitch knew everything and he expected you to know everything, too.

Lancey would do his Engine room walkthrough tonight and Final checkout tomorrow by LT. House. His concern was that, if he had a lot of 'Look-ups,' then there were only 2 more days to finish before he boarded the tug. He really wanted Scott to be the one to present him his dolphins.

"Dinner's on me, boys!" Lancey yelled, and everyone had a good laugh.

Tomorrow, they would be saying goodbye to the other two spooks and a doctor and some other guy would be coming aboard to fill in for Nichols. Just then, Mills and Oakes walked into the crew's mess and sat with Lancey. McCleary walked in right after;

"Gimme about ten of them lobsters, God dammit."

The old Senior Chief was smiling, a rarity in itself, and pretty much made his announcement for the amusement of the crew. A couple of gulps of "mouthwash" always made him feel better, and he could be downright pleasant for an hour or so.

The COB was busy stumbling around the Fan Room trying to get around the Spooks equipment while looking for that damn helmet and grounding rod for the helo transfer tomorrow. He had to chuckle at what was coming.

The Officers finished eating and Captain Scott suggested they all watch a movie. Quite different from the old days, when you had to deal with those big, heavy, green boxes of reel-to-reel movie film. Now, it was a thumb drive and a TV screen.

The CO could tell the death of their shipmate had hit them hard and they were trying their damndest to roll with it. "America never realizes just how young their front-line warriors are," he thought.

It's not easy to do this job when everything goes right. Submarining is a dangerous business, but having a crew member die was way out of the norm. He made a suggestion they watch a comedy and, since nobody ever disagrees with the Captain's choice of the movie, Chief Russell read off a couple from the index.

Doc Adams was busy sorting out the hypodermics and serum sent aboard during the last helo transfer that seemed a lifetime ago. He still hadn't figure out why they needed an actual Doctor to give shots…that was right in his wheelhouse. Had to be some political bullshit because of this 'pandemic.'

Submarines get message traffic once a day and he was about 24 hours behind the global status of Coronavirus. He read that thousands of people all over the world were dying from this thing. Businesses were actually closing down while more and more people all over the world were being forced to wear those masks.

"From a bat," he mumbled. He always thought it impossible for cross-species contamination to occur. Of course, he had yet to hear of Gain of Function research.

He kept reading about the Wuhan Lab and bats and a wet market. People were being told that if they wore the surgical masks, which he knew would not stop a virus, then they would be safe.

China was being blamed; people were even accusing them of doing this on purpose. People were having fun using names like the "China Flu, Kung Flu," shit like that.

The World Health Organization came out in strong favor of China while their detractors in Western Media made fun of them. The damn virus can be traced right to Wuhan; Wuhan is in China; the virus is China's fault. Failed, but convenient logic.

No one anywhere on planet Earth had any idea this all came from the vengeance of one old man. They still don't even know about the causes behind Chernobyl's meltdown. Who would have ever thought such a thing?

Imagine the disbelief if someone told him that aboard his very ship was the next step in the plan and a little girl, a fellow sailor, had been put aboard to kill them all, so they could STEAL THE BOAT?

Impossible, yet here we were. Hell was on its way and there were only 38 of them to stand in the breach.

22

Their 40-foot fishing boat was really getting pushed around by the morning waves. Jake Howard, in between spurts of puking his guts out, looked up when he heard a helicopter and saw the Royal Navy Blackhawk fly right over their boat. This was, actually, the very helo heading out to the DODGE CITY with Li Wei.

Jake had served aboard the Royal Submarine Superb back in the early 90s and still knew his way around. The American subs can't be THAT much different, he thought.

He knew how to dive one and get her back to the surface. That was all they wanted him to do except for the part where he and his 3 compadres would shoot the crew. If he had some time to look over the Control Room panels, he could certainly figure out the switches for the Main Vents and the Blow Valves.

If things went according to their loose plan, they'd be shooting these guys in about a day and a half. Christ, he hadn't ever shot a man in cold blood before, but how the hell hard could it be? He'd blasted enough of them Rag Heads over there; but never a Brit or a Yank. Still, it beats hanging from a bridge with your arms and legs missing.

Besides, if you were in good stead with a man who had the power and willingness to do THAT to somebody, then life could be pretty good. They were pulling in close to 50 thousand pounds a month NOW. Imagine if they became even more appreciated in this unholy outfit.

The Coppers, if they wanted their little extra every month, had learned to leave him and his brother alone. The clients paid up on time, and there was always product with which to make a fortune. This little favor would go a long way to cement their relationship with the Big Man and maybe open up new territory; perhaps all of England herself.

Of course, the Howard boys realized they had little to no chance of this plan actually working. It's not like they were going to back out now. Either the Big Man would have them dissolved in acid or this Wang character would just shoot them right here. He was an obvious zealot and there's no talking a zealot out of anything.

If this sea would just calm a little bit, he would be able to hold something down and maybe get some sleep. He thought about checking the weapons but he could hardly make his way across the deck let alone break out small arms and ammo.

He and his brother had "liberated" a case of AKs, ammunition, and hand grenades when they came back the last time from the Sand Box.

Their part of England was populated with a lot of surfers and tourists, so the threat levels were pretty low. Nobody in their own line of work would mess with them once the news of Roger's trapeze act spread across the area. Most people thought THEY had done it to take over Roger's territory. No need to talk them out of it.

He preferred the AK, truth be told. You could bury it in sand, dunk it in water, clean it with a knotted boot lace and it would still fire. Sending those big 7.62s downrange was a lot more comforting than the little pebbles the Americans fired.

He played through the rough plan in his head…according to that big Pedo from the Admiralty, the crew were going to transfer from the sub to the tug along with their gear. We were going to get them all standing in one area of the deck while we told them to get their bags and then "WHAM."

In theory, only those left below deck would still be alive and our man on board would hold them at bay until Wang and Joey could get down there and take command of the control room.

"What then?" he asked no one in particular. Someone would have to come and get this thing, he figured. If a message was sent, the entirety of the NATO forces would descend upon them and that would be that.

No way would NATO or the Americans permit one of their front-line Nuclear subs to get stolen. We're looking at the possibility of World War 3, here.

Must be the Chinese. Who the hell else could it be? Maybe this was the reason behind setting this pandemic loose on the world; cover for this operation?

Well, he had no way of knowing that China had nothing to do with any of it. Yeah, they weren't getting along with the Americans much these days, but they sure as shit weren't about to start a World

War.

They had their own issues at home, just like other countries. They had political squabbles, just like other countries. They had a percentage of their populace that followed directions and a percentage that were always complaining, just like other countries. Didn't they have their own submarines? Yes, they did.

Why would they just start world-ending problems with their biggest market and customer? The Chinese were businessmen, now. Put an end to the unlimited flow of money? Doubtful.

Another three hours of tossing and turning and the sea started to calm a bit. At this very moment, out on the sub, preparations were being made to rendezvous with the helo.

Joey walked out on deck and laughed at his brother's seasickness. "How the fuck did you serve in the Navy if you get seasick?"

"That's why I went submarines; nice and calm down deep."

They both laughed, a little too nervously.

"Are we going through with this, Joe?"

"How do we get out of it? That big bastard will kill us."

"Not if we kill him first. Call it an accident. He fell overboard. Happens, you know."

"You want to hang from the bridge? These people don't take 'no' for an answer."

"We can let ourselves get took, can't we? Spill our guts later?"

"They'll reach us in prison, Jake. They're everywhere."

23

"Surface the ship, Diving Officer."

"Surface the ship, Aye Captain"

"Chief of the Watch, on the 1MC, Surface, Surface, Surface."

"On the 1MC, Surface, Surface, Surface, Aye."

Graves made the announcement and energized the Low-Pressure Blower.

"62, 60, 58, 56, 54, 52, Broach!"

Everything proceeded as normal, the ship stabilized on the surface and two men headed up the trunk to the Bridge.

Captain Scott stayed on Number 2 scope and swept the horizon for a helicopter.

"Hold an airborne contact at 220 degrees, two four thousand yards. Bearing rate zero" the BPS-15 operator announced.

Once the bridge suitcase was plugged in, Scott told LT. House in the bridge where to look.

At eleven miles, it was a little hard to see the helo with binoculars, but Scott had him in high power.

"Senior Chief McCleary, secure as Diving Officer and relieve me on the scope."

"Aye, aye, Captain."

Scott turned the scope over to Pappy and made his way up the Bridge trunk.

"Captain coming up!"

Once he got to the bridge, he sent House below to coordinate getting the forward escape trunk hatch opened and the helo transfer team ready to go topside.

The Captain watched from the top of the Sail as the hatch opened and 4 of his men scrambled onto the deck. The COB and Sweetwater were the first two, then Lemon with the helmet and grounding rod. The Blackhawk was about 6 miles out, now.

"Radar?" Scott called on the 7MC.

"Ten thousand yards, zero bearing rate, Captain."

Scott pulled the radio out of his jacket pocket and established comms with the pilot. They exchanged a few pleasantries as it was the same crew as last time.

5 minutes later, they were hovering over the deck and dropped their hook with a couple of harnesses for the passengers to don. This was not the safest of all ways to transfer personnel, but SUBLANT and the Admiralty really wanted this doctor on board ASAP.

Down below, under that hatch, Mills and Oakes were waiting for the word to go topside. Mills was all smiles as he hated submarine deployments and preferred to see the ocean.

Oakes, on the other hand, was visibly nervous and clutched her parachute bag. She had only been pulled up into a helo once before and remembered how tightly the harness squeezed her thighs.

She clamped her hand around that plastic bag in her foul weather jacket pocket. Certain death for her and everybody else if she dropped it in the boat. Her plan was to throw it out the helo door once clear of the boat and over the sea. After that; no idea.

Russell stood nearby, as the escape trunk was in the very aft end of her messdecks. She hated when the seawater would splash down and wet the deck or splash onto some of the dry stores right next to it.

She hadn't said two words to Mills the whole time he had been aboard. Seemed like he slept at every opportunity. She could tell Oakes was having a hard time with something, though.

"You OK?"

"Yeah, just nervous about the transfer up. Hate this kind of thing."

Just then, two khaki legs were climbing down the ladder. They kept coming and coming.

"Jeez, this must be a big motherfucker," she thought to herself. Just then, the guy got to the bottom and turned so she could see his face.

"YOU!"

Then, a bellow of a laugh rang though the whole of the mess hall.

"It was CORNWALIS! All six feet nine of him, dressed in his newly promoted Chief's khakis and a Type 2 Foul Weather jacket. His face, clean shaven this time, was chiseled and rugged. He was a good looking bastard under all that beard, I'll tell you that.

"Sonar Supervisor Cornwallis, reportin' fer duty," he stood with a mock salute and laughed out the words; each one burred in his

168

classic Scottish way.

"Let me get outa the way; man coming down."

Kitty was stupefied into silence and just stared up at his handsome face in utter disbelief.

Right then, a little Lieutenant Commander hit the deck and turned around.

He looked at Chief Russell and motioned her to move forward a bit with him out of earshot of the others.

"I'll have that powder."

She just looked at him.

"The powder you were given. Give it to me before you leave."

Her face must have totally crunched up in confusion. What the hell was this guy talking about?

It was then that Oakes moved from behind Cornwallis who had been blocking her from everyone's view.

The "doctor" looked at Oakes and then back to Russell, who said, "You must have the wrong girl."

They all looked at Oakes who had gone white realizing this guy had thought he was talking to HER. He must be part of this whole mess. She quickly turned and passed her bag up into the trunk so Sweetwater could pass it on up to the deck.

To her credit, she never missed a beat, "Bye, all" was all she said and started climbing the ladder.

The lead balloon in the air was heavy and thick and Wei looked from Russell to Cornwallis and back again. He was thinking quickly…

"Seasick powder. Do you not have seasick powder? I am quite ill."

"He looked green the whole way out. Never said a word," Cornwallis offered.

"I don't have seasick powder, sir. Is there even such a thing? You'd better see our Doc."

"Forgive me…my English is sometimes lacking."

Oakes and Mills had left the ship and were waiting to be hoisted into the chopper. Mills went first and Oakes thought this was the longest wait she would ever make in her life.

Any second, they would grab her and bring her back below with questions. She thought of the Brig, being labeled a Traitor, and what it would feel like when the firing squad's bullets tore into her.

Her mouth was dry and she was wobbly on her feet. Were it not for the tornado of the rotor blades and her face half hidden behind the sunglasses, someone might have asked her what the fuck was going on.

FINALLY, Mills gets into the helo and the hook comes back down. The COB helps her tighten her straps, snaps the hook, and the hoist yanks her off the deck into the air. Five full minutes they hovered until the body of the once LCDR Kennedy was lifted off the main deck and shoved to the rear of the helo. Lines in, hoist retracted, helo banks left and out to sea away from the sub,

"Here he is now, sir" Russell points the "doctor" to Adams who has entered the mess hall to meet him.

"Doc, the Commander here was asking if we had any seasick powder? We do have stuff for seasickness, right?"

She said these words in such a way that let Adams know she felt something was weird about all this.

"Well, we haven't done Seasick powder in a long time, doctor, but I can give you a Scopolamine motion sickness patch for behind your ear. Is that OK for you?"

Doc Adams was torn between being respectful of an Officer and a Doctor at that, and calling bullshit on this guy. They both walked forward out of the messdecks and into Doc's office in the 3-inch launcher space.

"Here ya go, sir."

Wei looked at it, turned it over in his fingers, and handed it back to Adams.

"I'm actually feeling a little better already. I'll try to go without it."

Doc Adams was really looking this guy over now. It was as if he had never seen one of these things before. Every sailor knew what these were; hell, some of the queasier guys even wore two.

Russell and Cornwallis moved more into the crew's mess and got out of the passageway as the topside detail made their way down.

The COB came down first and the others brought down the doctor's bag, all the other gear, and closed and secured the hatches.

"Welcome aboard, Chief Cornwallis!" The COB sang out. The few other guys in the crew's mess were just staring.

"Thank you, Master Chief. When I heard the call for a Sonar Supervisor, I couldn't resist. Besides, the Royal Navy has disowned

170

me for losing the Boat Race, so I have nowhere else ta go."

Laughter all around as the COB explained to whoever was listening that Chief Petty Officer Cornwallis was Nichol's replacement as the rest of their own crew had already returned to the States. He's the only available qualified BQQ-5 Sonar Supervisor on this side of the Atlantic who volunteered to serve with us.

"Chief, I think our longest bunk is about 6 and a half feet," the COB said with a question in his voice.

"Well, if ye give me two mattresses, I can fashion a pallet in the Torpedo room. It'll do me just fine."

"We don't have a Torpedo Room in the way you're thinking…maybe we can arrange something in Lower Level berthing. The COB took their new man through after berthing and they grabbed a couple of unused mattresses. Sweetwater helped them carry them down to the lower level.

"How about just grabbing a piece of the deck between the bunks?"

"You'll have your own Berthing Compartment and Head. Our female Spook rider just left on your helo and she was the only one down here."

"Gets better all the time. Any chance I can get a look at the Sonar Suite?"

"We call it a Shack."

"Aye, the Shack, then."

"Stop in with the Doc and get a dosimeter, grab a coffee, and head up there whenever you like. You're in Underway watch Section 2."

Other than a tour of DODGE CITY when she got to Portsmouth, Cornwallis had never seen a 688 before. Not all that much different from other modern-day subs in the British Navy, but different enough.

He dropped his bags on the bunk next to his sleeping area and took off his outer gear and boots. Slip-on deck shoes for him when at sea, and he preferred his own uniform to one of those blue coveralls lots of other guys wore.

He was just too big for clothing like that. Just getting the damn thing off in the toilet stall when he had to take a shit was tough enough. Much easier to drop his pants and still have a little room. Had to be practical about these sorts of things.

He tucked in his shirt and tentatively moved through the berthing area and up the ladder just forward of the AMR. He wanted to head up to Sonar to stand the rest of the watch for a refresher. He knew the Q5 backwards and forwards, so he'd be able to hit the ground running with a couple of hours to look things over.

"Coffee," he mumbled with a hint of disgust. He always brought tea with him just in case, but maybe they had some passable tea aboard. English Breakfast was probably the only type of tea an American could name other than Lipton.

Funny thing about this whole tea thing is that Thomas Lipton was a SCOT and even English Breakfast was invented by the SCOTS. A popular tea in Scotland is actually Scottish Breakfast designed to mate with the soft waters of his dear homeland. Let's see one of these Yanks spew THAT kind of trivia even about their own swampy Coffee.

He wondered how the crew would take to him. Due to the Artificial Intelligence built in to this ship, there were very few crewmembers aboard. Most were mature, senior men who probably weren't prone to childish games and witticisms, anyway.

He had virtually no knowledge of the protocols and etiquettes aboard Yank boats. Did they request permission to enter places? Were there hierarchies at meals? NO alcohol on Yank boats; he knew that. How the hell did grown men go to war without a bracer or two?

Well, they asked for a replacement and here he stood. Open to instruction and correction, he was, and was excited at the newness of it and all he might learn. The truth of it was that he was the ONLY qualified operator of this type of sonar system between here and the States, so they would have made him go anyway.

Volunteering may sound magnanimous, but the Admiralty were going to send someone, like it or not. His standing up voluntarily just guaranteed him a ribbon on his return.

In the face of an emergency request from an American warship, the Royal Navy would certainly NOT demur. It would be unseemly and possibly bring discredit on the Crown. Riding to the rescue with a hardy "Aye, aye" would give the boys in Manning a point or two over evening tots.

Besides, and he would never speak aloud of it, he had volunteered for this assignment because of HER. It wasn't the professional aspect of it that motivated him to speak up when the request was made. It was the GIRL. It was Russell. His mind ran back to her each day since the night of the Boat Race.

At least once a day, he would picture her standing, bent at the waist, looking at him as she wiped the corner of her mouth. Empty tankard upturned, wry smile on that perfect face. He liked the thought of her bent over that way.

They shared their little ditty as though in that movie, and she walked out scant moments later. He had hoped for some time alone; to chat and feel her energy. He watched as she had made her way through the lot of yanks that congratulated her and narry did she turn to look at him.

He may have been speaking and laughing with others, but his eyes knew where she was in the room every second of her time there. His heart fell a bit when the Argyle doors closed behind her.

"Well, bugger this," he mumbled under his breath and made up his mind then and there this would not be the end of things.

The call for a Sonar Supervisor was a sign from God that this pairing must happen and he jumped at it as a man reaching for a lifeline from a sinking ship. He didn't know if anyone else might be chosen, so he was going to raise his hand and make SURE he was the one to be with her at sea.

Even this late in the game, he didn't know if she was married or anything important about her. This would be the longest deployment EVER if indeed she was a Missus. He had felt a twinge or two over one bonnie lass or another over the years, but THIS was different.

He remembered looking in her eyes that night and seeing something; some message, or possibly at least some interest? He hoped he wasn't just bullshitting himself and hadn't just become a puppy seeing what he wanted to see. Hopefully, it was something real. He already envisioned introducing her to his grandmother. He went on and on with his happy thoughts until...

"Chief! Cornwallis isn't it?"

"Aye!" he responded cheerily.

"I'm Petty Officer Adams, the Corpsman aboard. You can call me Doc like everyone else. I've got a dosimeter for you."

Every man aboard a nuclear-powered vessel wore a dosimeter to track how much radiation he had been exposed to, or DOSED with. These things were read every month or so and exposure would be documented in a sailor's health record.

In reality, if a man spent a year submerged aboard a nuke boat, then he would receive LESS total radiation than had he played volleyball on the beaches of California.

Wooly Boy undid his web belt and slid the dosimeter just left of the buckle.

"Thanks, Doc!" Again, cheerily as he wanted to be a positive addition to the crew and not That Guy from the Boat Race.

Mere feet from the Galley, he saw a chance to speak to Russell…

"The Master Chief ordered me to get a tea and make my way to the Sonar Shack. Will I have any luck with that?" he may have said a little too loudly to feign innocence.

She smiled as her eyes lingered on that magnificent face a second longer than they should have. He noticed.

"First of all, you'd do better calling him COB, for Chief of the Boat…we have English Breakfast, if that will do?"

"Aye! My lifelong favorite," he smiled broadly as he lied and waited while she dug a box out of the same storeroom they had stood next to but moments ago.

She showed him the hot water spigot on the coffee machine and he filled a cup in silence. He didn't want to appear too eager to chat was what he told himself, but the truth of it was he had no idea what to say; another first.

She stood by the galley door for a half second too long and watched him. She told herself it was to make sure their guest was taken care of, but she also just didn't know what to say. She walked into the galley just as the awkwardness started to grow out of control.

As he walked forward to the ladder leading up to the XO's stateroom and Upper Level, the Doctor that came out on the helo with him was just being escorted from the Wardroom back to Doc's.

"I'll leave you in the good hands of our Corpsman," Homes said.

"Ah, Doctor, your dosimeter."

Wei held it in his hands and gave it the once-over. Back on the Chinese boats, they had had the old Film Badge type dosimeters, not these new ones.

"Quite the change from the old badges," he spoke to no one in particular, but wanted to sound as though he had some history with such a piece of equipment.

It seemed weird to Adams as there hadn't been Film Badges in years and years. First the "seasick powder" and now this.

"They got you set up with a Stateroom, sir?"

"Yes. Very hospitable." Wei tried to smile and act friendly, but inside he was a nervous wreck. His mouth was dry and he was sweating like a pig.

"Well, you'll get two nights aboard before we transfer you to the tug with the crew that are leaving."

"Quite the adventure," Wei offered.

"Captain wants us to get started with shots in the morning, if that's OK with you. It'll give me time to organize everything and you'll be able to take a look around and settle in a bit. First time aboard a submarine?"

"First time," Wei lied.

He was trying to plan ahead and come up with some excuses should his behavior be questioned. Any slip-up that was noticed by another officer might lead to interrogation and discovery. He was NOT going down easy.

"Doctor, I'm the XO, Lieutenant Commander Berns. I'm going to escort our guest to meet the Captain, Doc."

"Aye, sir," from Adams.

"Lieutenant Commander Kellogg; nice to meet you," Wei offered.

Li Wei was actually experiencing a full panic at this moment as he could not remember what his phony first name was.

He had a feeling these officers, other than the Captain of course, were on a first-name basis and he couldn't remember this guy's name… ROBERT, it was Robert. He audibly exhaled.

"You, OK?"

"Yes, sir. First time on a sub. They yanked me out here with just a few hours' notice. Still catching my breath, I guess."

Li Wei was actually very impressed with himself right now. He had reacted quickly and come up with plausible excuses and his English was really holding up. Better not get cocky.

They made their way forward through middle level and up the ladder past the XO's stateroom and aft to the CO's.

"Captain Lazarus Scott, I would like to present our esteemed guest, Lieutenant Commander Kellogg of the Royal Medical Corps."

"A distinct honor," Wei volunteered.

"The honor is ours, Doctor. We are all caught up in this

175

spreading disease and figuring things out as we go. Glad to have an expert aboard."

"Far from an expert, Captain. I think I was the only Medico available when they searched."

"Too humble, certainly. Either way, you've met our Corpsman?"

"I have and he promises we'll be administering shots starting in the morning."

"Excellent. If there's anything you need, have the Doc speak to the XO immediately."

"Yes, Captain."

Berns could tell the Captain was done with the pleasantries so he wrangled "Kellogg" toward the Wardroom area.

"Your bag is on your bunk. A stateroom all to yourself. Evening meal in an hour and then we'll all get some needed rest.

Wei wanted to be pleasant but not arouse suspicion. He would just keep as quiet as he could get away with.

"Thank you, sir. I just may rest my head a short while. I was terribly ill coming out here."

"Jesus, don't tell me you've got this damn thing, too."

"No, motion sickness more than anything."

"Let's hope so…we'll have someone come get you for dinner."

"Thank you. I've not had many helicopter rides, and I'm not a fan." He tried smiling but he just didn't feel convincing. Wei closed his stateroom door behind him and bent over the bunk trying to steady himself.

He was totally alone aboard an actual United States nuclear submarine as a saboteur and pirate. He was certain to be killed instantly if he gave the slightest hint of his real purpose.

He had to get a hold of himself and wait for the software program that OTHER girl should have loaded into the ship's system to make itself known. How were there TWO women on this fucking submarine! Didn't that fat bastard Rothington think to tell him that?

Another thing for him to worry about…what WAS going to happen to clue him into performing his end of the ship takeover? Tianzho wo.

For the thousandth time, he checked his shaving kit for the snubnose.

24

Wei had no idea what to do with himself as he waited to be called for dinner. He washed his face and took a couple of aspirins. He didn't want to be cornered into a conversation with any of the officers as the slightest perceived slip-up was doom for him.

A knock at the door. It was House with a cheery "Commander, dinner!" Wei took a deep breath and opened the door.

"Please, call me Bob."

"Bob it is! Hope you're hungry. We have one of the best Mess Divisions in the entire Navy. You're in for a treat."

The entered the forwardmost door to the Wardroom and House motioned to a seat next the Captain's chair.

"For our honored guest."

"The honor is mine." Wei was really taken with himself at this point as he just felt like he was doing so well in this subterfuge. Saying all the right things at the right time. *Maybe I can actually pull this off.*

Wei was brought out of his daydream when the XO said "Gentlemen," as the Captain entered the Wardroom. All the officers stood and sat again as Captain Scott situated himself at the head of the table.

"Good evening, everyone."

"Good evening, Captain," en masse.

Scott turned and said to his guest: "Commander Kellogg. May I reiterate how happy we are to have you."

"I assure you, sir, it is a much greater honor for me." He was hoping this back-and-forth dance of proper commentary was ending now.

"So, how bad is it out there?"

"Sir?"

"The spread of the disease. How bad is it getting?"

Wei was a little taken back by this question. He hadn't gotten ahold of much info regarding the disease. His attention had been focused on what he was supposed to be doing on this submarine.

THE WRONG GIRL   MIKE DeROSA

Time to tap dance.

"It's serious. Spreading everywhere. The consensus is that we must combat it early in the process or it can be fatal."

"Fatal? People are dying?"

"Mostly the elderly, from what I hear." That was the only thing he had heard on the telly. Old people were kicking off left and right from this thing.

"The Admiralty believe we must treat immediately so, here I am. Quite the rush in the pharmacy world to develop a vaccine, I can tell you. These things take time, but I hear the Americans are moving at Warp Speed."

First of all, he WAS talking to "the Americans," so the joke was kind of a lead balloon. Secondly, these chaps hadn't heard about the Warp Speed initiative the President had going, so he was talking to the wall, as it were.

"Couldn't our Corpsman have handed immunizations? It's just a shot, right?"

"Captain, ours is not to reason why. They tell me GO and I WENT."

Well, that got a chuckle out of everyone at the table. This would be the last time so many DODGE CITY officers would be sitting together. Underway meals were usually catch-as-catch-can unless for a special occasion.

Wei kept repeating to himself, one more day of underway routine and then the rendezvous with the tug…

Which was, at this very moment heading due West at 13 knots when their Helmsman saw the red flare. Radar held a small surface contact 010 Relative at 6500 yards.

Dinner on DODGE CITY proceeded smoothly enough. The Captain was an excellent and charming host who engaged his guest in pleasant conversation. Much of the talk was about world events, sports, with complete absence of this submarine's operations or capabilities.

It had been made clear to him that he did not possess the proper level of security clearance to enter the restricted parts of the sub. His duties were to be carried out in the "Forward" part of the boat; everything outside of the Engine room and Weapons spaces to include Sonar.

At every opportunity, Wei made sure everyone knew that he was completely out of his element onboard a nuclear sub, just in case his overall ignorance was called into question. He always had THAT excuse to fall back on.

He also tried to act impressed with all the goings on around him. He hopes that each officer would take his turn trying to show off his knowledge and, therefore, carry the conversation leaving less chance Wei would say something self-incriminating.

Chief Russell had made several appearances in the Wardroom to serve and clear plates. She only spoke when asked a question and made the Captain the prime focus of her attention.

She seemed to be held in high regard by these officers; something rather uncommon in his Navy. He always assumed the enlisted people were looked down on by officers as many he knew were from some well-connected family, or highly educated, or just pompous bastards by nature.

She was never given direction by anyone at the table, either. He was of the opinion that enlisted people, and women in general, had to be told everything and rarely demonstrated any initiative or ever went out of their way to go over and above.

When he was in the service, he was actually rather low on the totem pole and didn't interact with senior enlisteds, so he really had no idea what he was talking about.

Anyway, as dessert and coffee were served, Chief Russell did ask him if he preferred tea, which he declined. He had learned to like coffee during his time in Boston, and he hadn't had any since he made his quick getaway back to the safety of Bolin Li.

That same Bolin Li who, at this very moment, was screaming at Zhang.

"I don't know is all you can say to me, right now!!? I ask for a status on our little adventure and all I get is 'I don't know'? So, who knows, then? Point me to someone who knows!" Li yelled sarcastically.

Zhang was standing in front of the fireplace clock as it chimed 1 AM and tried to hide the smile that wanted to burst forth. He had been on the receiving end of his dear friend's verbal assaults more times than he could count. They were usually born of frustration instead of anger, but it was better to remain silent until the mood passed.

Over the years, other men had dared to try and explain

themselves. It was a trait that Bolin Li regarded as insubordinate and disrespectful. THAT's when the anger would boil up and somebody was going to get hurt.

Even in his 80s, Bolin Li could swing a poker or throw an ashtray. He once pulled a Makarov from the belt of one of his many "grandchildren" and put a hole in the head of someone who spoke when he should have listened. This man was not to be trifled with.

"I want to know where the sub is, where the Howard brothers are, and whether or not you have established communications with our software to determine if it has been loaded into that computer."

For the millionth time, Wei, who was enjoying fresh Apple pie alamode and coffee, was wondering the same thing. "Is that damn software loaded, and how will I know when Uncle has taken control of the boat? What shall I do when that moment comes?"

Bolin Li: "What of Rothington? The last I heard, the girl was taken off the submarine and my nephew was put on board. Anything new?"

As Zhang took his first step toward the door, he said "I will contact him directly and get the latest information." Li watched him leave the room and shook his head. "Zhe shi yīgè zāogāo de jìhuà," he muttered. "A bad plan, indeed. Too many risks, too many things to go wrong, too much left to chance."

He swirled the Vodka in his glass and wondered if they should just kill everyone involved and let things go by the wayside.

Yes, it would have been great to capture an American submarine. Doubtful his friends in government would even accept the gift. It would make them seem complicit in the eyes of the Americans, let alone the entire world.

Maybe some other regime somewhere else would appreciate the gift. He didn't really care who destroyed his enemies as long as they were destroyed. NATO forces would eventually get to that submarine and destroy IT, which would keep him out of the spotlight.

Besides, it seemed it was only he who held onto the hatred and desire for revenge all these years. All those who were children with him, who suffered through the war and watched their country evolve to take its rightful place on the grand stage, had become rich and complacent, or grew too old and died.

Did they see their dead parent's faces every day in their dreams?

Could they still smell the smoke and burning flesh of their villages as he did? Probably not.

They comforted themselves in the money, whores, lavish estates, and drugs as they suckled from the teats of the empire he, HE designed. Perhaps it was time they were all reminded to whom they should bow. He reached into his pocket and rolled the Zippo between his fingers.

At the very same moment, the Blackhawk touched down at Cornwall and killed the engines. The flight in from the DODGE CITY had started out rough as hell, but the winds died down and it appeared the storm would miss them.

A little past 2000 hours now, so they had missed chow at the mess hall. The guests, Mills and Oakes, jumped down and took off their headsets.

"Thanks for the lift," Mills smiled as he handed the equipment to the flight engineer and reached in for his bag.

Oakes was silent as she kept her hand on that plastic bag in her pocket. She had wanted to throw the damn thing out of the helicopter while it was over the sea, but the rain and wind had gotten so bad as they left from over the DODGE CITY, that the flight engineer slammed the door almost immediately.

She threw her duffle bag over her shoulder and carried the parachute bag in her other hand as they all walked off the flight line. The Ambulance for Kennedy passed by them on its way to the helicopter.

There was a red-haired Able Rate with a clipboard and Motorola radio waiting just inside the door to usher them to their ride to the hospital.

They rode in silence as fatigue had crept in. Military people seem to make the most of ANY opportunity to sleep, and Mills was snoring and leaning onto her right side. She let him be and stared out the window as the raindrops moved diagonally along the glass.

She fought back tears as she wondered just what the hell she was going to do now. Her thoughts ran to her mother as she imagined every terrible fate she might be going through at the moment. She felt the nerves jumping in her stomach and an old conversation surfaced in her mind.

It was sixth grade and she was a member of the school soccer team. This one game in question was against a rival school, inasmuch as 12 years olds can be sports rivals.

The game had ended in a tie and the teams were taking penalty kicks to determine the winner. None of the other girls had managed to score and only she was left. Miss and the game ends tied, but score and her team would be victorious, she the heroine.

The ball was placed on the spot, she took her position and eyed it and the goalkeeper. Her mouth was dry with fear and the butterflies were going nuts in her stomach. Her legs were weak and rubbery with the fear of failure.

She stepped out, ran toward the ball, and managed a weakly rolling, hopeless shot that missed the post by a full yard. Never a hope of scoring, no chance to even force the keeper to move. It was utter failure.

The crowd, mostly parents, cheered graciously in the way one would expect, everyone left the field, and she walked toward where her family were standing.

Grandpa Saragian, her mom's father, was slowly walking onto the field toward her. Everyone else in the family called Grandpa "Sarge," playing off their last name AND the fact the he had been 30 years in the Marines and retired as a Sergeant Major.

"Sorry, Grandpa."

"For what?"

"For not winning the game."

"That's no reason to be sorry. You're not going to win every game no matter how hard you try. Sometimes, the other guy is just better that day."

Grandpa stopped talking, stopped walking, and turned to face her directly. She stopped, too, and looked up at the serious face with the smiling eyes.

"You should be sorry for giving up. You felt the pressure and you folded. Tell me if I'm wrong."

He was looking at her in such a way that she felt pinned to the ground like some bug in a science class. She couldn't speak. He knew what she had felt.

"You had the game in your hands, you were the center of attention, you felt the weight of the whole team counting on you, and you chickened."

Grandpa had such a way with words; brutally direct, but beautiful in their truth.

"I'm not trying to make you feel worse, I'm trying to show you that it's your interpretation of your feelings that is wrong."

She looked up at his face and saw the serious look in his eyes. She knew he wasn't angry or disappointed. She could feel the love and the kind of honesty of a moment she may seldom experience in life.

"I'm sure you felt butterflies in your stomach and they were just too much. Right?"

"Yes, Grandpa."

"WRONG!" he blasted out loudly.

Oh, oh, the Sergeant Major had just shown up and the lesson was about to begin.

"Whoever told you those were butterflies was full of shit! Weak people may have butterflies, but strong people, people like me and MY GRANDDAUGHTER, we don't have butterflies; we have ALLIGATORS!"

He shot his right hand out and pointed one finger right at her belly.

"Those are YOUR alligators and they will be woken up by whatever it is you're about to go through. They will be awake, stomping around in your belly, and they are ready to back you up and attack the second you TURN THEM LOOSE!"

This was one of those moments in life that people never forget. This was a moment when life becomes crystal clear and all doubt has been removed.

"The next time you find yourself in a situation important enough for that feeling to arrive in your stomach, I want you to say to yourself 'Alligators,' and never ever EVER again think that you, MY DEAREST GRANDDAUGHTER, have wussy little butterflies that are afraid. YOU HAVE ALLIGATORS READY TO ATTACK!!"

Her eyes were filling with tears, and God dammit, so were his.

"Now, let me hear you say Alligators."

"Alligators."

"I CAN'T HEAR YOU!"

"ALLIGATORS!!!"

"Now, let's go home," he said with the biggest smile on his face and a big grandpa hand on her head.

At this moment, she could have run through a brick wall; she could have lifted a car off a trapped kid; she could have beaten the shit out of Muhammad Ali.

Her last thought before being greeted by her mom was "Gimme that fucking soccer ball."

25

So, here she was, thousands of miles away from home, getting out of a Royal Navy van, rain on her face and that feeling in her stomach once again. She knew what had to be done and she was NOT going to wuss.

"Alligators."

"What'd you say, Oakes?"

"Nothing, Millsy, just thinking out loud."

They walked as a group through the entrance to the hospital and were ushered through the Emergency Room and down a short hallway to a ward that had been designated for those potentially exposed to the virus.

On the long table against the wall, there was a kettle of boiling water and some pastries. Mills was already over there checking out the goods.

"Greetings, all, I am Doctor Guinness. You'll be medically screened for this God-awful virus going around. As we get results from the tests, you'll either be let go or admitted to hospital for treatment. Clear?"

A bunch of 'Aye, sirs,' and a general shambling over to the kettle as jackets and helmets were removed and piled on the far table.

Oakes put her bags down by the door but kept her jacket on and her hand in the pocket.

Doctor Guinness held up a plastic jar and announced with true aplomb "For our American friends!"

It was instant coffee.

"Yay," said Mills and he made a cup for himself and one for Oakes who had a cinnamon roll in her mouth as she pulled out a chair.

"Sugar?"

"And creamer, please."

"That's not coffee, that's a milkshake."

"Shut up, Mills," she faked a smile.

They ate their pastries and drank their coffee. They wondered where that Navy was sending them next and if they would go together.

"Well, according to Senior Chief, it's supposed to be the LINCOLN for us both," she offered.

"Yeah, but that's if we get out of this place together."

She was about to respond when the Ward door opened and all eyes turned to see.

Well, holy shit, it was Nichols! He of the recent meningitis attack and medevac. Warrant Officer Watson was with him and they both walked over to Doc Guinness.

Since they had both been vaccinated, they were deemed safe from contracting the illness, so they were allowed to stay. The doctor pointed to the table where Oakes and Mills were sitting and over they came.

"Hey, you guys! Nobody else from the boat come with you"? Nichols asked

"Hey, man. Good to see you made it!" Mills shook Nichols' hand and Oakes gave him a thumbs-up.

"No, the plan is to off-load another half or so of the crew and engage the AI. I think they're getting on a tug tomorrow."

"How's my boy doing?" Watson was asking about Cornwallis. He's from my boat remember?

"We saw him for 2 seconds before we were loaded aboard the helo."

"Well, your COB and I have become close mates and I feel a sense of kinship with DODGE CITY now, ya know."

"He's not really OUR COB; we're just riders, but I know what you mean." Mills again.

"So, how are you feeling?" Oakes asked Nichols.

"Great. The meds have done their magic and I'm ready to get back."

Watson, now, with a hand on Nichol's shoulder, "Yer no going BACK, lad. You're here to recuperate; takes time. Wooly Boy will keep yer seat warm."

They had heard the nickname before, but never saw him before he came down the Escape Trunk. Neither Mills nor Oakes had been present at the boat race.

Oakes had been watching Watson. He had a cool, confident demeanor. He looked everyone straight in the eye as a strong man

186

might do, but he had a kindness toward Nichols he wasn't afraid to show. Kind of reminded her of an old Sergeant Major.

"Any chance you and I might speak. Privately?"

Watson was taken aback.

"You and I? Now?"

"Very important."

She had had enough of the fear. Enough of hiding. Enough. Alligators.

They both rose from their seats. Watson eyed her very closely as she led him across the Ward to another table and chairs.

Her eyes were starting to fill and she looked at Watson and whispered:

"DODGE CITY is in danger."

Watson leaned back a bit and squinted his eyes.

"Oh?"

"There is so much to be told, but right this second, there is a saboteur aboard. The Royal Navy Doctor that was sent out to do whatever with this vaccine is an impostor. They are trying to commandeer that submarine."

All the moisture drained out of Watson's mouth and an audible gasp escaped his mouth. He had his doubts.

"How do ye know and why are ye telling ME?"

"I was blackmailed into being a part of the plot. My mother is being held hostage. I have a plastic bag of poison cyanide powder and a thumb drive in my pocket they gave me to use. I should have said something sooner, but I was afraid for my mother's life. I didn't know whom to count on. I didn't want to be labeled a traitor."

Watson sat in stunned silence.

"Well, lass; I should say Petty Officer. You've

done the right thing, now."

Mills and Nichols were sitting across the way observing the interaction between Watson and Oakes. They could see her wiping her eyes, then standing and straightening her uniform.

Watson tore into a box of surgical gloves and

put on a pair.

"Give me that powder."

She slowly pulled the bag out of her jacket and

held it out toward Watson. It was the size of a tennis ball and he reached out a hand very slowly.

187

Before he took the bag, he remembered the jar
of jam on the other table and quick stepped over to get it. He
screwed open the lid and dumped the jam in the wastebasket.

Everyone was looking at him and then over to
Oakes and her plastic bag.

"Put it in the jar."

She did as she was told and he screwed the lid
on tight.

"Lads, everyone back out of this room. There's
cyanide powder in this jar!"

The entire group seemed to move as one and
cleared the room in one second amid "What the fucks" and Holy
shits."

Dr. Guinness was the only one to remain. He
pulled his key ring out of his pocket.

"Here, Warrant!"

He motioned Watson over to the Hazardous
Materials Locker and keyed the lock. The locker was airtight
when closed and in went the jar.

"Where in the Holy Fuck did you get THAT?" he
said to Oakes as he grabbed her hands to look at them.

"You were handling cyanide in your bare hands?
Do you realize how deadly that shit is?"

"It was in my jacket pocket and I kept my hand
over it so it wouldn't get out and hurt anyone."

Guinness dragged her over to the sink and said

"Get that jacket off" as he pulled a Red HAZMAT bag from the
locker.

"Put it in the bag and get soap and water on
those hands right away!"

"Warrant, did you touch the bag?"

"No, sir, opened the jar and the Petty Officer
placed it in. Doctor, is there a Royal Navy Police office at this
hospital?"

"Aye. Go to the duty desk out front and tell them
who you want."

In 25 minutes, a Sergeant from the Royal Navy
Police and a Special Agent from the U.S. Navy NCIS was
standing in front of Petty Officer Verona Oakes with ears wide open

and a tape recorder running.

She was put in handcuffs and loaded into the
Duty van. Watson rode with her.

"I'm going to stay with you as long as I can, lass. The cuffs and rough treatment thus far are certainly precautional and must be protocol until they can start sorting this whole mess."

She nodded and looked at the floor of the
vehicle. She had given them the three-minute version of the story. Disney, the hair, the big English guy, the fear and confusion, the poison, and the thumb drive, both of which were now in NCIS custody.

26

A few hundred miles west, the Navy tug was closing on the contact shooting red flares. It was almost time for the fourth guy on the fishing boat to make his appearance; maybe they should just go down to berthing and wake him up.

Sometimes in life, we make friends with people we'd never thought we'd get along with. The great weightlifter and shooter of defenseless women, Wang, was one of those guys that no one really liked, OR they were just intimidated and would rather agree than risk finding out if their fears had merit.

The guy sleeping below was introduced some months ago to the Howard brothers as a friend of Mr. Wang's and, consequently, a friend to the organization. He would be available, at Mr. Wang's request, to support them in their endeavors in any way he could.

His predominant value was logistics insomuch as he managed their cadre of delivery vehicles and drivers throughout the British Isles and reported directly to Mr. Wang. He also interfaced with the blokes on the docks and had a unique ability to get things done. What kinds of things? Things.

Beyond that, Wang liked to joke that his friend, here, was an expert at delivering Long Range Justice to those who were a threat to the organization. The Royal Marines had taught him how to do that very thing and Long Range meaning anything pretty much up to 500 yards.

Wang, although legally a Chinese citizen,

spends most of his life in Great Britain as an ambassador, so to speak, for the interests of Bolin Li.

His absolute loyalty was invaluable to a man like Li, who sometimes asked his people to do things the common employee would not, or was incapable of doing.

He was the kind of man that, when you saw him walking toward you on the street, you found a reason to cross to the other side. He had an aura that people just wanted no part of. Muscular and scary, he was also cursed with a pair of soulless eyes that observed the world as a place to maximize opportunity rather than a place to find joy.

So, here he was one evening a couple of years ago, in gray and rainy Edinburgh. He had, just moments ago, finished a successful 'staff shuffling' shall we say, crushing the skull of one Freddy Domino.

Domino, a vulgar and uneducated brute had just spewed out his last words on Earth: "…and fuck you AND your mother, you slanty eyed cocksucker…."

Imagine! Wang had just made clear to him the organization's need to either increase profits or minimize costs as Freddy's area was not meeting goal. A reasonable request; a purely business decision and dumb ole Freddy had to respond emotionally and rudely.

Wang, after all, was merely the messenger. Those in authority, and we know who HE is, sent word for middle management to make some changes for the good of all.

The ruckus had not been a quiet one, and the noise had gotten the attention of the driver waiting out back in the alley. Opening the door slowly, Wang's soon to be new friend entered the warehouse and slowly walked over to the prone Mr. Domino.

"You work here?"

"I did. Apparently, I no longer have an employer."

"You do. I am your employer just as I was the employer of this gentleman."

Waldo Michael Quinlan laughed at that one. Freddy Fuckin' Domino was no gentleman. He was a pig, a disgusting wife beater and was always trying to get over on somebody for something.

"I take it that YOU have an employer, as well?"

"I do; the same gentleman who employs us both as well as many others around the world."

"I've heard that story."

"Would you care to continue your employment with our organization?"

Man, this guy really made an effort to sound like one of those super-villains in the movies. Thick Chinese accent and everything. Waldo wanted to call him Dr. No, but didn't think this the right time. Men who've just killed someone have their blood up for some time and this guy's hands were still wet.

"Well, this 'gentleman,' as you say, was a terrible boss and paid me like shit. I'll stay but I'd like to make more money."

Wang liked a man that worked for a living. You never had to wonder about his motivation. Nothing ideological, just pay.

"He had me driving a truck, but I have other skills an outfit like this might appreciate."

Wang wondered if there was a veiled threat in that remark.

"Care to discuss it over a drink?" Wang asked as he snapped his flip-phone shut. "Now would be a good time as I just reported finding this body to the Police."

"Fine. No Coppers for me, thank you."

The evening went exceedingly well as Wang and Waldo discussed his military service, politics (which was something neither man cared for), and the two blondes at the bar.

Wang was impressed with Waldo's supposed skill with a rifle and even more impressed with the fact that he used a 300 Win Mag now as his military rifle was unaffordable for him.

"I may have something further up the organization for you if you pass your test."

Waldo wasn't too sure he liked that sound of that, but was in serious need of money. These last few years saw an unimaginable decline in the custom motorcycle market. He watched his business shrink and shrink.

As times got tougher, very few people wanted to spend 40 thousand pounds on a custom chopper anymore. So, three years ago, he invested his own money and opened two more shops: one in Cornwall and the other in Brighton, both upbeat resort towns.

His hope was to grow a motorcycle rental business aimed at the tourist trade, but so far, it had been a lead balloon. Sadly, he borrowed heavily against what was left of the bike building business as he needed cash.

After all, he did have a "silent partner" whom he had to provide for. No way was he ever going to admit that he had lost it all; Fergus' part of it, too.

He had used the inheritance from Big Bob to buy some Japanese bikes as rentals. He bought them outright which was much riskier than taking out insured bank loans.

The drunken tourists crashed and damaged a few of the bikes; two were actually stolen and the losses came out of his pocket. The deeper he got, the more he borrowed until it got so bad, he went over to the Dark Side and borrowed money from the wrong people.

In another of those coincidences the Universe has in store for us, Waldo, having been turned down by the banks, had borrowed money from a Mr. Roger Echelson. Yes, the same Roger Echelson who had fallen out of favor with the Bolin Li organization.

Wang made a very clear and straightforward presentation about how Mr. Echelson needed to be replaced. If Waldo were willing to support this endeavor, let's call it a 'test,' then all his debts would be forgiven and he could embark on a new and very lucrative career.

One tranquilizer dart later, Waldo had Roger rolled up in a tarp from his shop in Cornwall and thrown into the back of a Mercedes bound for parts unknown. Bolin Li's 'specialists' took charge of the medical proceedings and Mr. Echelson ended his days as a bridge ornament and warning to all who dare mess with the master.

In the two years hence, the Howard brothers were promoted and Waldo Quinlan accepted a well-paying spot offered by Wang.

He managed to sell off the motorcycle business in toto explaining to Fergus and grandmother how demand for such pleasantries had declined. He presented Fergus with a check three times larger than that which he kept for himself.

He threw himself into his new role moving product all across the British Isles; he even got a congratulatory phonecall from Zhang himself and a nice bonus check for Christmas of over a hundred thousand pounds.

If it weren't for the dicey extra-curricular jobs that came along every now and then, things were great. So, here he was, hung over and sleepy, tossing around in the bunk of a smelly old fishing boat. Just another one of those damn extra-curricular jobs offered him by Wang.

Oh, there was always a good check at the end of it, but there was also a veiled assurance that, if the opportunity was refused, there would be no more opportunities to do anything; anything at all.

This was way beyond the beating the hell out of a guy, or collecting money, or the usual goon squad stuff. The trank dart was one thing; after all, he didn't know what was about to happen to Roger. He just handed the guy over to put an end to the debt AND the exorbitant vigorish that bastard was charging him.

He would have been glad to slug it out and settle the matter like men, but that bastard Echelson had threatened to tell Fergus about the sad state of Waldo's business. He just couldn't have that, so he paid and paid and paid until he got the chance to get out from under.

What happened to Echelson after that was not his business. Wang asked for him to do it, Zhang outlined his payment as it were, and he did it. Never mentioned it, never ratted, never caused anyone to wonder about him. The trust factor was what kept Waldo alive and gave him a whole new line of work.

27

Given the hour, it took some time to get The Admiralty, COMSUBLANT, NCIS, and the MOD all on the same page. FLASH traffic was sent to DODGE CITY and the tug NEPTUNE. Two Royal Navy Blackhawks were scrambled; one with the same crew that had already been out there twice.

2200 hours in London put it at 1700 at COMSUBLANT. The duty sections were manning the offices as the workday ended an hour and a half ago. Checklists were opened and thrown on desks, VIPs were called one after the other, and the DODGE CITY was punching holes unaware a killer was in their midst.

NEPTUNE had closed to within a thousand yards of the Howards and their pals when they got the emergency message. Bad form to leave a stranded boat; one of those "law of the sea" things.

Chief Petty Officer Dillon was standing in the wheelhouse when he was told about the DODGE CITY.

"This must be some kind of exercise." He muttered. "Gotta play it straight."

"Raise that fishing boat on the UHF."

"This is the tug NEPTUNE. We are unable to effect rescue. We are radioing for an additional asset to rendezvous your position."

The Howards looked at each other with a "Holy Shit" expression on their faces as they watched NEPTUNE turn away from them and head East.

"This is good and bad, Jake."

"I know. We can't be blamed for not making the transfer AND we won't have to go up against the whole of NATO."

Wang came up from below and they filled him in. "When the tug moves off, start engines and follow," he commanded.

In the hours that had passed since being put in handcuffs, Oakes had told her story to 8 different people. She knew some of them were trying to find discrepancies in it to determine if she was lying. Others were the type of super cop that had to hear the whole story told to them first hand.

She must have described the big Oriental in the video ten times. Once real slow to a forensic artist. How the hell do you describe a guy like that? A guy you've seen for a minute, maybe.

About this tall, dark hair, dark eyes, Oriental. Jesus, what they hell could she tell them? The same with the big pasty guy that gave her the powder. The interesting part of that description was the smell.

She described him as tallish and overweight looking. An odor of shitty tobacco and Body Odor. She could even smell his horrible teeth; you know that 'lack of flossing' smell?

The NCIS guy was most interested in the fact that he had met her right outside the Billeting Office on base. Obviously, he had to have some kind of authorization to physically get on the base. Could he actually be Ministry of Defence?

The cyanide and the thumb drive had been taken somewhere and she assumed they were trying to get some info from them. She was sitting, handcuffs chained to the table, in one of the NCIS interrogation rooms allowed them by the Royal Navy Police.

Inspector Healey was now sitting next to the NCIS agent, Frank Evangelista. They were kind of just staring at her; sizing her up as it were.

"So," Evangelista started, "you've had your hand on top of a lethal dose of cyanide for the last few days?"

"Not every second of the day, but, yes."

"Because you didn't want to deploy it too early, right?"

"No, because I didn't want to hurt anybody. I didn't know what to do! I didn't know if I was the only one those guys sent. There might have been someone else ready to kill me AND the crew."

The two LEOs looked at each other.

"The thumb drive; what's that for?"

God damn. She's answered this 5 times already, but this is the game cops play.

"It's supposedly a software upload to take over the sub. Stick it in the USB connection, it loads, they have the boat. That's all I know."

"Did you try to deploy that?"

"Yes. I stuck it in the connector, but the Marshal rejected it."

They asked her who the Marshal was. She didn't know if they knew about the AI or not. Were they going to hang a charge of spilling secrets on her, too? She tried to stay strong.

"Alligators."

"Excuse me?"

She just told them everything. That happened from the Mail Buoy to letting Schiano touch her so she could try to insert the thumb drive.

Watson had wanted to sit in on the interrogation, but the NCIS guy threw him out. He was the kind of guy whose team meant the world to him. They were his family; the people who stood with him in the gravest of times, and he didn't like seeing how alone and broken Oakes was looking.

Her interrogators were giving her a good going over, but that was their job and years of experience taught them how to treat a suspect. Even he didn't know the whole story and she might very well be a terrorist bent on bringing death and destruction to his side.

He looked through the window in the door and sized her up as she answered questions. His life experience said to him that she was being truthful. Her facial expressions and body language gave him no hint of deception, but what did he know.

The cyanide and the thumb drive had been securely boxed and carted out of the building and were on their way over to MOD headquarters where U.S. and British reps were waiting to tear into them and try to glean some Intel.

Everyone else that had been in the ward had been moved to a different part of the hospital and were being screened for poisons.

His thoughts went out to the DODGE CITY and his newest friend, Joe Durocher. Jesus, they might all be dead, for all he knew. His own mate, Wooly Boy, might be laying among them. Oh, he hated feeling helpless.

Meanwhile, miles and miles out to sea, dead west from here, The Howards started engines and headed in the same direction as NEPTUNE. That was when Wang made his first bold move, firing the flare gun into the bilge below the fishing boat's diesel.

He had drained some fuel and set it alight knowing smoke would billow out the hatch. He climbed out of the Engine room and launched another flare into the sky knowing NEPTUNE would see it and the smoke.

"Radio an emergency," he commanded Jake who did so. NEPTUNE turned around.

Chief Dillon kept muttering, "I don't like it."

"What, Chief?" It was QM1 Hobbs.

"The sudden fire and flare on that fishing boat."

"We can't leave a burning craft at sea with souls aboard, Chief."

"Must be some kind of exercise to see if we'll go off orders."

"We can pick up those people and still get back on original track. Wouldn't go over too well if just let them burn and sink."

"Yeah, I guess so. Any word from the sub?"

"Not yet."

Hobbs went back to his chart and laid in the heading they would need to go to the rendezvous point.

"We've got plenty of time to rendezvous, Chief. Let's pluck these guys out of the water."

"OK, radio it in to the Admiralty. If they tell us no, then we'll be free of the consequences."

"Aye, Chief."

Dillon had the binoculars on the fishing boat and saw three men at the rail waving their arms. He didn't see the fourth man looking back at him through the rifle scope.

After receiving a compliance message, NEPTUNE put the rudder over and came along side, putting the fishing boat in her lee. Heaving lines went over. Three sailors on NEPTUNE tied her to the fishing boat and one held out his hand to help someone cross over.

The first rifle shot went right through the wheelhouse window and Hobbs' chest; the second dropped Dillon.

All three Seamen looked toward the sound of the shots and Wang executed them each with shots from his pistol. They had been told to expect an eight-man crew and already 5 were dead.

Jake and Joey each climbed aboard NEPTUNE with their AK47s and searched the rest of the tug. They found one in the Engine room, one sitting in the mess area having a coffee, and one asleep. They herded them together at the dining table, gagged and tied them up with a heaving line and some zip-ties they found.

Jake was the engine guy and Joey knew about steering and radios. Joey put on a green foul weather jacket and NEPTUNE ballcap. He took his place in the wheelhouse.

Waldo had thrown the bag of ammo and weaponry onto the deck of the tug and cut the lines once he was aboard. The fishing boat drifted away as the flames got higher and higher.

Jake went down by the throttles and answered Joey's EOT order for a Standard Bell. He was trying not to puke his guts out. They had just murdered 5 Americans. AMERICANS. He couldn't believe it.

Wang climbed the ladder to the wheelhouse and handed Joey the piece of chart Rothington had given him. 2 hours to go, so they headed to the rendezvous point.

Wang had Waldo throw the bodies overboard including the three he just killed in the mess hall. Waldo had seen how emotionless and deadly this guy had been several times before, but executing young sailors who were bound and gagged was a new low even for Wang. God, he wanted to just cry. How the hell did his life become so fucked up.

Must be about 2 or 3 hours to rendezvous., he thought to himself.

28

Doc Adams had been mentally replaying his entire interaction with Doctor Kellogg. From the seasick powder to the Dosimeter to the way he looked at the hypos to his oddly total unfamiliarity with Navy life in general; he was really bothered by this guy.

Then, he had an idea. He went to find Dusty.

"Dusty, Dusty, wake up."

"Doc, what's wrong," Hochstetler croaked from the dark reaches of his bunk.

"Dusty, can the Marshal pull up files on military personnel?"

"Huh?"

"Files, files. Can the Marshal show me a Service Record for someone?"

"He's got files of everything DOD already loaded as well as NCIC and INTERPOL. We update them periodically via satellite. If the info is in a database accessible to the Marshal, he can show you anything current; up to the second, actually."

No matter how tired or preoccupied Dusty was, any opportunity to talk about his Marshal would get him to talk endlessly.

"Get up, Dusty."

"Dammit."

15 minutes later, Dusty was sipping the coffee Doc got him and they were standing in the computer room at the Marshal's keyboard.

"Show me whatever you have on a Doctor Robert Kellogg, Royal Navy Medical Service."

"Is that the guy that came out here yesterday?"

"We'll see."

It took less than a half second for the photo and records of some guy they had never seen before to pop up on the screen.

"Print that out; blow up the photo."

Doc took the information and, with Dusty in tow, left the computer room and headed to the Chief's Quarters.

Two knocks.

"Enter."

"COB, I have something to show you. I think we're in trouble."

"For fuck's sake, what now?"

Doc put the picture in front of him.

"Who's this guy?"

"That's the problem. This is the official Royal Navy photo of Lieutenant Commander Robert Kellogg, 34, Royal Navy Medical Service"

Durocher looked at Adams a little quizzically.

"This is supposed to be the Doctor they sent out here. It looks nothing like him. Yeah, the only similarity is they're both Asian, but the guy we've got is definitely younger. It's obviously a different person."

Dusty explained how they got the info from the Marshal and how he could access data bases all over the world or just the files he has stored.

"Where's this fucker right now?"

"I saw him in the Wardroom sitting with House about 20 minutes ago."

"Before I get the Captain involved in this, I want you to get your cellphone and take a picture of the guy in the Wardroom. Dusty, can the Marshal scan the photo and cross reference this same database?"

"He can do anything. If this dude's in a database, then the Marshal will snag him."

In seven minutes, Dusty was handing his COB an NCIC mug shot from the Boston Police Department of a Li Wei, now 26, Chinese National, arrested for rape and assault. There was a murder investigation mentioned, but the suspect was repatriated to his home country as a direct official request from the Chinese Embassy.

Wei was listed as family to an Embassy member and a former Boston med school student. Diplomatic Immunity was extended to him and he was immediately released.

Of course, the Boston PD had no way of knowing that Bolin Li's organization was behind that request, but they let Wei go and he was bound for parts unknown.

So, what in the hell was an imposter doing here and where was the real Robert Kellogg?

"FLOODING IN THE ENGINE ROOM!" was announced over the 1MC followed by the collision alarm.

"FLOODING IN THE ENGINE ROOM!"

Doc, Dusty, and the COB all looked at each other and they heard the Emergency Blow system engage. The deck pitched up under their feet and the boat headed for the surface.

The CO was running a drill to give Lancey his last practical factor of Emergency Surfacing the ship from the BCP.

They would be meeting with the Navy tug, soon anyway, so it was a good way of getting everybody up and around as well as surfacing the boat in preparation for the rendezvous.

They felt the boat broach and drop back down into the sea, returning again to the surface and settling down.

The COB hurried up the middle level ladder and fast walked the length of Upper Level into the Control Room.

"Hang on!" House had said to Wei Li as the boat lurched upward.

Wei's thoughts were all over the place as he figured this must be the sign that Bolin Li had taken control of the submarine. No one else seemed to be ready for this event. He watched House and was certain the boat was surfacing on the command of Bolin Li.

He must get up to the Control Room and get the hatch open to receive Wang!

The forward door to the Wardroom opened.

"Don't move, motherfucker!"

It was Durocher who, after briefing the CO, had been ordered to the Wardroom to subdue Wei Li. He might have used a different strategy had he known that Wei Li was armed.

He had sent Sweetwater to the Small Arms locker to get a 45 and some handcuffs and meet him at the Wardroom.

At this same moment, Russell had been handing coffee cups to LT. House and Wei Li who put his hand on the snub-nosed in his jacket pocket.

Sweetwater burst in the Wardroom After door and pointed his pistol at Li who pushed House away and fired a round into his side from inside his pocket. He slid back in his chair, grabbed Russell by the collar, and pulled her down to shield him. He pushed the hot revolver barrel against her neck, right below her right ear.

"Back away! Get away from me or I'll shoot her, too!"

As though to emphasize his point, he cocked the pistol. She heard the noise, but wasn't sure of what he had just done. It was a standoff as Sweetwater looked at his COB for some kind of direction.

Cornwallis then showed up at the door right behind Sweetwater. He looked between the door jamb and Sweetwater's head at Russell's predicament. He just wanted to rip that little bastard that held her to pieces.

He looked at her face and realized she looked more pissed off than scared. He started signing to her.

The hammer is back.

She knew it! Cornwallis saw her eyes narrow a bit and then she shot her hand up to the gun. She grabbed it from the top, clamped her hand on the cylinder, and just got the web of her thumb and forefinger in front of the hammer as Wei Li pulled the trigger.

The hammer snapped into her flesh and she pulled downward on the gun twisting it right out of his hand. She backhanded him with it in the face and blood spurted from his nose.

Three enraged Navy men dove across the Wardroom table and wrestled Li to the deck. House had fallen to the deck and was holding both hands over the wound in his side as Doc Adams put pressure.

"Help me get him on the table!"

Blood was everywhere as Doc tore open House's shirt and reached into his medic bag for bandages.

Russell made her way into the galley and put a wet towel on her neck where the barrel of Li's gun had burned her.

Li was frantically trying to get out of the Wardroom and Cornwallis pinned his arms to his side and thrust him up into the overhead slamming his head into one of the lights knocking him unconscious.

Sweetwater cuffed him and they threw him off to the side while they looked after House.

"Thanks, Doc" House muttered.

Doc had a compress against the bullet hole as the blood pumped all over the two of them and the Wardroom table.

Adams held his stethoscope to House's chest as his shipmates watched in stunned silence. He stood up straight and pounded his fist into House's chest.

"C'mon! C'mon!"

Stethoscope again.

He slowly put a hand over House's face and shut his eyes.

"Jesus Christ. He's gone."

Sweetwater looked over at Wei Li on the deck and pounced on him. In less than a second, he was wailing the holy shit out of him and Cornwallis had to pull him back and try to calm him down.

Chief of the Boat now, "I cannot believe this shit. What in the FUCK is going on?"

LCDR Bern's was taking pictures with his cellphone. He wanted to document everything that had happened, He was writing notes about times and events; trying to remember the sequence and who did what when.

"Doc, go check on Russell; she's in the galley."

He went to the deep sink in the scullery area and tried washing all the blood off his hands. He was covered up to the elbows and had some splatter on his face.

Russell was standing off to his left with some ice against her neck. She was staring down at the deck. She still had Wei Li's gun in her hand.

"Let me see your neck."

She showed him the circular burn mark from the hot barrel.

"I'm fine. Really. My hand hurts worse than my neck."

Doc took a Ziplock bag off the counter, "Put that in here."

She dropped the gun into the bag and he zipped it shut. He took a look at the hole punched in her skin by the gun's hammer. He pulled her hand under the faucet in the sink and dried it off with a Kimwipe.

He looked in her face and saw no tears. No fear, no angst. This was one tough bitch.

"Took some balls to do what you did."

"Only had one option. I wasn't going to let that little prick shoot me, too. No way was I going out like that."

"How did you think to block the hammer?"

"I thought I heard him cock the gun, but Cornwallis signed to me that the hammer was back. If I could be quicker to get my hand between it and the gun than he was to pull the trigger, then I knew I had him. Surprise alone would help."

"Signed?"

"Yeah. We found out we both signed that LAST time he came out here when we off-loaded Nichols. He signed to me from the chopper."

"Well, if that ain't a one in a million."

Bern's came into the galley asked if everyone was alright. He took pictures of Russell's wounds and also commended her on getting that gun away from the "Doctor."

Doc turned again to Russell, "House didn't make it."

"Oh, goddammit." She looked down again and shook her head.

The XO spoke up and said "Chief, that guy might have shot a few more people if you hadn't done what you did. You risked your life going for that firearm."

"Well, thank God for that, anyway."

Doc handed his XO the bagged-up weapon.

Some weeks later, they would find out that the bullet had pierced LT. House's descending aorta and he bled out very fast. Sad as it was, it helped Doc feel less guilty about House's death as there was no way to save him.

Also, Chief Petty Officer (Submarines) Theresa Russell would be recommended and approved for the Navy and Marine Corps Medal, the highest non-combat award for valor.

29

By this time, Oakes had been getting interrogated for almost 7 hours. She had been completely forthright in all her answers and shown no annoyance at having to answer the same question a hundred times.

She not only had to answer the same question a hundred times, but she had to answer it for several different organizations who each sent their own interviewer.

NCIS and the MOD were the predominant forces trying to extract information. They had sent the cyanide and the zip drive who-knows-where to try and get even more in formation from them.

MOD had also backtracked every move from the time the helicopter left Cornwall including who, how, and when every person got onboard.

Individually, each piece of info stood alone, but when one investigator looked at all of it at once, the picture started to clear. The virus, the vaccine, the doctor, the manifest for the people on the helo, and the written directive from Planning.

They even downloaded every tidbit from Oakes' cellphone from her carrier's servers to get a look at the video she said showed her mother in extremis.

It took less than three hours to get officers to Kellogg's home and find him and his girlfriend lying dead in the tub. Natalie, the cat, was put in a carrier and dropped the nearest veterinarian.

They dusted the whole place for prints and, low and behold, they got a hit for someone in the Admiralty itself. He would be at his office that very minute, so, off to see him they went.

The tricky part was the zip drive. They were afraid to load it up on some laptop as it may self-destruct. They had no idea what program was used to code it, so they decided to get an expert to dig in as deep as possible rather than risk ruining the damn thing.

Enter Isabella Mastrangella, MI8, Signals Interception and Communications Security. Born in Rutigliano, Italy, 30 years ago, she had become a British subject after her parents were killed in a car accident in Bari on a shopping trip.

Shortly after the crash and the settlement of the estate, she turned 22. Her parents had left her a rented home, which was unaffordable on a computer nerd's wage, so she would give it up at the end of the lease 2 months away.

Her family fortune amounted to a treasure trove of almost 7500 Euros combined with the parents' savings and the sale of all the furniture and household items.

So, feeling like nothing was left for her in Italy, she decided to spread her wings as it were and go live somewhere else. Since she spoke some English, she toyed with the idea of moving to America, but it seemed too big and expensive to tackle at this point in her life. Instead, she opted for England.

After all, she could also emigrate to America once she mastered the language and gotten a little more confident in herself. She had only one marketable skill, and that was coding.

Her mom once told her that some people could make a living on their beauty, but she must remember that she is beautiful ON THE INSIDE. Thanks, mama.

The years since had seen some enhancements, though. She reduced her "WOW" nose, as she liked to call it. It stood for Wicked Witch of the West; most people referred to it as a 'Roman Nose.'

Some filler here, nip there, boobs of course, and she emerged a new woman. She liked looking in the mirror, now, and took second fiddle to no one. She sauntered into a meeting room or restaurant with consummate confidence these days and put many a man back on his heels.

Not to mention her unusual skill with tech. She invented a zip drive that could be loaded telemetrically something like a wireless cell phone charger. If you plugged the USB end of the drive into a laptop, her circuitry was designed to completely erase all the information.

She included a timer into her programming language that would revert a modified code to the original if the drive were plugged into a USB connector. Only her own telemetric readers could access or change the coding.

In the months before the accident, she had worked coding for a large, private hospital in her home town and sometimes hired herself out to other 'private' enterprises. There was a surprisingly large

market out there of people who needed computers RE-
programmed, or codes massaged in order to get the results they
needed.

Once settling in England, she had been hired at the first place she
applied, HSBC Holdings, England's biggest bank. She was an
absolute wizard with computers and, once she realized she could
never get by on her crappy salary, she went big.

Within four months, she had managed to recode all the online
transaction programs so that she was able to skim, to her own
accounts, 0.01% of the banks 100 Billion or so Pounds of wire
transfers.

One hundredth of a percent may not sound like much, but for
the mathematically challenged, it equals Ten Million Pounds Sterling.
This went swimmingly well for quite a while. The days came and
went, then months, then a few years. Nobody noticed and nobody
questioned when the little girl in coding gave two weeks' notice and
left her situation.

She had gone from living in a flat in the poor area of Newham to
purchasing an apartment on Welbeck Street, Marylebone section for
about 2 Million pounds.

She had manipulated every necessary database in London and
Italy to STOP being Isabella Mastrangella and START being
Maxime Mastrangella, a person whose entire life she constructed
except for the name; her mother's.

She spent the next two years modifying databases and codes
wherever she could to please her very wealthy clients. Some, the not
so savory types, had tried, on rare occasion, to avoid paying through
intimidation.

A few hours of keyboarding and these people were usually
plucked from the street for crimes too heinous to mention. They
eventually found their way into His Majesty's Prison Wakefield,
better known as "Monster Mansion."

Sorry, sorry, please forgive me and promises to serve would
sometimes see them released on technicalities or dismissals or
whatever else she could program into the system; at double the
original bill.

She even once changed the flight pattern from Heathrow to stop
planes from annoying a client by flying too close to his summer
home.

Her reach became global and, for three years more, she was coding her little heart out changing, improving, deleting, whatever it was that made her money.

She had developed a way to modify source codes by introducing a time aspect. The original source code for wire transfers, for example, would be enhanced with a code sequence that would automatically return its configuration to original if accessed by anyone other than her.

Once entered, the modified coding that skimmed her 0.01%, would return to original within 3 picoseconds. Once she had made the changes, the financial systems would transfer funds to her right along with all the legitimate clients.

If someone decided to take a look at the coding, well it would just revert to original and look innocent until such time as the interloper clicked off, as it were.

It was the concept of "too many irons" that eventually caught up with her. She had been looking forward and enjoying the amazing flow of money from so many financial institutions, that she neglected to look behind her and see if anyone was sneaking up. Well, they were.

Long story short, the Bank of England had a pretty good accounting outfit who, after a lengthy forensic audit of wire transfers, found the 0.01% anomaly. Of course, it's only little when you're talking percents; it's BIG when you're talking actual money.

When she was standing in the dock behind the well of the court waiting for her sentence to be read, the judge's condescending lecture about right and wrong and whatever else he needed to say to get his mug on the telly made her think about "paying one's fair share."

The Americans loved to say that whenever they wanted to raise taxes on rich people. They pulled their hair and pounded their chests at how a billionaire's PERCENTAGE was less than a secretary's or a teacher.

True, but the amount of DOLLARS paid into the treasury from the billionaire far exceeded those of a normal person. Not to mention that many of those billionaires own big companies. BIG in this context usually means lots of employees ALL paying taxes they would not be paying had this billionaire not given them a good job.

Whatever; she was pretty well screwed and very scared. She had never been in trouble before let alone something this big.

"My own fucking fault," she muttered. She hoped to wind up in a Class D prison somewhere to at least not serve her time with the worst of the worst.

In her daydreaming, she missed the first part of what the judge was saying, but she clearly heard him say "His Majesty's Prison Channing's Wood," though. Then, for a little salt in the wound: "For a period of no less than 10 years…" her knees buckled and she slipped to the floor.

Her mind was trying to rationalize and commiserate with itself all at the same time.

"Jesus God. It's just a white-collar crime. I didn't hurt anybody."

That's not the way the bank saw it. The bank that donates so much to political campaigns and has friends at all the best clubs in England. Oh, you're not going to make us look bad without paying a big price, young lady.

The two court officers picked her up back onto her feet. She didn't think anyone saw the small pee puddle she'd left on the floor when all hope and control left her body.

She was trying not to cry even though tears slowly rolled down her cheeks. She had seen enough prison movies to believe it was time to look tough. The prison dykes would be sizing her up the second she hit the sally port.

A feeling of utter hopelessness engulfed her as she realized she had nothing now. Her parents were gone, she had no other family, the government had confiscated her apartment and all the cash she had in the bank. Her car had been seized and probably sold, by now. She didn't have many friends before this and certainly had none now.

In this moment, at the lowest point a person could find herself, God decided to show up and offer a hand of redemption.

"Hello, Isabella. My name is Bond. James Bond."

"Look, I'm really not in the mood for jokes."

"No, that really is my name. I just say it like that to lighten the mood." He smiled and put out his hand.

She held up her handcuffs the three inches they would travel. Mr. Bond looked at the guard to his right who immediately undid the cuffs.

"Seriously. My name is James Bond and I work for MI8. Heard of us?"

"Ministry of the Interior something?"

"Correct. Signals Interception and Communications Security. We were part of the group that caught you."

"What am I supposed to say? Nice job? I'm going to prison for 10 years. Not too happy right at the moment."

"I understand and I am not here to rub your nose in it. I'm actually trying to help."

What could this guy want? She looked him over a little. Seemed in relatively good shape. Nice suit. Nice smile with straight teeth. She looked down at the shoes; shoes were supposed to be the giveaway about a man…

"Those are bespoke by Cleverly, actually. 700 Pounds Sterling."

Thus far, she hadn't gone as far as having her stuff custom made. She had laid low for a while to see if anyone was going to come knocking at her door. Then, about 4 years into the scam, she bought her apartment, the car, and the rest is, as they say, history.

Bond had been researching everything about her since they pulled the plug. He knew the whole story of the family, the coming to England, and the development of her management of computer codes.

She was unmarried, unattached, and fully ripe to become a willing and loyal slave to the Crown. All she had to do was grab at the apple.

The guard steered Isabella in behind Bond as he walked into one of the side rooms of the court. She gave Isabella a slight backward push and she fell into one of the chairs at the long table. She shook her hair back from her face and gave a defiant look at her gentleman caller.

"OK, I'm here to save you. All you have to do is agree to serve and we take off the cuffs and walk out the front door."

"Seriously? Just like that?"

"You must not realize just who we are, Miss Mastrangella. To review; I am from MI8. I represent the Minister of the Interior, the Prime Minister, and His Majesty the King. In this moment, you may as well be talking one on one with His Royal Highness, so carefully choose your words and contemplate your situation."

She was listening even though her mind was one big tornado. She had a bead of sweat on her forehead and was rubbing her wrists where the steel had been chafing these last few weeks.

Bond looked at his Omega and, without looking up, said:

"Lunch service begins in 25 minutes at Café de Channing's Wood. Shall we reserve you a seat OR would you care to swear allegiance to King and Country and come work for me?"

"That's it?"

"Well, except for the chip we'll shoot into your butt cheek to keep track of you along with the promise of reinstatement of sentence PLUS whatever the penalty for fucking up in the future."

"Also, as a part of your penance, you will integrate all your designs and strategies into all English based banks and Ministry of Defence programs, for no fee of course, as well as make a promise to keep an eye on and update the programs as new strategies became available."

"That's what caught you, by the way. We got smarter over time and you just stood still, so, whammo!" He wasn't smiling.

"Actually, it was a very lengthy accounting task that counted every penny and pound for about a 4-year period. Someone noticed a little shortfall, but no one could find it. That was because of your outstanding timer integrated into your codes. All the programming looked perfect, but YOU made it that way. Remarkable. It was old fashioned pencil and paper that put us on the right track."

"Besides, I know you'll do a good job because you're capable of doing a good job; you LIKE doing a good job, and the profilers say you need the warmth of validation from your family."

"I don't have a family anymore."

"We're your family, now, Isabella. Just give us a chance. It took the best people in England over 5 years to catch you. Even then it was because you got lazy."

"You'll be great at this and a great life will follow you. We'll be giving you back the apartment, the car, everything. You'll enjoy protection, status, an exciting career, all for doing important work for your country. You should thank God for this opportunity."

"Don't believe in him."

"Oh, why not?"

"I tend not to believe in things I can't see or feel."

"Like gravity, love, evil, joy, stress? Stuff like that? Yeah, good argument. Well, what's it going to be, then? There's a shitburger waiting at Channing's Wood with your name on it."

"Let's get out of here."

"Good girl."

30

DODGE CITY was on the surface, now. All the dances had been done, the Bridge was manned, both scopes were up, and they were making 3 knots in a relatively calm sea. Captain Scott and Demzer were standing on top of the sail together looking at the water in silence.

The Captain has assumed the Deck and the Conn while Demzer had binoculars as the Lookout and an M16 as Bridge watch in case someone fell overboard. Below, the Wardroom was being cleaned and sanitized and they were loading House into the second body bag of the run.

Scott had read the Emergency Traffic from the Admiralty too late. Yeah, he knew NOW they had a saboteur. The message hit the printer 7 minutes after House died.

God damn. He knew that guy a long time; another shipmate back on the old ALBUQUERQUE. One of his most reliable officers and a guy he hoped would command his own boat one day.

Now, they've got some Chinese rapist and potential murderer in cuffs and leg-irons under guard in Kennedy's old stateroom. The spook, Oakes, had been aboard with a pocketful of cyanide destined to wipe out the entire crew.

A thumb drive with programming designed to take over his ship! What an unbelievable story this was. He shook his head. Was he in the middle of some international incident?

The son-of-a-bitch that shot House was Chinese; could it be that China was trying to steal an American Submarine? This was World War Three shit, right here.

Just before climbing up to the bridge, he had met with the Chief of the Boat and Senior Chief Lancey to brief them about Oakes. The two old Chiefs just sat quietly and listened.

The message said that she was in custody and being interrogated. NCIS and MOD had the cyanide and the thumb drive; that's all he knew.

The message he just sent in reply would really get the chairs

213

sliding and the feet stomping at both Norfolk and Whale Island. Another dead Naval Officer, a saboteur in cuffs; boy, if somebody had it in for Lazarus Scott, they really could slam the coffin lid on his career.

He wasn't thinking about that. He was thinking about House's family, what had to be done next, and the radar blip just reported from Control. The tug was at 8100 yards, making 12 knots, relative bearing 350 with a zero-bearing rate.

Joey Howard had ripped the message off the printer in the wheelhouse and read it out loud to Wang and his brother.

"Well, they know about Wei, but they don't know about us. No time for these guys to have gotten a MAYDAY off, so we're in the clear, so far."

"How long until we get to the sub?" Wang looked at Joey.

"At this speed, about 20 minutes."

"Faster."

Jake went below and gave it the gas. A few minutes later, they were maxing out at 15 knots cutting their arrival time by a few minutes.

"NEPTUNE. NEPTUNE. We hold you visually at 7000 yards. We will tie you to Starboard in our Lee."

"Tie to Starboard in your Lee. Roger."

Joey tried to sound official and confident while minimizing his accent. Jake shifted throttle control to the wheelhouse and joined Wang in the messhall. They put on U.S. Navy dungaree pants and green foul weather jackets as a proper crew would wear. Wang put on a black Balaclava to cover his face.

"Bridge, Control." It was the XO who was acting as Navigator.

"Recommend All Stop, Right Standard Rudder to new course Three Five Zero."

"Very well. Helm, All Stop, right 15 degrees rudder, come to Three Five Zero."

"Captain, Helm. Answers All Stop, Rudder is Right 15."

"Very well."

"Passing Three Three Zero."

"Very well."

"Passing Three Four Zero."

"Very well."

"Captain, Helm, Steady Three Five Zero."

They had reeled in the Floating antenna and the Towed Array before surfacing, so if they drifted astern with the tug tied up, then nothing would get cut.

The tug was 515 yards away. The Forward Escape trunk hatch was being opened for the transfer of personnel to the tug, including LT. House.

Joey pulled back the throttles and slowed to a crawl. He had done this maneuver a few times tying up to a dock with fishing boats, but never with THIS kind of craft under these circumstances.

He slowed some more and took a quick look at the sub's Bridge and the guy up there with the rifle. Demzer had been the Bridge Rifleman for a few Swim Calls, you know, just in case a Great White wants a piece of a sailor. Those Five Five Sixes won't do anything to the shark, but they sure make the crew feel better.

He had passed his rifle familiarization firing when he first got to the boat, about 2 years ago, and had never fired one of them again. Now, he had no idea that he was the only armed military man standing between the good guys and bad.

Quinlan saw it, too. He was prone on the tug's main deck covered by tarps and the black netting he kept in his gun case. He looked through the scope at the two on top of the boat. He sized up Scott. He saw a certain hardness in the eyes and a strong relaxed posture typical of the man in charge. The Captain was unarmed, so it was the other guy that was the threat. He'd have to go first.

He swung left a bit to the man with the weapon and zeroed Demzer's head. Not yet. The last plan they all made was for Wang to jump to the deck once the mooring lines were over as though he wanted to help pass gear to the tug.

He'd try to get below down the hatch once all the sailors were out of the boat. If they tried to stop him, the Howards, with their AKs and he, with the rifle, would open up.

Joey stayed on the throttles a little too long and slammed the tug into the submarine. They heeled over a bit. Wang, in his Balaclava and Navy clothing, threw one end of the After line over to Tripod who put it over the centerline cleat.

Wang hustled forward on the tug and threw the other line, which also found a place on the cleat right behind the sub's Sail.

The crew had dutifully brought House's body topside with Cornwallis straddling the hatch and pulling the body bag up and out.

With his size and strength, he gently laid the Lieutenant on the non-skid as easily as if he were a piece of luggage.

"What in the fuck?" Joey mumbled to himself as he figured out there was a body in that bag. The message said nothing about a body. It must be Wei Li! Once he moved on them, they killed him and stuffed him into a body bag!

Wang had the same thought as he jumped to the sub's main deck and started to throw seabags onto the tug. He moved along the row of men and bags trying to get to the hatch.

"We need a gangplank!" Cornwallis yelled to Wang.

"We have to carry him across," he said pointing to the body bag on the deck.

Wang was standing across from Cornwallis, with the open hatch between them. He looked down and saw the ladder was clear all the way to the deck. He would knock this big redhead overboard and get below as fast as he could.

He shot his left arm out and grabbed Wooly Boy by the belt. Wang's powerful right cross hit Cornwallis fully on the left side of his face. The big Brit Chief's head snapped to the right, came to a stop, then turned slowly back. His eyes stared straight at Wang and the corners of his mouth turned up in a slight smile at a suddenly clear-headed and shocked adversary.

Captain Scott was watching all this through his binoculars from the Bridge and started yelling to the men on deck to get their attention.

"Demzer! Repel Boarders!!"

Demzer just looked at his Captain after hearing something he never thought he'd hear.

"1MC! Repel Boarders!" Scott repeated as he pointed to the Bridge suitcase below them in its usual mount. Demzer jumped down and screamed, "REPEL BOARDERS" over the 1MC in the suitcase.

Everyone below was standing and looking at each other. 'This can't be happening' was probably the thought that went through everyone's mind.

They had to get to the Small Arms locker and get weapons. Who has the 231 key for the padlock?

LT. House had one as Weapons Officer, but where the hell could it be now? The COB's got one, but he's topside. The OOD's got one, but the Captain's got the Deck and he's on the Bridge.

The XO ran into his stateroom and took the Snubnose from the Ziploc in his safe. This was the only weapon they had to repel borders. 4 rounds. The 4 .38 Caliber rounds left in this gun were all they had to protect the most advanced submarine in the NATO inventory.

Oh, and the M16 in the bridge. How much ammo did he have? One magazine of 20 rounds. That's it; 20 rounds of rifle ammo plus 4 pistol rounds.

To make it worse, no one below decks had any idea how big the threat was. Berns put the pistol in his belt and grabbed number 2 scope. He tried to look around, but the tug was too close to see the whole deck.

In the same microsecond that all this was going on, Waldo Quinlan had been watching Wang to get his cue to open fire. He saw him punch the big bastard standing in front of him.

It was in that moment that his rifle scope framed the face of the other man. It was a face he hadn't seen in a long time. The smoothly shaved face of Fergus Lowell Cornwallis, the boy he loved who had become a man. The son of the guy who brought him into his family and gave him some purpose.

Sad how his life had taken more wrong turns since then. Sad that he had come to this day with other allegiances and other battles to fight. He knew there was no choice. He fired.

The shot entered right below the big man's left eye and carried away the entirety of the back of his skull. He was less than 30 yards away, so the energy from that round was fully transferred from gun to head.

So powerfully had the bullet destroyed him, that he just stood there for a full second more before falling to the round hull and sliding into the sea.

Cornwallis watched as the corpse of the once powerful Haoyu Wang sank out of sight when he heard the crack of automatic rifle from the tug. The Howards had taken Waldo's shot as the signal to commence firing and they raked the whole of the sub.

Scott had jumped from the top of the sail into the Bridge as soon as he heard the very first shot.

"Open fire on that tug!" He yelled to Demzer who stood and blasted out the wheelhouse windows with his first burst.

Joey Howard had taken one to the throat and was choking out his life as Demzer went single fire to cover his shipmates all trying to get back below.

Jake emptied his first magazine and stood up to change, but Waldo put one in his back and blew him completely over the tug's gunwale and into the sea.

At this moment, the two Royal Navy Blackhawks that had been dispatched from Cornwall, entered the airspace above. The Reaper drone assigned to watch over DODGE CITY's surfacing and subsequent op with the tug, had sent back close up video of the shocking gun battle at sea.

The Blackhawks, cleared to fire from The Admiralty, engaged the tug with all four 7.62mm machine guns and turned it into junk. Waldo was hit several times and said one last prayer to beg forgiveness for a life gone astray.

The helos were BINGO fuel and headed East. The five guys who hid behind the port side of the sail tentatively came out and surveyed the damage. Scott leaned over the side of the sail and told them to cut the tug loose.

The forward line had gone slack and easily came off the cleat, but the stern of the tug had swung out enough to make the line taught. The COB's TL29 cut her free. They threw the remaining bags down the hatch and all went below.

"Leave that hatch open a minute," the COB said when he got to the bottom.

"Get Russell out here."

"Yes, COB."

"Here." He held out a Camel and she gave them the that ain't allowed look.

"They can kiss my ass."

She hadn't moved, so he lit his up, took a long drag and handed it to her.

"Now, people will say we're swapping spit."

They both tried to laugh, but it wouldn't come. Two drags later, he sent Sweetwater up to close the upper hatch and throw his butt overboard. Sweetwater took a couple of drags, too.

31

Months later, Cornwallis would find out that his "uncle" and former business partner, Waldo Michael Quinlan was on board that tug. It had been he who saved his life and the life of others by shooting Wang and the one Howard brother. It didn't make any sense, but it was all on video.

There was an inquiry, to be sure, as to why a Royal Navy Chief Petty Officer was once business partners with a known criminal. Why was this business partner on THAT tug? Was there any connection between Chief Cornwallis and the plot to steal a submarine. It took weeks, but the truth was sorted out.

What also had been sorted was the thumb drive. Isabella Mastrangella, England's top computer magician, had first cloned it to keep from destroying the only copy, then read it using her own technology.

If there was one thing she learned from her own experience getting caught, was that you couldn't let your tech get old. In the age of computers, "old" could mean hours. There was always something newer and better coming down the pike.

The whole job of the program was to upload an external control executable file and establish communications between the host computer and the controlling transmitter. It appeared the initial program had been using some kind of RF or Infrared technology which was subsequently replaced with Bluetooth.

Bluetooth came along about mid-1999, so somewhere in the life of this obviously proprietary program, it was made Bluetooth to satellite phone compatible. Once uploaded, the executable program could be initiated by the satellite through any one of the cellphone carrier servers anywhere in the world.

One of these thumb drives inserted into a USB terminal would upload a program that would allow the host program to be fully controllable by an external user through satellite phones, cell carriers, and Bluetooth in any order at any time.

They just never updated the program which made it discoverable by someone skilled enough who was actually LOOKING. Once loaded into the host, no one would be the wiser as there would be no warning until the host was attacked.

Unbelievably, the programming she was looking at in this thumb drive was from about 1985. It was simple, straightforward, and would certainly get the job done as long as there was nothing in place to deter it. A program developed in 1985 must have been developed to do some particular job, she thought.

What had happened back then that must have been done remotely? What could have been so important and so dangerous that it had to be controlled from afar?

"Let's try to reason this out," her alter ego spoke. "What kinds of events were happening back then?"

"If the program was developed late 1985, what happened in 1986?" Let's ask Google…

"Soviet MIR is launched into space; probably no. The World Cup is going on in Mexico; no. Oh, fuck! Chernobyl!"

So, who did it, why, and where are they?

Isabella poured over the language. It had all the expected construction, but there was an interesting syntax at play in the programming. If one assumes that a programmer's computer language syntax is the same as his native tongue, then one might expect Left to Right characters for, say an American programmer.

When examined Left to Right, the programming in this thumb drive made no sense. Using a Japanese Tategaki type syntax, or Top to Bottom, made more sense in the way this drive was programmed.

She started ticking off in her head bits of evidence, we have an Oriental programmer; Japanese or Chinese? Mandarin, after all, is a Left to Right oriented language, BUT that wasn't always the case. Before any European influence, the Chinese read from Right to Left and Top to Bottom, but that was WAY before the language in this program was developed.

She liked to talk to herself when she was thinking something through as though she were someone else. It was almost as though you had a completely different person to bounce things off.

"Well, we have in custody one Wei Li, Chinese citizen. We have fingerprints at the murder scene of one Doctor Robert Kellogg, Chinese by birth, belonging to a former Chinese Olympic Caliber Weightlifter who had been listed as a member of the Chinese Team in 1984. We are looking at computer language with an antique Chinese syntax. I say we go with China."

What she didn't know was that another office in MI8 had Rothington's satellite phone. Once they identified his fingerprints at the Kellogg murder scene, they descended on his home and found it hidden in his dirty clothes hamper. The phone was covered in his prints.

Coincidentally, police had been called when a body had been found sitting in his car outside a downtown pub. A quick check of the license plates and the documents in the man's possession, identified him as a Mr. Lawrence Rothington, late of the Ministry of Defence.

Autopsy revealed that a slender object, something like an icepick, had been rammed into his right ear puncturing his brain and also through his right eye. Autopsy also revealed the presence of saliva and feces on his penis. Authorities surmised that he had been engaged in some kind of sexual deviancy in his vehicle when attacked.

As the attacker may have been the person with whom he was so engaged, the search was on to connect the DNA with the second person. As luck would have it, there was no match from the biologic evidence taken from Rothington's body filed in any database.

Sadly, this second person would not be found as he was, at this very moment, submerged and decomposing in one of the large diesel fuel tanks that feed the engines at Waterloo train station.

The satellite phone easily gave up the signal routing, times, locations, and receivers of calls. It seems there has only been one person to whom every call from this satellite phone had been made or received; a Mr. Zhang of Zhang Enterprises, Hon Mun, Vietnam.

Further investigation revealed that Mr. Zhang was a Chinese National who had purchased about a thousand acres on the beautiful island of Hon Mun almost 45 years ago. The transaction had been approved personally by the then acting President of Viet Nam, Nguyen Huu Tho.

She pulled up satellite photos of the island and, lo and behold, a large compound overlooked the ocean. Her check of real estate and tax records filed in Hanoi showed that this Mr. Zhang had invested a sizeable amount of money into constructing a 12,000 square foot home on the easternmost side of the island directly across from

Debbie's Beach.

Since the date of purchase, the island itself has become the epicenter of the famous 30,000-acre Hon Mun Marine Protected Area.

Make no mistake, despite the official records, Bolin Li was the de facto owner of the residence on Hon Mun. He also owned all the infrastructure necessary to carry utilities like power and water from the Vietnamese coastal town of Nha Trang.

Of course, there were backup systems for everything. Backup electrical generators, solar and wind powered generators, sea water desalinization equipment, security personnel and physical barriers/deterrents to keep the hordes of tourists away from him.

The entirety of the one road leading from the tourist beaches of the island up the mountain and on to the residential compound was replete with cameras, ground vibration detectors, and buried anti-tank mines.

Although the coastline below the residence was very rocky and without a beach, there was a helicopter pad to the south. Yep, a global financial and pharmaceutical enterprise that made it all possible, but Bolin Li's greatest asset was his friends who would do anything for him should he merely ask. Verona Oakes and the late Lawrence Rothington could certainly attest to that.

Isabella also learned that another of Mr. Zhang's dearest friends, Mr. Haoyu Wang, the former weightlifter, was the owner of those fingerprints at the Kellogg home. Agents of MOD and NCIS showed his picture to Petty Officer Verona Oakes who confirmed he was the man in the video of her dear mother being set ablaze.

The Vietnamese were also briefed on the entire matter, but refused involvement as Mr. Zhang was NOT one of their citizens. He was a friend to their government and multi-decade owner of a private residence for which he paid A LOT of property tax.

The political machines went All Ahead Full on deciding a course of action. The Crown insisted that, since Mr. Zhang was a Citizen of the Chinese Republic, their embassy in London needed to be consulted.

The Chinese showed great appreciation for the West's diplomatic respectfulness. So much so, that they regarded this as such an opportunity to bring the global community closer, they wanted to bring something tangible to the table.

So, through back channels, China suggested all nations concerned hold a very discreet meeting in London. They also suggested that the World Health Organization and America's CDC also be represented, which really piqued everyone's interest.

At any other time, a thumb drive, a satellite phone, a nuclear submarine, and a handful of dead Englishmen might not instigate an international meeting of the highest secrecy? So, why now? Because of the second thumb drive.

32

Thankfully, every bigwig in the world has a staff. Those staff are able to pack a bag, get on a plane, and get more done by dinner than the bigwigs can do in a week. This is true because one type of meeting requires posturing and posing, presumption and photographs, formal outfits, and chefs.

The second type of meeting requires a sense of urgency, beer, finger food, and the courage to actually act. It was during this type of meeting that two shocking pieces of information were revealed: the existence of a thumb drive that held First, the chemical makeup of a vaccine that would save the world from this COVID pandemic and Second, the name Bolin Li.

The government of China would NOT reveal this thumb drive if its existence were to be made public. They were fighting a big enough blow to their public image since this virus had been falsely connected to them.

The only reason they were willing to offer it up to this secret, back channel international meeting was to shed light on the existence of Bolin Li. For many years, he had become a thorn in their side.

Of course, they were well aware of his machinations on the world drug trade. They were also quite amused that Western Law enforcement was completely Unaware.

They regarded Bolin Li as an anachronism given his motivation for revenge for world events from the last century. They did, however, appreciate his magnanimous financial contributions and respected his formidable allegiances all over the world. Also, as individuals, they did not want him angry at them.

Their part in bringing him to justice would have to remain secret and they did not want any hint of their involvement to be known. In fact, it was their suggestion that the problem be eradicated WITHOUT involving the justice system or the press. A small team could be formed and direct intervention against Bolin Li's forces of evil could be managed completely under the radar.

Of course, China's actions of bringing the existence of the thumb drive to the world's attention AND providing two men as advisors to the assault team, would continue to cement China's place as a world leader.

Since the West had orchestrated the direct action against such dark forces, they would be blamed should there be a leak to the press or if the mission failed. Good strategy was to prepare contingency statements for any eventuality.

After all, without the second thumb drive, the West would have continued to stumble forward completely unaware of the true culprit behind the pandemic.

At this very moment, Bolin Li and Zhang were sipping some relatively cheap wine as they sat in lounge chairs looking out at the sea. They had been silent for the last 20 minutes, each lost in thought as to what must have happened to their plan.

There had been no word from Wang or Wei. They must assume the worst in that the plot has failed and their people have been caught. If that is true, then they would spill their guts either through torture or drugs.

"How much might they know?" Zhang asked Li.

"We should believe they know it all. I doubt Wang will go quietly. You were wise to authorize that English pervert be killed once Wei went out on the helicopter. If they would have gotten Rothington, then he would have told them everything."

They could not have known that the English had Rothington's satellite phone. They also had no knowledge of Isabella and the extent of the information she had gleaned from the thumb drive.

They also had no idea that a team of Special Operators would be showing up at their door in less than 24 hours.

"Shall I double the guard for the next few days, just in case?"

"You don't seriously think they'll show up here?"

The international, secret, back-channel meeting ended and the agreed upon course of action was taken back to London, Washington, and Beijing for approval. Two hand-picked operators from each country would be sent in. The right people had to be picked, briefed, outfitted, and transported to Hon Mun Island ASAP. Extraction had to be planned and coordinated, too.

The Brits and Americans had Special Operators throughout the Pacific, but would have to get moving as their people had to fly longer distances to meet up with their Chinese counterparts. They had to keep the operation quiet and involve the fewest people possible. Who were the best guys to send, let's ask someone with plenty of experience.

"Warrant Officer Watson!" General Von Milspaugh, Commandant of the Royal Marines greeted him. The General's family emigrated to England right after the Big One back in 1919.

There was little left in Germany on which to grow a family and build a future, so they packed up and headed West. Two generations since and both had served the Crown.

"I know you had NO notice, but thank you for coming."

"Anything for you, General. We go a long way back."

"Aye, we do. I was a mere Major when that round went through yer arse," they both giggled a little. "I've replayed that scene many times in my mind. The helicopter crashed and burned, the RPGs, all of it. You saved a bunch of men, that day, Warrant."

"T'was my privilege."

"Let's get down to cases, shall we?"

Von Milspaugh laid out the whole circumstance as he knew it. Bolin Li, the virus, the drug empire, the thumb drive, Rothington, and the rest. He had spilled blood with this man and he knew him to be the most trustworthy soldier you could find. He had the operational expertise in the Special Boat Service, too, and the General wanted his input.

Since there would be 3 teams of 2 men each, Watson suggested each have its own piece of the operation rather than try to coordinate efforts on one detailed plan without any time to practice.

One team assault the island residence from the West and two from the East; HAHO drops probably so the noise from the opening of the chutes would not be detected and they could fly in from 25 miles away.

Have them land in the water and swim in meeting the West team or have a separate place to enter the compound. Hell, they could even use the Helo pad if the LZ was secure enough.

The SBS could easily coordinate with the SEAL team; it was the unknown factor of the Chinese People's Liberation Army Oriental Sword guys. We wouldn't know what they were planning until the meetup on the C130 in Hong Kong.

Five minutes later, Von Milspaugh had the U.S. Navy SEAL Commander and the Chinese interpreter on the scramble phone.

Time and place for meetup and flight out of Hong Kong were agreed upon. The basic bones of the mission were discussed and it was agreed that the teams on the ground would work out the details on the way.

"It's quite the hurry we're in, General."

"Aye, Warrant, but we can't risk him pulling the trigger on another world-wide disaster. We're guessing a bit here, but we think this bastard's responsible for the Chernobyl melt-down. If he did that one, then it's also a possibility he did something else we're not aware of, yet."

"Remember, he's reliving World War Two. He's trying to make the guilty pay. USSR, Japan, maybe a Western City next?"

"I understand, General. I wish I were going along."

"Too far away, Warrant. We've got 2 of our best guys enroute."

Isabella had just cracked the second thumb drive. A lengthy chemical equation that, when examined by actual medical and chemical researchers, was the formula for this pandemic sweeping the planet.

The programming language was different from the other drive. It was modern and Western in its syntax. It was so simple to read, that she was convinced it was planned that way.

An hour later, she was on the phone with James Bond to update him on what she found. She suggested they get their best biochemical guy out of bed and over to his office at the Francis Crick Institute. What good was having the premier biomedical discovery institute in the world right down the street if you couldn't give them an emergency to resolve?

By midnight, the Head of the department that prevents, diagnoses, and treats illnesses had printed out the chemical equation for a vaccine that appeared a perfect solution in every way. What they didn't know was that they were playing directly into Bolin Li's hands.

The COVID was one thing and, yes, it made people sick. It made weak people die; weak either from other health comorbidities or just from old age. The vaccine would negate the effects of the initial virus, but the BOOSTER was the actual bioweapon.

The human body could assimilate and manage the amount of vaccine introduced, but the booster shot was too much and bodily systems would start to shut down. Seemingly without explanation, the overall number of heart attacks might spike worldwide. People may start stroking out. Wherever the booster could attack the host's weakness, it would.

All Bolin Li had to do was turn on the evening news and rejoice in the global retribution he was spreading. He had access to news channels from all over the world via his satellite dishes. He would pour a Chivas Regal and turn from one to the other as the death tolls were revealed each night.

In the U.S. from COVID alone, 2000 elderly people were dying out of every 100,000.

"How does it feel, America?" he would say to the TV.

"Take your vaccines, everyone!" He'd say with a laugh.

The vaccines would ameliorate the spread just enough to get the pundits to push for a booster. He had people positioned everywhere, in every government, in every news room, who would popularize the booster idea. They would do it, or they would face the consequences. Oh, what joy the next few months would bring!

33

While he was watching his 82-inch TV, Bolin Li was unaware that a group of special men were taking off from the airport in Hong Kong. 2 American SEALS; Peterson and Dalby; 2 Brits of the Special Boat Service, Rode and Waldie; and 2 members of China's Oriental Sword Special Forces Group, ONE and TWO.

Yep, no names; just ONE and TWO. They both spoke English; they were both very young men; no more than 22 or so. They were sitting in the shoe shine chairs outside the tea kiosk by gate 211.

When they saw the 4 white guys with full sea bags walking their way, they both stood, picked up their own bags, and walked directly to the first man and offered a salute.

Peterson was a Navy Lieutenant and was the ranking man of this mission. As they all made their way to Gate 202, Peterson put out his hand and introduced himself to the Chinese team having already done so to the Brits back inside the terminal.

"Lt. Peterson, Navy SEALS."

He held out a hand. The taller of the two Chinese first saluted, then shook Peterson's hand and said, "I am ONE. He is TWO. We are soldiers in the People's Liberation Army."

It was easy to see that the Brits were upbeat and chummy while the Chinese were very serious and quiet in their demeanor. ONE took a quick look at TWO who nodded.

"We are happy to serve with you gentlemen."

The Westerners answered in kind and were each inwardly impressed with ONE's command of the English language. At least they wouldn't have difficulty communicating the plan. They wouldn't talk about anything more until they all got on the C130.

Gate 202 was empty and they all walked right through the door, down the jetway, and down the stairway at the end. Their plane was running engines and pointed out toward the taxi way.

Each man carried two bags, but the Brits and Americans' bags were MUCH bigger than their teammates. HAHO equipment calls for helmets, breathing equipment, insulated suits, radio, a raft on your right leg, and weapons, not to mention your chute.

The Chinese guys had two duffels about 36 inches long.

"What ya carryin' there, mate?"

ONE bent over and opened the first bag. The parachute pack was obvious with the 7-strap system and all. There was an NVG integrated skull crusher and goggles and two small bottles for breathing.

This equipment sat on a black pile of cloth underneath. ONE pulled out the parachute pack, placed it on the deck and then out came the pile of cloth. It was a Wingsuit!

The other 4 men looked at each other while TWO put his head back and laughed. For the remained of the two-hour flight to the island, everybody checked and donned their gear and got comfortable with the upcoming sequence of events.

The only pieces of equipment the U.S. and UK teams had in common were the communications units on their throats and the P226 sidearms. Peterson gave ONE and TWO each a set of comms units to stay in touch with the group.

The Brits were carrying their C8 Carbines with the 10-inch barrels and 30 round magazines, while the SEALS had their H&K 416s with suppressors.

TWO looked over his Western friends' weapons and then pulled a weird-looking thing out of his second bag. It was a firearm, but nothing like the other guys had seen before. It looked a little like that vibrating massager a barber will use on your head after a haircut.

TWO's hand and forearm slipped through the closeable clamp and his fingers closed around a tube-like handle. The main body of the weapon was held fast to the back of his hand. It had no sights but two stubby barrels about four inches long and two inches apart.

He then pulled something out of his bag that had two curved parts that attached to, what looked like, two oversized tuna cans. These cans were actually drum magazines that secured to the underside of the forearm and fed rounds through the curved guides to the barrels. It fired 22 Magnum ammo fully automatic.

"This is Zaoshang Hao," TWO said. "Means Good Morning!" He laughed and laughed as he held his hand about a foot in front of the barrels and made a buzzing sound then shielded his eyes.

"Zaoshang Hao!" and he buzzed again, laughing.

"Likeable sort," Rode said to Waldie and held up his hand for

TWO to high-five.

"I hope we get to see that thing in action," Waldie commented.

TWO slipped his arm thru the brace and wrapped his hand around the bar-shaped grip. The thumb end had a button that TWO wiggled his thumb over and said "Trigger. 15 rounds per second each barrel. Bullets cross at 7 meters. He flexed his fingers over a spring-loaded lever on the front of the bar; safety. Pull safety, press button, Good Morning!"

TWO could tell from Sgt. Rode's face that he was impressed. TWO smiled.

He pointed at the cans, "Drum magazines. 200 each. 6 extra drums in belt."

"Hmmph," offered Waldie.

The 22-magnum round was small and light so a guy could carry a bunch of them. It had pretty good ballistics, too, and at 30 of them a second through two barrels, it could flat fuck some people up.

The two Brits noticed the weapon went on the left, or off hand. The shooter also wore what appeared to be a flame-proof glove. Depressing the safety and thumbing the trigger would force the shooter's hand into a fist. The barrels protruded far enough past his knuckles to keep his hands safe while he fired. Who the hell thought this thing up?

So, the plan was for the Americans and Brits to exit the plane at 32,000 feet 30 miles East of the island. Open their Ram Air chutes at 25,000 feet and fly toward the island entering the sea 2 miles out. Drop the flight gear, get in the rafts, climb the rocks, and hit the compound at first light.

The Chinese team were to stay with the plane and divert to the Southern side of the island and exit at 12,000 feet. They would wingsuit to the West, turn Northeast and guide on the tourist beach. They would fly in and down to 250 feet, pull up and stall, deploy their chutes and drop onto the tourist beach and bury their gear.

They would then work their way up the mountain road, disable the microwave antennas there, and take out any sentries quietly. Once at the compound, they would traverse the helipad and cover the landing of the rest of the team.

From that point on, the mission was to locate Bolin Li and take him into custody. A Blackhawk would be on the helipad for extraction 20 minutes after the Reaper drone's video confirmed that the entire team inserted. Once the sun rose, the tourists would be all over that place, so they had to be over the crest of the hill and out of sight.

For the entirety of the flight, intel was sent to them accrued from the Reapers over the target and satellite surveillance of emissions from the house. The place seemed quiet; no radio or microwave signals were being sent and the video cameras showed no guards walking the property.

They were all standing around the map on the lighted table when ONE suggested to LT. Peterson that they modify their insertion.

"We fly right to helipad. Pull up, deploy chutes, and drop on pad."

"Isn't that too dangerous to expose yourselves?"

"We get in fast. Out of equipment fast. I cover front doors, here," pointing to the latest photos. TWO cover rest of team coming up from sea."

Peterson looked at the other men and everyone nodded.

"We'll go with that plan unless new intel tells us something different."

0415 hours. 30 minutes to first team deployment.

Bolin Li had been asleep but that same nightmare woke him. He always smelled the burning of the homes. It had been said that you don't smell things in a dream; Bolin Li knew this to be false. He smelled his house burning and the dead villagers each time.

He got out of bed and padded to the bathroom for a morning pee. These last few years, even peeing had been hurting him. Just getting out of bed and walking the first few steps hurt. His eighties had not been kind.

He flipped on the screens over his desk and scanned the security camera feeds. Nothing moving. No hits on the time-lapse motion detectors. No courtesy notifications of suspicious aircraft from the sea sweeping radar on the Vietnamese coastline.

It was going to be another fine morning in one of the most beautiful places in the world. In fact, he had chosen this spot because it WAS so beautiful. His personal relationship with the President of Vietnam had sealed the deal for him. The man liked his vices and Bolin Li was able to see to it that he was well supplied with everything he desired for a guarantee of peace and anonymity.

In that very moment that he stretched, as Jung's concept of

synchronicity would have it, Peterson exited the plane with Dalby and the two Brits right behind.

The C130 banked left and started a 6-minute descent to 20,000 feet. 16 miles from the island, ONE and TWO went out head first. Each team leader kept one eye on his indicators; compass, altimeter, and breathing air remaining.

The Western team had opened within a minute of leaving the aircraft and were all under canopy with 27 miles to fly. The world is deathly silent at these altitudes; there was only the rippling of the Hi-5 chutes, but the jumpers' headsets blocked it out.

There was a text on Bolin Li's phone from his contact at the Nha Trang weather radar station:

"Aircraft 34 miles East of your location. Turning South. Descending. Probable Tourist traffic."

Depending on the time of year, he would get more or less notifications. He was always wary that someone with a grudge might mount some incursion of his little piece of paradise. Sometimes, you can't kill them fast enough and they try to get you, first. No one's come close in all these years, he mused.

34

It was almost straight up 0500 when ONE flared up short of the coastline just over the museum. He arched his back quickly and repositioned his body from a horizontal "Superman" aspect to one as vertical as possible. This maneuver had the effect of stalling the wingsuit.

He pulled his ripcord and his canopy sprung out of the pack and caught air at just over 100 feet. This altitude was way below the minimum recommended, but these guys were something else.

ONE's boots hit the concrete of the helipad and he heard TWO's chute pop open. They were both down, out of their suits, and running. ONE made his way near the front entrance while TWO turned right to the rocks above the coastline. He could see the rafts still about 500 yards offshore.

The ground vibration sensors were triggered which automatically turned on the cameras and the floodlights. The security roll shields came down on all the windows and the guards were turned out of their accommodation.

They didn't really charge the field with the requisite enthusiasm as they had had false alarms go off before when a big turtle would drag its ass across the sidewalk. Never in their lives had they imagined what was about to happen.

There were only 4 permanent staff on the island. Two security sergeants, a cook, and a housecleaner. The other 8 guys admitted to being indebted to Zhang or the other old guy for one thing or another. Most had done time; only two had ever been in the military, but all were Chinese. Zhang didn't want any communication problems.

Plus, these guys had no idea where they were. So, when their three-month stint was over, they were shipped far away and couldn't tell anyone where they'd been. Each man signed up for a 3-month stint which really wasn't that bad.

Lodging in the bunkhouse, food, and one day off a week. Don't ever get caught drunk or unable to take your shift, though. That one guy from Anhui did and he was gone the next day. Although they weren't certain, they all had a bad feeling that his punishment was worse than just getting fired.

There were 6 men posted around the island each night which left the other 6 in their bunks. They were wakened by the alarm that accompanied the motion detectors, dressed, and drew weapons to take a look around.

The sergeant radioed the other posts for a status report, but no one had seen anything. The floodlights revealed nothing, but the light could be seen from the bottom of the black cliffs where the SEALS and SBS guys had stopped climbing.

Bolin Li and Zhang watched the camera feeds from his respective bedrooms. 15 minutes later, having seen nothing untoward, Zhang asked Bolin Li if he could raise the shields and stand down the men. Bolin Li took another sip of his tea and told Zhang to go ahead. Both men returned to their beds.

It was barely a minute when "Chuang ru zhe!" came over the intercom. Intruders had been spotted entering the compound from the cliff area. The guards had their weapons at the ready and were waiting for orders.

It was then that Zhang's satellite phone went off. He ran to Bolin Li's room before answering and held the phone up as if to ask what the old man wanted done.

"Answer."

Zhang just depressed the button when:

"Mr. Zhang. This is INTERPOL. Our agents are there to take you into custody for crimes against humanity. Please surrender peacefully."

Isabella tried to sound as friendly as possible. Then, one of the staff from the Chinese Embassy repeated the message in Chinese.

"Gai Zoule." Bolin Li said and Zhang bolted from the room to get dressed.

The charges went off in sequence: first, the helipad, then mines on the road to Debbie's Beach, then, the claymores in the trees.

The SEALS and SBS guys were crouched below the boulders at the top of the cliffs, but ONE and TWO were at each of the two front corners of the residence. ONE was hit in the leg and face with a few steel balls from a claymore.

He looked around the corner to check on TWO, when three of

the guards came out of the building. They were sweeping in all directions and started firing when they saw him. He pulled back and waited a couple of seconds for them to empty their magazines.

Then he jumped forward on to the ground, held up his left arm, and said Good Morning with a 4 second burst of 22 magnum fire. He made a small circle with his arm and everything in a 20 foot radius got peppered.

One of the guards made it back inside, but the other two were dead. TWO came out from behind his corner and ran toward ONE.

"OK?" Quick nods. TWO wrapped a bandage on ONE's thigh and gave him a compress to hold against the side of his face.

The SBS guys ran up to the front door and, with the SEALS as rear guard, they attached a breacher strip, then backed off.

Peterson gave a pounding motion with his hand and the breaching charge took off the entire door. The SEALS and SBS teams made entry as TWO helped ONE to the door.

One of the interior doors opened and shots rang out from the inside. The Brits opened up with the C8s as the SEALS swept the room in case of a diversion.

The Brits entered the room, but the one rifleman had been killed. They cleared the rest of the room and bathroom.

"One four mikes to LZ," sounded in their headsets. It was the extraction Blackhawk.

"LZ hot. Damaged," Peterson said into his throat mike.

ONE sat on the floor with his back against the couch and covered the front door opening as the other five cleared the rest of the house.

More explosions from the back of the house! It was Bolin Li's bedroom where his communications equipment and files were kept. Everything was backed up in one of his other houses; he just didn't want anything to fall into the hands of INTERPOL.

A hand grenade flew into the front door and came to rest a foot from ONE. He rolled but not in time to avoid injury. He took most of the blast in the back and it threw him over in front of the bar.

He poured 22 magnum fire all over the front door opening in the event someone was coming through. The rest of his team was crouched at the back of this greatroom and, when the two guards rushed in, they killed them both in a hail of 5.56.

The sun was coming up and the rental boats from the mainland would be heading to the island soon. There was enough smoke in the air to warrant attention from the authorities, but just who were the authorities around here, anyway?

"5 mikes. Clear?"

"Roger. Cleared to land. Alpha, this is Papa. Objective Not in custody. Repeat NOT in custody. Continuing. Roger?"

Everyone in the INTERPOL war room were listening on the speakers. Isabella looked at Bond who nodded.

"Papa, this is Alpha, Roger."

Peterson intended to have his guys continue to look for Bolin Li by searching as much of the island as they could before taking off. That old bastard had to be here somewhere. He made a circular motion around his head and the other 5 went into the brush.

The Blackhawk popped up over the cliff and came down softly on the blasted helipad, but the ground was only slightly tilted. The pilot throttled down and two other U.S. Marines got out. They had headphones, as well, and signaled to Peterson they would look into the brush.

Peterson waved one over to him and told him to load ONE into the helo. The Marine checked his leg and the bleeding had stopped. He pulled out a morphine syrette from his pack and ONE waved him off shaking his head.

Smoke was pouring out of the house, now. Peterson was afraid there might be other charges that might explode, so he ordered everyone back for extraction.

The Brits came out of the jungle with the last two of the guards in handcuffs. They walked them toward Peterson and he motioned to the helo. All the others came back in sight and he did a sweeping motion over his head and a "Let's go" into the mike.

As he was almost ready to step into the helicopter, a shiny object on the ground caught his eye. The really old Zippo went into his pocket.

EPILOGUE

By the time Captain Scott had the tug cut loose from DODGE CITY, the entire Reaper drone video of the occurrence was on its second play at the Admiralty and at COMSUBLANT. Shortly thereafter, Isabella would crack the thumb drive and the satellite phone, and the chase would be on.

Scott brought the remainder of his crew below and they submerged. Three men topside had been hit during the firefight with the tug, but they would be alright. LT. House's body was in the freezer and he would be carried off the boat by his own guys.

Scott had requested direct transit to SUBASE, Groton, but the Admiralty suggested Portsmouth ASAP and COMSUBLANT overruled Scott.

In the following months, Verona Oakes had been prosecuted for spying, which was dismissed because she was not attempting to obtain information and convey it to a hostile party.

They tried to prosecute her for any one of a number of offenses from Article 121, Larceny and Wrongful Appropriation for trying to steal a ship, but she never actually did anything, so they opted for an Article 15 for Adultery since she messed around with the married Petty Officer Schiano.

She wound up in the Norfolk Naval Base Brig for 30 days and got busted to E-1. Her lawyer had a shit fit about it and reminded the court that she risked her life to keep that crew safe from the cyanide. She had to choose between her mother and the Navy,

"How would the gentlemen here, today, have chosen?"

But they had to get her on something, so they did. She served her time, and accepted a General Discharge under Honorable Conditions which allowed her GI Bill benefits. Once her separation was complete, she applied for, and was accepted to, Law School.

DODGE CITY returned to Portsmouth. All injured personnel were admitted to St. Mary's Community Health Campus, nursed back to health, and released none the worse for wear except for some cool battle scars.

Captain Scott insisted, and COMSUBLANT concurred, that his current crew, with the full assistance of Matt Dillon, sail her to

Norfolk. DODGE CITY remained in Portsmouth for 5 more weeks before getting underway. COMSUBLANT and COMSUBRON 8 were planning a hero's welcome replete with the Navy Band, Medals, and Commendations where warranted.

Wei Li was charged with International Terrorism; the Chinese made no effort to have him returned with Diplomatic Immunity. He was returned to Boston and, since there is no statute of Limitation on murder, the old case of the dead coed was reopened.

Despite an intensive global manhunt, Bolin Li and Zhang were never brought to justice. Some said they must have had a secret escape route on the island. Others said they had somehow gotten into the helicopter, but drone video showed no such thing.

Unless they were dead and rotting in the jungle somewhere on the island, the best bet was that they had made their way down to Debbie's Beach, blended in with the tourists, and hopped a tour boat back to Nha Trang.

Chief Petty Officers Cornwallis and Russell made it a point to get to know each other better. Many an evening were shared discussing their mutual love of orange cats and Panhead motorcycles (Uncle Johnny's was a 1965).

Theresa was also impressed with Fergus' cooking skills. He credited his grandmother's influence; a person whom, from the minute they met, Theresa felt she had known her whole life.

One Sunday evening at Grandma's, after the dinner dishes had been washed, and Elizabeth and Grandma had gone to bed, Fergus walked Theresa out to the garage.

He brought out two Anisette nightcaps and they sat at the workbench looking at his bike.

"Do you know what today is, by chance?" he asked.

"Ah…. no."

"Here's a hint: 'Well, I've never been beaten, let alone like that'." He cocked his head and gave her a slight smile.

"That was tonight?"

"Aye. The Argyle. Do you remember what you first said to me?"

"You don't have a chance and you're messing with the wrong girl." They both giggled nervously.

"Aye…and I said?"

"May I have the honor of your hand and the pleasure of your name?"

"Correct, Lassie!" More giggling.

He stood, reached into his back pocket, and went to one knee before her.

"I love ye. I've loved ye from the first second. Eternity will end before I stop lovin' ye. For me, yer the Right Girl. May I have the honor of your hand and the pleasure of you taking my name?"

He held out a simple diamond ring. She had trouble focusing on it through the tears.

"This was my mother's."

She slipped her finger through and whispered "Yes. I'll love you forever and honor you always."

Funny how life works out, sometimes. Fergus and his now missus, Theresa Cornwallis, both ended their military service the same year, as the time apart for sea duty was unbearable.

Together, they opened a Navy-themed restaurant called The Ship's Galley. The entire décor was that of an actual mess hall on a Naval vessel. There were metal trays to scoot along the serving line. The "cooks," wearing Navy Dungarees and White Dixie Cup hats, would scoop your selection onto your tray just the way it's done on the big battleships.

They served meals prepared from the actual 1940's U.S. Navy and Royal Navy cook book recipes. Military announcements and alarm sounds would play in the background.

The restaurants were decorated with pictures of real Navy warships, flags, knotted ropes, and bells, too. SO many customers just loved the food and theme SO much, that they opened 9 more restaurants in Great Britain and the United States before five years were out.

As though life couldn't be better, on one of the anniversaries of the crash that took Fergus' parents, they welcomed to the world twin, orange haired boys: Bobby and Toby.

The End

About the Author

Mike DeRosa is a 24-year veteran of the U.S. Navy Submarine Force and a retired High School Teacher. He has been married to Sharon, the love of his life, for 20 years. They spend the summers in North Dakota and the winters in Arizona, but they're moving....

His first book was a motorcycle-themed kid's story: The Adventures of Olive Pearl and Hammy Davidson.

Printed in Great Britain
by Amazon